EDUCATIONAL ASSESSMENT IN A CHANGING WORLD

This timely book takes stock of the wide range of developments in society, education and assessment and offers conclusions and strategies that are necessary for the future of educational assessment.

Drawing on examples from the UK, Europe and USA, the book will dissect cultural, political, psychological and ideological ideas on society, education and assessment and foreground pressing issues relating to artificial intelligence, social justice and climate change. Acknowledging its predominantly Western perspective and providing context on the evolution of educational assessment, the book will bridge the gap between theory and practice to progress debate and discourse on creating a culture of assessment fit for the future and rethinking strategies for the path ahead.

Ultimately, the book will provide insights and key takeaways for the field of educational assessment along with an evidence-based agenda that will be relevant for education professionals, the assessment industry and policymakers interested in higher education, international and comparative education and testing.

Isabel Nisbet has held senior roles in the regulation of qualifications and assessment in the UK.

Stuart Shaw is Honorary Professor of University College London in the Institute of Education – Curriculum, Pedagogy & Assessment, UK.

EDUCATIONAL ASSESSMENT IN A CHANGING WORLD

Lessons Learned and the Path Ahead

Isabel Nisbet and Stuart Shaw

LONDON AND NEW YORK

Designed cover image: © Getty Images

First published 2025
by Routledge
4 Park Square, Milton Park, Abingdon, Oxon OX14 4RN

and by Routledge
605 Third Avenue, New York, NY 10158

Routledge is an imprint of the Taylor & Francis Group, an informa business

© 2025 Isabel Nisbet and Stuart Shaw

The right of Isabel Nisbet and Stuart Shaw to be identified as authors of this work has been asserted in accordance with sections 77 and 78 of the Copyright, Designs and Patents Act 1988.

All rights reserved. No part of this book may be reprinted or reproduced or utilised in any form or by any electronic, mechanical, or other means, now known or hereafter invented, including photocopying and recording, or in any information storage or retrieval system, without permission in writing from the publishers.

Trademark notice: Product or corporate names may be trademarks or registered trademarks, and are used only for identification and explanation without intent to infringe.

British Library Cataloguing-in-Publication Data
A catalogue record for this book is available from the British Library

ISBN: 978-1-032-38663-8 (hbk)
ISBN: 978-1-032-38661-4 (pbk)
ISBN: 978-1-003-34616-6 (ebk)

DOI: 10.4324/9781003346166

Typeset in Sabon
by Apex CoVantage, LLC

CONTENTS

About the authors — *vi*
Acknowledgements — *viii*
Authors' preface — *ix*
Foreword — *xi*

1 Introduction — 1

2 Developments in education and assessment — 17

3 New priorities and an unexpected shock — 58

4 Changes to thinking about society — 96

5 Changes to thinking about education and assessment — 122

6 The moral compass — 170

7 Lessons learned and the path ahead — 191

Afterword — *208*
Index — *210*

ABOUT THE AUTHORS

Isabel Nisbet's academic training was in philosophy, with her tutors including R.S. Downie in Glasgow and R.M. Hare in Oxford. Her professional career has been in government and regulation in the UK, including posts in government departments in Scotland and England and senior roles in the regulation of medicine and postgraduate medical education. These led to a Director role in the Qualifications and Curriculum Authority in England. Isabel was the founding CEO of Ofqual, the statutory regulator of qualifications and assessments in England. From 2011 to 2014, she worked for Cambridge Assessment in South East Asia, based in Singapore. Isabel has served on the Board of Qualifications Wales and has been governor of four universities in England. She is currently Vice-Chair of the Board of Governors of the University of Bedfordshire. In 2021, Isabel was appointed to a panel carrying out an Independent Review of Education in Northern Ireland, and their report was published in December 2023. She is a member of the National Statistician's Data Ethics Group, and she contributes regularly to national and international conferences and seminars.

Stuart Shaw is Honorary Professor of University College London in the Institute of Education – Curriculum, Pedagogy & Assessment. Stuart has worked for international awarding organisations for over twenty years and is particularly interested in demonstrating how educational, psychological and vocational tests seek to meet the demands of validity, reliability and fairness. He left Cambridge Assessment (now Cambridge University Press & Assessment) – where he was Head of International Research, in January 2001 to pursue work as an educational assessment consultant. Stuart has a wide range of publications in English second language assessment and educational/

psychological research journals (including a number of books). Stuart is Chair of the Board of Trustees of the Chartered Institute of Educational Assessors (CIEA). He is also a Fellow of the CIEA. He is a Fellow of the Association for Educational Assessment in Europe (AEA-Europe), an elected member of the Council of AEA-Europe, and is Chair of its Scientific Programme Committee. Stuart is also an elected member of the Board of Trustees of the International Association for Educational Assessment (IAEA) and Chair of its Communications Committee. He is also the Chair of the e-Assessment Association "Research" awards.

ACKNOWLEDGEMENTS

We are very grateful to the following people for comments on draft chapters:

Eleanor Andressen
Ben Colburn
James Conroy
Catarina F. Correia
Martin Johnson
Nick Hillman
Paul Newton
Elisa de Padua
Mick Walker
Lesley Wiseman

The content of the book has benefited from the comments of participants who attended the 2023 conferences of the Association of Educational Assessment, Europe, and the British Educational Research Association; and events held by the Chartered Institute of Educational Assessors; the Institute of Education, University College London; and Cambridge University Press & Assessment.

AUTHORS' PREFACE

This book has been prompted by our shared awareness of the need for the rather specialised world of educational assessment to look outside its familiar spheres of reference to changes in the world and in education and re-assess where it should go next. We came to this conclusion from different backgrounds – one from detailed participation in research on educational assessment in theory and practice; the other bringing an academic training in philosophy to a professional career in policy and regulation covering education and assessment in a wide range of contexts.

We had collaborated before, particularly on fairness in assessment (Nisbet & Shaw, 2020), and contributed to conferences and seminars for assessment researchers. During the Covid-19 pandemic, many of these events had to be held remotely, and this gave us the opportunity to participate in discussions in the USA, as well as in Europe and in the different constituent parts of the UK. We were particularly struck by the contrast between the preoccupations of conference delegates on the two sides of the Atlantic. Our US colleagues used their coffee breaks and plenary discussions to talk animatedly about difficult and controversial issues – notably race – which dominated their perception of the context in which they had to work. Some of them were very worried by the bitterness of the public debate around areas of their work and about the use being made of the assessments that they had helped to produce. In European events, there was certainly the feel of a community of practice meeting each other and producing – and critiquing – high-quality detailed work. There was an awareness of the national policy contexts in which they practised, but not the same preoccupation with challenges from the world beyond assessment.

We came increasingly to the view that, as we approach the end of the first quarter of the 21st century, it is time to stand back and survey educational assessment in context. That context includes developments in society and education, as well as developments in *thinking* about society and education. We have attempted to cast our net widely and bring together source material from different disciplines and very different subject matter. Synthesising such a wide range of material can be uncomfortable for assessment researchers used to detailed analytic work, but it reflects the intertwining of different factors in the real world where assessment is situated.

The wide scope of the material that we have sought to include in our synthesis has made this project very challenging for us. It also means that we have had to be selective. Some readers may find that issues of particular interest to them have not been covered. But we hope that the questions we have asked and the approach we have taken will be relevant and helpful. We are also limited in that almost all of the source material we have used has been in the English language.

We hope that this book will be of interest not only to assessment researchers and academics but also to newcomers to work in educational assessment, to policymakers and to workers in government and regulation affecting educational assessment. We also hope that students who are seeking to deepen their understanding of assessment in context will use the many references that we have provided to follow up topics of particular interest to them.

We have expressed our own views throughout the book, particularly in the final chapter. We expect that some readers will disagree with us. Indeed, we would be disappointed if that were not so. For us, the importance of this exercise is to use its wide scope to raise important questions for assessment as we move into the second quarter of the century. Twenty-five years later, it will be time to take stock again.

Isabel Nisbet and Stuart Shaw
May 2024

Reference

Nisbet, I., & Shaw, S. D. (2020). *Is assessment fair?* SAGE Publications Ltd.

FOREWORD

History, it might be argued, is about considering both change and continuity within the scope of human existence. Reflecting on who we are, how we live and, in the case of this book, how we are educated, matters if we are to understand and learn from what has been and to consider what might be in the future. Research and writing about educational assessment might seem, to a casual bystander, to have little relevance to daily life once we have left formal education. However, that is not the case. Assessment is crucial in terms of understanding what we know, reflecting on experience and, perhaps most importantly, applying these things to our lives.

The history of assessment demonstrates that very little actually changes in terms of either policy or practice. We tend to privilege and trust certain types of assessment, notably those resulting in a grade or mark from an examination result. Such forms of assessment are not bad or wrong, but they have limitations that are often ignored. However, their use continues despite the body of evidence emerging from research from the latter part of the 20th century onwards, advocating new ways of assessing learning that are inclusive, focused *on* learning and which drive student motivation in more ways than simply chasing the highest grade. But the question remains: Is there an appetite for any change, for other ways of thinking about assessing learning?

What this book does is to engage with key issues that are not, on first sight, obviously linked to assessment and deftly interrogate how and why they *should* matter to all of us in education. The authors admit to the somewhat daunting challenge of such a task and, in doing so, provide a sound argument for seeking more than technical "solutions" for how to manage the challenges in assessment. Their approach is not to ignore pragmatic resolutions but to use deep thinking, genuine reflection, and a range of examples to interrogate the breadth and reach of assessment issues we currently face.

Assessment is a frequent feature in global news media, and this reflects a sustained public interest where grades and other assessment outcomes claim to characterise the success (or otherwise) of education systems. The Covid-19 pandemic revealed the limitations of national testing systems based on ancient and embedded beliefs that require students to sit in examination halls for finite periods of time in order to "show their learning". For example, in England, Norway and the Netherlands, examinations were cancelled completely during the height of the pandemic; in China, Hong Kong and Spain, national tests were postponed; and in the USA, entire test systems were rewritten at speed to create something that worked in a socially distanced world. Alongside these cancellations were hasty enactments of assessments that relied on incomplete sets of data and school-level reporting. What followed from this was a global wringing of hands about whether national test results (and similar assessments) were fair or even accurate. This in turn revealed anger and fear on the part of students who felt their very futures were in peril. The fallout from the pandemic is unknown in terms of its impact on education and it will be perhaps decades before we have anything approximating a good understanding of what has unfolded as a result of school closures, lost learning and, in the case of assessment, lost experience of test taking. But what we have learned is that students are taught from a young age that assessment outcomes, particularly examination results, really matter and this message means that they become a part of a learner's identity. In turn, teachers know that assessment outcomes will reflect on their practice, both in the classroom and as leaders of educational institutions. What this book ponders is how it is time to consider the value of inculcating such beliefs in our education systems. It is very rare to see philosophical considerations of the moral and ethical implications of assessment and their inclusion here is to be welcomed. For many of us in the assessment "world", such writing may not make for comfortable reading, but it is *necessary* reading. Well-being is now a common part of public discourse, and here its links to education (and assessment) are laid bare, in terms not simply of the mental stress resulting from testing but of a global notion of well-being. This holistic view can be seen in terms of creating sustainable societies that are able to understand and manage the human and artificial challenges unfolding in the 21st century; education has a vital role to play if we wish to assure our future. There are no absolute solutions to the issues presented in this book, but this is not the point because the authors are not attempting to do this. Rather, they are shining a light on what has happened and presenting some thoughts about what might be.

Assessment requires an open mind to afford continuous engagement in reflective practice. It is this openness that allows us to spot the potential to learn from experience and perhaps to improve the human condition. This is not easy as it challenges that very human wish to take the well-trodden path, but we stop being curious and attempting to tackle the thorniest of problems in education at our peril and, importantly, at the peril of those who follow us. Many of the recent debates around education are highly polarised and critics often take the easy route and present just two sides to each story. This book presents ways we might move beyond a binary argument towards more nuanced ways of talking about education and assessment; let the debate begin.

Mary Richardson
Professor of Educational Assessment
IOE, Faculty of Education and Society,
University College London

1
INTRODUCTION

Some readers will remember the millennium. We certainly do. It prompted much reflection and looking forward. The western world celebrated half a century of comparative international peace and marvelled at the opportunities offered by worldwide travel and speedy communication. Participation in education had increased in most countries of the world, and this was seen as closely linked to economic prosperity and growth. There was an industry of writing about "21st century skills", with an emphasis on creative thinking, working together, and using the opportunities presented by technological advance.

There was a short-term panic about risks to computers from the "millennium bug" – the fear that computers that only registered the last two digits for dates would either treat the year 2000 as 1900 or, worse still, shut down altogether, with catastrophic consequences, not least for education. In the event, that fear – which was very real at the time – failed to materialise.

But more lasting concerns remained – about inequality between and within countries, about poverty and hunger, and about worrying signs of climate change. However, many shared the largely optimistic spirit of the millennium speech by the American President Bill Clinton:

> Never before have we known as much about each other. Never before have we depended so much on each other. Never before have we had such an opportunity to move toward what the generations have prayed for, peace on Earth and a better life for all. We must both imagine a brighter future and dedicate ourselves to building it, and I ask you all here today to reaffirm the clear understanding that we must do it together.[1]

DOI:10.4324/9781003346166-1

There was also reflection on where matters stood in the world of educational assessment. As the 20th century began to draw to a close, Professor Caroline Gipps wrote *Beyond Testing: Towards a Theory of Educational Assessment*, in which she reflected on developments in assessment during the 1990s. She examined technical issues about the effect of assessment on curriculum and teaching, the relationship between performance assessment and assessment by teachers, and she began the book with these words:

> This book is written as part of the attempt to reconceptualize assessment in education in the 1990s. There has been over the last decade an explosion of developments in assessment and a number of key actors have been reconceptualising the issues. The aim of this book is to bring together much of this work to discuss and synthesize it in an attempt to further our understandings and practice in educational assessment: to develop the theory of educational assessment.
>
> *(Gipps, 1994, p. 1)*

In our book, written some thirty years later, we are seeking to take up the baton offered by Gipps. We believe it is now time for a rethink about educational assessment, taking into account recent developments affecting assessment practice and developments in thinking about education and assessment, and looking forward towards the mid-21st century.

In this introductory chapter, we set out the approach taken by the book, and we briefly describe the content of the subsequent chapters. In conclusion, we offer a scene-setting account of some of the dominant themes in education and educational assessment at this time. These themes will be explored in greater depth throughout the book.

An introduction to the book

Our approach

The size of the challenge that we have taken up has required us to bring together a wide range of sources and academic disciplines – including, in addition to education and assessment, psychology, public policy, information technology, law, science and moral philosophy. Such synthesis is required, we suggest, as the issues we discuss are essentially interdisciplinary (requiring an integration of contributions from several disciplines),[2] as is the real world in which they are situated. However, it does have the drawback that, by necessity, we have had to be selective in the examples we discuss. Readers may have particular interests that are not covered. We hope that they will be encouraged to explore these further themselves and apply some of the questions we have posed here.

Both authors are based in England, though they have worked elsewhere. The book draws on examples from throughout the UK, but also from the USA and Europe. Our adoption of an interdisciplinary approach may be of particular interest in the USA, where academic thinking on assessment is now much more influenced by other academic disciplines than it was previously. The book also draws on publications by international organisations such as the Organisation for Economic Co-operation and Development (OECD) and the World Economic Forum (WEF). Almost all our source material is in the English language.

In Chapters 2–6, we explore developments and changes to thinking about education and assessment. Many of the examples we have cited merit much longer and more detailed discussion than has been possible for a book of this scope. Our purpose has been to rise above the details and draw lessons about the implications for assessment. However, we have offered references at the end of each of these chapters, which should enable readers to follow up in more detail particular issues that interest them. That has resulted in a contrast of styles between different parts of the book. Chapters 2 and 3 are grounded more in the literature, while Chapters 4, 5 and 6 emphasise more theoretical issues, examining developments in thinking about society and education and debating the issues that they raise.

Our use of terms

Definitions of concepts such as "education" and "assessment" could be discussed at length.[3] However, at this point, we confine ourselves to saying what we mean by those terms in this book. By "education" we refer to all processes that lead to learning or the acquisition of knowledge, skills or understanding. Our use of "processes" here may be seen as too narrow, but for our purposes it is sufficient to point out that we are not confining our consideration to formal education in schools or colleges (we are not using "education" as a synonym for "schooling").[4] We return to some of these definitional issues in Chapter 6.

We are using "assessment" to denote "a judgement based on evidence",[5] drawing on the Latin derivation from *ad sidere* ("sitting beside"). This allows selection judgements and diagnostic processes and conclusions to be included as forms of "assessment". By "educational assessment" we mean all such evidence-based judgements in educational contexts.[6] "Assessment", as the term is used in this book, is not confined to "exams" or "tests" but does not exclude either.

Structure of the book

Each of Chapters 2–6 describes and discusses developments and concludes by posing and attempting to answer the question "What does this (the development discussed in the chapter) mean for assessment?" Emerging conclusions are brought together in the final chapter. The assessments discussed in the book are largely educational assessments. However, many of the issues discussed are also relevant to assessment for entry to – and advancement in – employment and the professions, although we do not discuss these applications in depth.

Chapter 2 ("Developments in education and assessment") offers an overview of important educational reviews and educational assessment initiatives taking place around the turn of the 21st century. In the latter decades of the 20th century, many countries sought to articulate the educational needs of the next generation, described by the US National Commission on Excellence in Education as a "Learning Society" (NCEE, 1983). There followed an overabundance of lists of "21st century skills" – the competences, skills and learning dispositions identified as being required for success in 21st-century society and workplaces, with linked guidance on curriculum and assessment (e.g. Trilling & Fadel, 2009). The chapter also describes a developing focus on what it means to be "competent" in modern-day society (European Commission Education & Culture, 2007; Vitello et al., 2021), and the implications for the curriculum – and related assessment – in formal education. Finally, Chapter 2 refers to developments in technology, including digital data systems, "deep" and transformative technologies, computational intelligences and smart automation, concluding with a discussion of the impact of generative artificial intelligence (AI).

In Chapter 3 ("New priorities and an unexpected shock"), the two priorities that we identify and discuss in detail are climate change and well-being. The "unexpected shock" is the Covid-19 pandemic. The "new priorities" are not new developments, but the priority now given to them is a highlight of the first quarter of the 21st century. Climate change has very quickly aggravated environmental and social concerns (in both developed and developing countries), as well as directly and indirectly affecting all organisations, institutions and areas of life during the early part of the 21st century. And the two "new priorities" are linked by the reported increase in anxiety and stress about the future of the planet. Questions about the implications for educational assessment are raised and discussed in the chapter. Well-being and mental health, including that of young people, are increasingly seen as important objectives of education and offer a template to hold against educational assessment: Does assessment focus on the right things and do its practices and institutions promote well-being?

Covid-19 was undoubtedly a shock, though many governments had prepared for such an eventuality to some extent. We are only beginning to understand the impact of Covid-19 on teaching, learning and the content and practicalities of educational assessment. What is clear is that the pandemic has created a fissure in long-term thinking about education and assessment:

it is not possible to chart continuous straight-line development through the first quarter of the century.

Chapter 4 ("Changes to thinking about society") seeks to identify trends in thinking about society and public policy that have come to the forefront in the 21st century and that are particularly important for education and assessment. Views about the purpose and content of education are at the heart of debates about society and values and arguably have become more contested and divisive (Putnam & Garrett, 2020). "Culture wars" have been reflected in conflicting views about assessment and the use of assessment for selection. This has played out most notably in the United States (Campbell & Manning, 2018) but has reverberations in Europe, and perhaps particularly in England. The chapter considers the theoretical challenges presented by critical theory – and, in particular, by Critical Race Theory – and then presents two case studies: the debate in the USA about whether the law should allow race-conscious college admissions policies; and the agenda for "decolonising" the university curriculum in the UK. All these theoretical developments have implications for assessment – for what is assessed and how, and how the outcomes are used.

Chapter 5 ("Changes to thinking about education and assessment") identifies and discusses strands of thinking about education and educational assessment that are particularly powerful or important at this point in the 21st century. These include trends in thinking about the purposes of education, challenges to any consensus on constructivist views of learning and a revival of support for "knowledge". We consider the theoretical issues raised by the increased focus on "competence" as an aim of education and a construct for assessment. We also consider the challenges posed to the conceptualisation of education and assessment by the availability of "big data" and the seismic impact of generative AI.

Chapter 6 ("The moral compass") seeks to analyse moral questions about assessment in educational contexts. It starts with a brief account of the domain of "morality" and proceeds to address key, fundamental, questions: What is the moral justification for educational assessment? What moral challenges can be made to educational assessment, and are they persuasive? And what moral principles should govern practice in educational assessment?

In Chapter 7, we draw together lessons learned from the previous chapters and offer conclusions about the path ahead for assessment theory and practice. We indicate areas in which further work will be required. We give examples of what needs to be done, but we do not complete the tasks. For example, we argue that a reconceptualisation of the theoretical "assessment argument" is required, and we say why that is so, but it will be for others to follow our lead and complete the development of a new model argument. And throughout the book – and particularly in the final chapter – we express our own views. Readers may disagree with them, but our main aim is to invite readers to address the questions we have posed and decide what their own view is.

Before proceeding to give an introductory overview of these discussions, we would like to mention three examples of areas of assessment that we have not had space to discuss in detail in this book, but which we hope will continue to be taken up by others in the years ahead. The first is the role of assessment in the development of infants and very young children. There are two overlapping reasons why assessment in the early years is important. The first is to provide information as early as possible about children who are not progressing as might be hoped/expected in areas identified as important for their development. Common sense and research (e.g. Research in Practice, 2022; OECD, 2018) concur in advocating supportive early intervention. The second reason is that assessment in the early years can look forward to formal education (preschool, school and beyond) and can denote aspects of learning, health and well-being which most accurately predict future educational achievement. Information from longitudinal sample surveys is typically used for this purpose. With increasing recognition of the importance of motivation to learn and its interrelationship with mental health and well-being, the two purposes increasingly intersect.

The second area of assessment that deserves wider study than has been possible in this book is its role in relation to the education of learners with special educational needs and disabilities (SEND). The numbers of children and young people of school age who have been categorised by governments as having SEND can fluctuate because of definitions or changes in government policy, but in many countries, the trend in the 2020s has been steeply upwards,[7] with the highest numbers diagnosed as having autism, followed by speech and language difficulties (e.g. Lindsay et al., 2016). The questions raised for assessment are at least twofold: How can and should incidences of SEND be assessed? And how can educational assessments be made more equitable and accessible for learners with SEND?

A third area, which we mention here but do not cover in detail elsewhere, is the link between assessment and eugenics. Early eugenics, in the 1900s and before, sought to study ways in which the physical and mental characteristics of the human race might be improved. The most troublesome link with assessment was the use of testing to identify people with "inferior" genes (as evidenced, e.g., by their IQ test scores), with consequences including national measures to prevent or discourage them from having children. The horrendous implementation by Nazi Germany in the 1930s and 1940s of practices based on eugenic ideology is well documented. At this time in the 21st century, attention focuses mainly on the elimination of genetic disease. However, two questions remain pertinent for assessment: Is there any defensible and unbiased form of assessment that can be used to identify inherited attributes, knowledge, or skills? And second, should qualifications or evidence from assessments of levels of education achieved ever be used as a criterion for steering priorities in national (or international) policies on encouraging or discouraging childbearing? As late as 1986, Singapore guaranteed pay increases to female graduates when they gave birth to a child, while offering grants towards house purchases for non-graduate married women on condition that they were sterilised after the first or second child. In China, in June 1995, a law was passed making it illegal for carriers of certain genetic diseases to marry unless they agreed to sterilisation or long-term contraception. All couples who wished to marry had to undergo genetic screening. Although readers may easily conclude that such examples are not relevant to future decades in the 21st century, they do bring into focus difficult questions about the use of educational outcomes for social policy and the possibility of unbiased, standardised testing.

Why did we not cover these important issues – or others that readers may identify – in detail? The main reason is space and the need to be selective, given the wide sweep of the survey of issues in this book. However, we also consider that the issues that we have selected have wide relevance, beyond the context in which they first arose, for the world of assessment. For example, many of the theoretical issues about assessment discussed in Chapter 7 are as relevant to early years as to the assessment of older learners.

The remainder of this introductory chapter seeks to bring together some key features of our account of education and educational assessment at this time.

Setting the scene

Changing worlds, shifting horizons

The opening quarter of the new century has been defined by iconic moments and groundbreaking developments, all of which had varying impacts on education and assessment. The list includes a proliferation of wars: the US invasion of Iraq and the long-term impact on the Middle East; ongoing civil wars in Syria, Libya and Yemen; the Russian invasion of Ukraine; genocide in Congo and Darfur; the "Arab Spring" – a series of uprisings and protests against Arab governments; deepening concern over the rise of Islamic extremism following the 9/11 terrorist attacks on the USA; and conflict in Israel and Palestine. Economically, 2008 saw the worst global recession since the Great Depression in the 1930s; the rise of a global economy and Third World consumerism; the growth of international migration; and the acceleration of the global shift from working in agriculture to living in cities.

Developments in communications included the growth of online social media and networking services such as YouTube and Facebook; the launch of the first Android smartphone; the emergence of Global Positioning Systems;

and increasingly faster cellular technologies like the internet. The United States elected its first African American President; the UK departed from the European Union; and culturally many countries saw rises in nationalism, in contrast to the internationalism of communications available, and increasingly polarised differences of view ("culture wars"). And all of these developments are over and above those we have selected for more detailed discussion in Chapter 3, such as Covid-19 and the rapid increase in evidence – and awareness – of the threats posed by climate change.

Shifting horizons have been a prevailing feature dominating the first quarter of the 21st century: shifts in technology, resources, migration and demographics – from leveraging assets to accessing ecosystems; from the knowledge economy to the collaboration economy; and shifts in power from corporations to technology platforms.

As the 21st century began to unfurl, it was becoming increasingly evident that technological "connectedness" was not only beginning to pave the way for transformative changes in the way society and individuals functioned but also starting to disrupt almost every area of life. At the time of writing, generative AI is the world's fastest-growing "deep" technology,[8] and is demonstrating enormous potential to reform the rules of industries and organisations; drive significant economic growth; and transform all sectors of life, including education (HM Government, 2021).

In these changing contexts, educational assessment has itself been changing (e.g. Pellegrino, 1999; Bennett, 2002). A backcloth of growing diversity, increased migration, globalisation, the emergence of new players in the world economy and the explosion of information technology has meant that citizens of most countries need to upgrade their skills throughout their adult lives in order to keep abreast of changes in the requirements of modern living, both in the workplace and in their personal lives. "Lifelong learning"[9] has become the new mantra for all citizens in the modern world.

Education is expected to prepare learners for a fast-changing world in which technological, demographic, social, environmental, economic and political transformation are proving to be seismic. Assessment is increasingly expected to take account of the need to support all the developments described here, including increased participation in schooling and in university education (particularly in preparation for the increase in careers requiring a degree); "credentialism" (increased demand for formal qualifications); and the need for so-called 21st century-competencies (OECD, 2018).

Setbacks and unresolved issues

The early years of the 21st century saw a plethora of visionary initiatives, strategies, mandates and reform movements that set out key educational goals to be fulfilled by specific deadlines (see, e.g. UNESCO, 2000; World

Education Report, 2000; World Education Forum, 2015). However, a mere 15 years after 164 countries agreed to work towards "Education for All", the six goals set at the turn of the century were achieved by only one-third of them, and only half made universal primary education a reality.

The United Nations 2030 Agenda for Sustainable Development included a Fourth Sustainable Development Goal, which was to "Ensure inclusive and equitable quality education and promote lifelong learning opportunities for all" (United Nations, 2015, p. 18). Growing importance was placed on "lifelong learning", which had been championed in the latter decades of the 20th century. Lifelong learning not only seeks to enhance social inclusion, active citizenship and personal development but serves as a catalyst for competitiveness and employability. However, according to the OECD (Bollington, 2015), actual implementation of related policies was falling behind quite quickly, with some sources suggesting that adult participation beyond formal school years was low and has remained low (Smith et al., 2019; UNESCO, 2019).

Nevertheless, the importance of learning for the welfare of the nation and its citizens beyond formal schooling has continued to be thought to be crucial in fostering a learning culture fit for the 21st century. Empowering learners with "new" skills and competencies constituted a nation's human capital, upon which the 21st-century economy and society were seen to depend. Though not a new concept, the "learning society" (an educational philosophy backed by the OECD and UNESCO) increased in recognition and popularity with the proposal that lifelong learning is a condition for global economic competitiveness (superseding the former conception of it being a condition for democratic citizenship). However, there were important challenges to making lifelong learning for all a reality, not least of which was equitable access to learning.[10]

The "21st century skills" were thought to be essential for success in 21st-century society and workplaces. Lists of these skills were shared across the world, and education was seen as linked to growing internationalism across countries and multiculturalism within countries (European Commission, 2019). In reality, the skills learners needed for the 21st century were neither new nor qualitatively different from those required in previous times.[11] What was different, however, was the degree to which national and individual economic success was seen as reliant on the acquisition of such skills – even though there was never agreement on precisely what the skills were.

The ubiquity of increasingly advanced technology promised novel opportunities for teaching, learning and assessment. Voices throughout education made ambitious claims about the extent of change that technology would drive in education and the speed with which it would take place (Boston, 2005). In the world of educational assessment, technology was seen as opening doors to many new opportunities and promising much in terms of informed interventions, practice and policy. It seemed inevitable that technology would "force fundamental changes in the format and content of assessment" (Bennett, 2002, p. 2; Boston, 2007). However, in 2016, the OECD reported that the influence of digital technologies on educational assessment appeared "shallow" (OECD, 2016, p. 3)[12] and in many countries there continued to be a nervous reluctance to use digital technologies in high-stakes national examinations. Now, more than two decades into a new century, we see that while the availability of digital-based learning and assessments continues to expand, we are still on the journey towards being able to assert definitively that "we are making appropriate use of good technology" (Richardson & Clesham, 2021, p. 5).

As key assessment educators and organisations were increasingly coming to accept the inevitable union of assessment and technology, they were also becoming more aware of the ethical considerations that the development and implementation of technology-enhanced assessment practice would create.[13] Ethical issues were varied and far-reaching:

- Would technology-enhanced assessment lead to new social and educational divides?
- What would be the dangers relating to the collection, use and protection of huge personalised data sets and the ownership and control of information? Could – or should – assessment providers take steps to mitigate these dangers?
- To what extent could digital technologies support fairer assessment methods and greater involvement of learners in their own assessment?

Ethical concerns touched upon emotive issues: social exclusion, trust, individual autonomy, new forms of digital dividedness[14] and privacy as well as the increasing risks associated with "big" data and the rise of learning analytics.[15] We discuss this in more detail in Chapter 5.

The impact of advances in the cognitive sciences on educational assessment had already been a cause of some optimism in the second half of the 20th century. It was predicted that the potential of cognitive psychology would be "fully realized through item design" (Embretson & Gorin, 2001, p. 343). Aspects of cognitive psychology appeared particularly well-suited to psychometric traditions of theory and practice, where measurement and cognitive issues intersected. Any means of observing test-taker behaviours and the mental processes they employed in responding to and solving test questions were perceived as fundamental to construct validity (Snow & Lohman, 1989; Messick, 1995, p. 742; Knight & Silverstein, 2001).

Throughout the first decade of the new century, there was growing demand to make assessments more transparent about the cognitive processes they sought to measure (US. Department of Education, 2004). It was evident, for example, that the competencies required for "mathematisation" (OECD, 2004, p. 40) encompassed a number of cognitive activities and demands elicited in assessments for the OECD's Programme for International Student Assessment (PISA) in 2003.

Over the last thirty years, cognitive diagnosis has been increasingly influential in a range of educational contexts to measure and advance individual development. The question of how psychological constructs such as cognition and personality can be optimally related to observable behaviour was seen as central to psychometric measurement, particularly in the USA. Research was also beginning to focus more on theories of learning and their relationship with educational assessments (see, e.g. Baird et al., 2014).

Alongside cognitive psychology, the application of neuroscience to education was also gaining traction, helped by the emergence of innovative imaging technologies (Goswami, 2006). Neuroscience and the psychology of learning were demonstrating their potential relevance, legitimacy and possibilities when applied to educational assessment (Dhawan, 2014).

In the latter stages of the 20th century, talk of "assessment for learning" (AfL), as opposed to "assessment *of* learning", became prominent in discussion of educational assessment in many countries, with many at the time championing AfL as one of the most promising approaches for initiating improvement in student learning. In their highly acclaimed review of classroom assessment practices, Black and Wiliam (1998) suggested that increased adoption of and engagement with formative assessment approaches would lead to noteworthy improvements in standards of attainment and achievement. However, they also expressed uneasiness that progress had been slow-moving, primarily owing to the amount of effort afforded to the various developments of summative assessments. In England, the "Assessment Reform Group" (1989–2010) played a key role over the turn of the century in making the case that policy on educational assessment should take more account of relevant research findings. However, there were ideological and policy differences about education and the place of assessment in it, and the competing views had their academic champions.

In addition to conceptual confusions and definitional ambiguities, practical barriers to the integration and implementation of AfL classroom practices were beginning to be reported in the early research literature, even causing some to question the legitimacy of treating AfL as a type of "assessment" at all (e.g. Swaffield, 2009; Bennett, 2011; Didau, 2014; Fletcher-Wood, 2017; Brown, 2019). It was clear, at the turn of the century, that formative assessment was not well understood by teachers and was weak in practice.

Other theoretical disputes arose during this period. One in particular related to the scope of validity – a controversy that had been simmering since the late 1980s. In 1989, Samuel Messick's conceptualisation of validity widened the compass of validity inquiry by including social and value-laden aspects

12 Introduction

of assessments. He effectively extended traditional measurement boundaries into issues relating to policy – what Kane (2001) has termed the prescriptive part of a validity argument. However, almost immediately following the publication of Messick's (1989) seminal treatise on validity, his progressive matrix[16] (based on a foundation of construct validity) was subject to intense scrutiny and criticism (see, e.g. Shepard, 1993, 1997).

Although Messick's conception of validity provided the basis for what became a broad professional consensus over core validity concepts within the mainstream educational and psychological assessment community (AERA et al., 2014), discontent with Messick's approach has continued to be voiced. A new wave of validity theorists has decried the "absurdities of construct validity theory" (Borsboom et al., 2009, p. 135), rejected what they perceive as complicated validity frameworks, and contended that construct validity is unable to restrict the type and extent of test score interpretations to be considered.

What Newton and Baird (2016) have called "The Great Validity Debate" has continued over the years we are reviewing. Broadly, a major issue has been whether or not social consequences should be defined as an integral part of a definition of validity, with a "for" camp embracing the evaluation of social consequences (e.g. Linn, 1997; Shepard, 1997), and an "against" camp rejecting it (e.g. Mehrens, 1997; Popham, 1997). The debate continues.[17] In Chapter 7, we advocate a future direction for thinking about assessment, which has implications for validity as well as for the theoretical model for the "assessment argument".

. . . .

In this introductory chapter, we have outlined the approach and structure of the book and set the scene by describing and briefly discussing some of the main issues in educational assessment as we approach the second quarter of the 21st century. Our aim is to bring together disparate trends and intellectual disciplines, to identify and ask questions about them for educational assessment, and, we hope, to provide a reference point for similar reviews in the future. We hope that readers – whether policymakers, assessment practitioners or researchers – will be stimulated to follow up some of the issues we raise and develop their own ideas as assessment moves forward.

Notes

1 Bill Clinton at the "Millennium Around the World" Celebration, 2000 www.presidency.ucsb.edu/documents/remarks-the-millennium-around-the-world-celebration
2 See Manolakelli (2022) – Inter, Multi, Cross, Trans, & Intra-disciplinary: What is the difference, and why is it important? www.archpsych.co.uk/post/disciplinarities-definitions
3 As, for example, by R.S. Peters in the first chapter of his *Ethics and Education* (1966). Aspects of Peters's account were disputed then and remain so.

4 See Johnson and Majewska (2022) for a review of the literature outlining the characteristics, benefits and disadvantages of formal, non-formal and informal learning.
5 We have discussed this definition at greater length in Nisbet and Shaw (2020, pp. 7–10).
6 Mary James defines educational assessment as "all those activities that involve eliciting evidence of student learning and drawing inferences as the basis for decisions" (James, 2010, p. 163).
7 For a discussion of trends in the UK, including among young children, see www.educationalneuroscience.org.uk/2022/04/01/why-has-there-been-a-rise-in-number-of-sen-children-especially-in-the-early-years/
8 "Deep" technologies are grounded in important scientific advances and engineering innovations but which require a longer period of gestation and/or extensive capital investment prior to commercial application. Transformative technologies are technologies that have the potential to impact across many sectors of the economy (as opposed to a single sector).
9 "Lifelong learning" was a term coined by Leslie Watkins and popularised by Professor Clint Taylor of City Unified School in 1993. While not a new concept, it is one that has assumed a greater and new emphasis in the 21st century.
10 See the United Nations 2030 Agenda for Sustainable Development Goals – Goal 4: "Ensure inclusive and equitable quality education and promote lifelong learning opportunities for all". https://sdgs.un.org/goals
11 There also exists an ongoing tension in assessment around the conceptualisation of 21st century skills, that is, how knowledge is embedded in competence and how this can be recognised.
12 OECD (2016) was a background report to the second Global Education Industry Summit, held in Jerusalem on 26–27 September 2016, and covered the available evidence on innovation in education, the impact of digital technologies on teaching and learning, and the role of digital skills and the education industries in the process of innovation, using data from OECD surveys.
13 See, for example, Lowman (2013) for a discussion of the use of unproctored or proctored internet testing, p. 107.
14 See Coleman (2021) for a discussion of the digital divide in the UK post-pandemic.
15 See Timmis et al. (2016) for a discussion of the potential, the challenges, and the risks associated with technology-enhanced assessment.
16 Introduced to illustrate how the evaluation of scientific and ethical questions could be integrated within a common validity framework.
17 Chronicled by Newton and Shaw (2014).

References

American Educational Research Association, American Psychological Association, and National Council on Measurement in Education. (2014). *Standards for educational and psychological testing*. American Educational Research Association.

Baird, J. A., Hopfenbeck, T. N., Newton, P. E., Stobart, G., & Steen-Utheim, A. T. (2014). State of the field review: Assessment and learning. *Oxford University Centre for Educational Assessment Report OUCEA/14/2*. Norwegian Knowledge Centre for Education (case number 13/4697).

Bennett, R. E. (2002). Inexorable and inevitable: The continuing story of technology and assessment. *Journal of Technology, Learning, and Assessment*, 1(1). www.jtla.org

Bennett, R. E. (2011). Formative assessment: A critical review. *Assessment in Education: Principles, Policy & Practice*, 18(1), 5–25. https://doi.org/10.1080/0969594X.2010.513678

Black, P., & Wiliam, D. (1998). Assessment and classroom learning. *Assessment in Education: Principles, Policy & Practice*, 5(1), 7–74.

Bollington, A. (2015). *Business brief: Why isn't everyone lifelong learning?* OECD Yearbook. www.oecd.org/education/lifelong-learning.ht

Borsboom, D., Cramer, A. O. J., Kievit, R. A., Zand Scholten, A., & Franić, S. (2009). The end of construct validity. In R. W. Lissitz (Ed.), *The concept of validity. Revisions, new directions, and applications* (pp. 135–170). Information Age Publishing.

Boston, K. (2005). Assessment, reporting and technology: System-wide assessment and reporting in the 21st century. In *Tenth Annual Roundtable Conference: Strategy, Technology and Assessment*. Qualifications and Curriculum Authority.

Boston, K. (2007, September 25). Ken Boston: Big brother is testing you. *The Guardian*. Higher Education Profile. Higher Education. www.theguardian.com/education/2007/sep/25/highereducation.schools

Brown, G. T. L. (2019). Is assessment for learning really assessment? *Frontiers in Education*, 4, Article 64. http://doi.org/10.3389/feduc.2019.00064

Campbell, B., & Manning, J. (2018). *The rise of victimhood culture*. Palgrave Macmillan.

Coleman, V. (2021). Digital divide in UK education during COVID-19 pandemic: Literature review. *Cambridge Assessment Research Report*. Cambridge Assessment.

Dhawan, V. (2014). Education and neuroscience. *Research Matters: A Cambridge Assessment Publication*, 17, 46–55.

Didau, D. (2014, March 12). Why AFL might be wrong, and what to do about it. *David Didau Website*. https://learningspy.co.uk/myths/afl-might-wrong/

Embretson, S., & Gorin, J. (2001). Improving construct validity with cognitive psychology principles. *Journal of Educational Measurement*, 38(4), 343–368. https://doi.org/10.1111/j.1745-3984.2001.tb01131.x

European Commission. (2019). *Key competences for lifelong learning*. European Union.

European Commission Education & Culture. (2007). *Key competencies for lifelong learning – A European framework*. European Communities. https://op.europa.eu/en/publication-detail/-/publication/5719a044-b659-46de-b58b-606bc5b084c1

Fletcher-Wood, H. (2017, March 26). Is formative assessment fatally flawed? Confusing learning & performance. *Improving Teaching*. https://improvingteaching.co.uk/2017/03/26/formative-assessment-flawed-confusing-learning-performace

Gipps, C. C. (1994). *Beyond testing: Towards a theory of educational assessment*. The Falmer Press.

Goswami, U. (2006). Neuroscience and education: From research to practice? *National Review of Neuroscience*, 7(5), 406–411.

HM Government. (2021, September). *National AI strategy*. Presented to Parliament by the Secretary of State for Digital, Culture, Media and Sport by Command of Her Majesty. Command Paper 525. Published by the Office for Artificial Intelligence. ISBN 978-1-5286-2894-5.

James, M. (2010). Educational assessment: Overview. In P. Peterson, E. Baker & B. McGaw (Eds.), *International encyclopaedia of education* (3rd ed., Vol. 3, pp. 161–171). Elsevier. www.sciencedirect.com/science/article/pii/B9780080448947017139

Johnson, M., & Majewska, D. (2022). Formal, non-formal, and informal learning: What are they, and how can we research them? *Cambridge University Press & Assessment Research Report*. www.cambridgeassessment.org.uk/Images/665425-formal-non-formal-and-informal-learning-what-are-they-and-how-can-we-research-them-.pdf

Kane, M. T. (2001). Current concerns in validity theory. *Journal of Educational Measurement*, 38(4), 319–342.

Knight, R. A., & Silverstein, S. M. (2001). A process-oriented approach for averting confounds resulting from general performance deficiencies in schizophrenia. *Journal of Abnormal Psychology*, 110(1), 15–30. https://doi.org/10.1037/0021-843X.110.1.15

Lindsay, G., Ricketts, J., Peacey, L. V., Dockrell, J. E., & Charman, T. (2016). Meeting the educational and social needs of children with language impairment or autism spectrum disorder: The parents' perspectives. *International Journal of Language & Communication Disorders, 51*(5), 495–507. http://doi.org/10.1111/1460-6984.12226

Linn, R. L. (1997). Evaluating the validity of assessments: The consequences of use. *Educational Measurement: Issues and Practice, 16*(2), 14–16.

Lowman, R. (2013). Ethical issues related to personnel assessment and selection. Chapter 6. In *New directions in assessing performance potential of individuals and groups: Workshop summary*. National Academies of Sciences, Engineering, and Medicine (pp. 101–107). The National Academies Press. https://doi.org/10.17226/18427

Manolakelli, A. (2022, September 5). Inter, multi, cross, trans, & intra-disciplinary: What is the difference and why is it important? *ArchPsych*. www.archpsych.co.uk/post/disciplinarities-definitions

Mehrens, W. A. (1997). The consequences of consequential validity. *Educational Measurement: Issues and Practice, 16*(2), 16–18.

Messick, S. (1989). Validity. In R. Linn (Ed.), *Educational measurement* (3rd ed., pp. 13–100). American Council on Education.

Messick, S. (1995). Validity of psychological assessment: Validation of inferences from persons' responses and performances as scientific inquiry into score meaning. *American Psychologist, 50*(9), 741–749. https://doi.org/10.1037/0003-066X.50.9.741

NCEE. (1983). *National Commission on Excellence in Education (NCEE) A nation at risk: The imperative for educational reform*. NCEE.

Newton, P. E., & Baird, J.-A. (2016). Editorial: The great validity debate. *Assessment in Education: Principles, Policy & Practice, 23*(2), 173–177. https://doi.org/10.1080/0969594X.2016.1172871

Newton, P. E., & Shaw, S. D. (2014). *Validity in educational & psychological assessment*. SAGE Publications Ltd. https://doi.org/10.4135/9781446288856

Nisbet, I., & Shaw, S. D. (2020). *Is assessment fair?* SAGE Publications Ltd.

OECD. (2004). *Learning for tomorrow's world: First results from PISA 2003*. OECD.

OECD. (2016). *Innovating education and educating for innovation: The power of digital technologies and skills*. OECD Publishing. http://doi.org/10.1787/9789264265097-en

OECD. (2018). *The future of education and skills: Education 2030*. www.oecd.org/education/2030-project

Pellegrino, J. W. (1999). *The evolution of educational assessment: Considering the past and imagining the future* (William H. Angoff Memorial Lecture Service, Ed.). The Educational Testing Service.

Peters, R. S. (1966). *Ethics and education*. George Allen and Unwin.

Popham, W. J. (1997). Consequential validity: Right concern-wrong concept. *Educational Measurement: Issues and Practice, 16*(2), 9–13.

Putnam, R. D., & Garrett, S. R. (2020). *The Upswing: How we came together a century ago and how we can do it again*. Swift Press.

Research in Practice (RiP). (2022). *What is early help?: Concepts, policy directions and multi-agency perspectives*. Ofsted.

Richardson, M., & Clesham, R. (2021). Rise of the machines? The evolving role of AI technologies in high-stakes assessment. *London Review of Education, 19*(1), 9, 1–13. https://doi.org/10.14324/LRE.19.1.09

Shepard, L. A. (1993). Evaluating test validity. *Review of Research in Education, 19*, 405–450.

Shepard, L. A. (1997). The centrality of test use and consequences for test validity. *Educational Measurement: Issues and Practice, 16*(5–8), 13.

Smith, R., Egglestone, C., Jones, E., & Aldridge, F. (2019, December). *Adult participation in learning survey 2019*. Learning & Work Institute. https://

learningandwork.org.uk/wp-content/uploads/2020/04/Adult-Participation-in-Learning-Survey-2019.pdf

Snow, R. E., & Lohman, D. F. (1989). Implications of cognitive psychology for educational measurement. In R. L. Linn (Ed.), *Educational measurement* (pp. 263–331). Macmillan Publishing Co, Inc; American Council on Education.

Swaffield, S. (2009). The misrepresentation of Assessment for Learning – and the woeful waste of a wonderful opportunity [Online]. In *AAIA national conference, Bournemouth, 16–18 September 2009*. Retrieved August 29, 2018, from www.aaia.org.uk/content/uploads/2010/07/The-Misrepresentation-of-Assessment-for-Learning.pdf

Timmis, S., Broadfoot, P., Sutherland, R., & Oldfield, A. (2016). Rethinking assessment in a digital age: Opportunities, challenges and risks. *British Educational Research Journal*, 42(3), 454–476.

Trilling, B., & Fadel, C. (2009). *21st century skills – Learning for life in our times*. Jossey-Bass.

UNESCO. (2000). The right to education: Towards education for all throughout life. *World education report 2000*. United Nations (UNESCO Publishing). https://unesdoc.unesco.org/ark:/48223/pf0000119720

UNESCO. (2019). 4th global report on adult learning and education. *Leave no one behind: Participation, equity and inclusion*. UNESCO Institute for Lifelong Learning. https://uil.unesco.org/system/files/grale_4_final.pdf

United Nations. (2015). Transforming our world. *The 2030 agenda for sustainable development* [Online]. UN. https://sustainabledevelopment.un.org/post2015/transformingourworld

U.S. Department of Education, National Center for Education Statistics. (2004). *Stronger accountability: Testing for results: Helping families, schools, and communities understand and improve student achievement*. www.ed.gov/nclb/accountability/ayp/testingforresults.html

Vitello, S., Greatorex, J., & Shaw, S. D. (2021). *What is competence? A shared interpretation of competence to support teaching, learning and assessment*. Cambridge University Press & Assessment.

World Education Forum. (2015). *New vision for education: Unlocking the potential of technology*. www3.weforum.org/docs/WEFUSA_NewVisionforEducation_Report2015.pdf

World Education Report. (2000). *The right to education: Towards education for all throughout life*. UNESCO Publishing.

2
DEVELOPMENTS IN EDUCATION AND ASSESSMENT

Introduction

In this chapter and the next, we set out some of the key developments affecting education and assessment, both as seen at the turn of the century and as experienced in the first quarter of the new century. Our focus in these two chapters is on developments in policies, practices and events. Chapters 4 and 5, which follow, are more theoretical, discussing developments in *thinking* about society and education – and assessment. But whether we are considering events or theories, we shall periodically seek to draw out the implications for educational assessment. Here in Chapter 2, we offer an overview of key developments in education and assessment, concluding with a section on the impact of generative AI.

Before embarking on an overview of developments in policies and practice, a number of caveats should be mentioned. First, we have had to be selective and group the developments we are discussing under key headings that we think are important. We may have omitted important developments, particularly if they are recorded in languages other than English. Second, we have had to strike a balance in the amount of detail we give about particular developments. We hope that the references we have provided will help readers to explore further if they wish. And third, the time-periods that we allocate to some of these developments are only approximate. Many developments that became important in recent years had their roots in the 20th century or earlier. For example, the much-discussed "21st century skills" were by no means invented around the year 2000, as readers who are familiar with Bloom's taxonomy – or even with the works of Plato! – will recognise. The purpose of this chapter is to stand back and survey a range of developments in education and assessment, viewed from the vantage point of the mid-2020s, to trace

DOI:10.4324/9781003346166-2

some common themes and, where this has not been done sufficiently before, to draw out implications for educational assessment.

Developments in education

At the end of the 20th century, there was much reflection about the state of education and of educational assessment (Pellegrino, 1999). In April 2000, an international community assembled in Dakar, Senegal, to create an agenda for making progress in education by 2015. Despite significant subsequent successes, by the year 2015, just one-third of countries had achieved all six of the measurable "Education for All" goals (UNESCO, 2015). Against a background of a changing, challenged global education landscape and increasingly heated cultural and academic debate, the future of assessment was also being contested and discussed.

Discussion of education in the early years of the new century was characterised by an emphasis on preparation for rapid change. Andreas Schleicher (Director for Education and Skills, OECD) captured the zeitgeist succinctly:

> Today, because of rapid economic and social change, schools have to prepare students for jobs that have not yet been created, technologies that have not yet been invented and problems that we don't yet know will arise.
>
> *(2010, p. 42)*

That challenge was exciting as well as daunting for the education world. Technology and the ease of international travel were opening up new vistas of opportunity for new generations. Could education meet the challenge?

Globalisation, the "knowledge economy", and educational participation

By the start of the 21st century, it had become commonplace to talk of "globalisation" as a "given"[1] in the lives for which young people were being educated. What was less commonplace was clarity about what "globalisation" meant, but an article in the UK in 2001 by Michael Barber reflected many of the related ideas. It included:

> Students today are much more likely to compete in a global jobs market and work for global companies. They will also find themselves facing up to a series of apparently intractable global problems – conflict, the environment and poverty among them.
>
> *(Barber, 2001, p. 20)*

Barber appears to be saying at least three things here: first, that students will need to compete for jobs with students educated in other countries (hence their education needs to be as good as that of their competitors); second, that increasingly companies operate in several countries and are part of international supply networks (with implications for the skills required of workers at all levels, not just of high-flying top management); and third, that all countries share some major problems, which will affect a student's future life and work wherever he or she lives.

Linked to this thinking was the concept of "the knowledge economy" – an economic system of consumption and production grounded in human intellectual capital and knowledge-intensive activities. Building knowledge-based economies was seen to be vital for developed and developing countries in order to ensure their long-term growth and fiscal strength and to prepare to participate fully in an international economy (World Bank, 2019, p. vii). The knowledge economy called for a human workforce with higher-level thinking skills and more sophisticated communication skills than their parents and grandparents required, as machines were increasingly taking over routine and manual work (Levy & Murname, 2004), and more and more employment was expected to come from the service sector. The decades ahead were expected to see further rapid change, both in the economy and in society, and 21st-century citizens would need to be able to cope with that (Lynch, 2003, p. 13). In March 2000, the European Union's (EU) Economic and Social Strategy was launched in Lisbon. EU policy was to make Europe "the most competitive and dynamic knowledge-based economy in the world, capable of sustainable economic growth with more and better jobs and greater social cohesion" (Article 3 of the Lisbon Treaty, European Commission, 2003).

The knowledge economy had clear implications for education. In the 1980s, the US National Commission on Excellence in Education had reported on the need for a "Learning Society" (NCEE, 1983). The emphasis was on preparing students for fast change delivered through technological, demographic, social, environmental, economic and political transformation. Workers would need to upgrade their skills throughout their adult lives in order to keep abreast of the increasingly competitive challenges and new developments affecting their professional and personal lives.

Globalisation and the knowledge economy were both seen to make demands on education. There was a need for more creative, collaborative and critical thinkers who could work with international partners and were prepared to continue to learn throughout their adult lives. There was growing concern that 20th-century education was not preparing young people for 21st-century life: "Today's students are no longer the people our educational system was designed to teach" (Prensky, 2001, p. 1). Prensky argued that 20th-century education had had its "triumphant day" and that what was needed was a shift towards "Post-Education-Empowerment" – "a 21st century alternative to the 'education of the 20c' that takes a diametrically different approach" (Prensky, 18 August 2020). Humanity's needs (both individually and societally) had changed, according to Prensky.

Others shared Prensky's concerns about future generations of learners preparing for new challenges. A crucial requirement, for example, was seen to be for students to develop skills that future employers would want. Automation meant that approximately 15% of the global workforce (around 400 million) might be required to switch occupations and learn new skills by 2030: "in about 60 percent of occupations, at least one-third of the constituent activities could be automated, implying substantial workplace transformations and changes for all workers" (Manyika et al., 2017, p. 2). As Andreas Schleicher (2019) fittingly commented:

> Education is no longer about teaching students something alone; it is more important to be teaching them to develop a reliable compass and the navigation tools to find their own way in a world that is increasingly complex, volatile and uncertain. Our imagination, awareness, knowledge, skills and, most important, our common values, intellectual and moral maturity, and sense of responsibility is what will guide us for the world to become a better place.
>
> *(p. 1)*

It became increasingly clear quite soon into the Lisbon programme that educational changes in the EU were "falling short and . . . being implemented too slowly to enable the Union to attain the objectives which it ha[d] set itself" (Viviane Reding, European Commission, Press Release, 11 November 2003).[2] Nevertheless, the policy remained to build a high-value economy through a workforce educated at higher levels than before. Education was seen as a means of reducing poverty, promoting employment and earnings, ensuring equality of opportunities, improving health outcomes, promoting gender equality, enriching lives and well-being, and preparing for active citizenship. As we shall see in later chapters, the relationship between these things was later seen as much more complex, with education being a cause of some of the problems as well as part of the solution to others. However, more education is seen as a key to personal and societal advancement; the World Bank estimated that in 2016, there was a 10% increase in hourly earnings for every extra year of schooling (Patrinos, 2016).

Although there was much agreement about the benefits of schooling,[3] the early years of the 21st century saw continuing debate, particularly in Western Europe and the USA, about the level and content of education beyond school necessary or desirable to benefit individuals and society. *Is College Worth It?* was the title of one book in the USA, and the answer, for many people, was "No" (Bennett & Wilezol, 2013; but see also Willetts, 2017). However, against this scepticism – noticeably less visible in developing economies – figures published by the OECD supported the continued existence of an earnings "premium" for participants in post-secondary school tertiary education (compared with non-participants), although in some countries the amount of the "premium" decreased in the early years of the 21st century (Machin & McNally, 2007). But even in the countries where the sceptics were raising their concerns, one trend was clear: an explosion in participation in tertiary education (beyond secondary school/high school). In the UK, when one of the authors attended university in 1968, around one in twenty of her age cohort were doing the same. By 2000, one in three were participating in higher education (Mayhew et al., 2007); by 2018, that figure was approaching one in two.[4]

Literacy and basic education

According to the "World Education Report 2000", four out of five adults in the world at that time were estimated to have at least some simple literacy skills (UNESCO, 2000a, Table 3, p. 114). Although the absolute number of illiterate adults in the world in 2000 was larger than it was in 1948 (the year the Universal Declaration of Human Rights was first drafted), it was estimated to be falling, and the percentage of illiterate adults in every region of the world had significantly declined (UNESCO, 2000a, p. 19). However, the authors of the Report were uncertain as to how much real progress had been made. Were the purposes of Article 26 being truly fulfilled? Were people's literacy skills – whether in industrial or developing countries – sufficient to enable them to contribute fully to the political, economic, social and cultural life of their society?

The "World Conference on Education For All – Meeting Basic Learning Needs",[5] held in Jomtien (Thailand) in 1990, was a key event organised in response to the widespread concern over the persistence of functional illiteracy across the world. The Jomtien Declaration embraced six broad educational goals to be fulfilled by the year 2000, designed "to serve as beacons to guide and encourage countries in their own goal setting" (UNESCO, 1990, p. 3.)[6] The Jomtien decade undoubtedly witnessed major achievements, including the organisation of global action to advance and improve education. However, throughout the 1990s, commitment and stakeholder involvement were uneven and in some countries education reform remained static (or worse) (UNESCO, 2000b, p. 11).

A decade later, the "World Education Forum" (Dakar, Senegal) reaffirmed the vision set out in Jomtien, but it was clear that the goals set ten years earlier had not been met. Consequently, the Jomtien deadline was postponed until the year 2015. In 2015, UNESCO reported[7] that only a third of countries had reached the global education goals set in Dakar.[8]

The year 2000 also witnessed the approval by world leaders of eight Millennium Development Goals (MDGs). These included halving extreme poverty rates, promoting gender equality and female empowerment, reducing environmental degradation, providing universal primary education and arresting the spread of HIV/AIDS. All eight MDGs were to be accomplished by 2015. Although many or all of the MDGs are relevant to education, the stated educational priority was universal primary education. That aim proved elusive, even though more children registered for primary school than ever before – in 2012, the global figure stood at 90%, up from 83% at the turn of the century – there were still some 58 million children aged between 6 and 11 not attending school. And in 2015, UNESCO opined that the "focus on universal primary enrolment meant less attention to other crucial areas, such as education quality, early childhood care and education, and adult literacy" (UNESCO, 2015, p. xv).

In a press release in 2000 (SOC/4543), the United Nations reported significant progress in many parts of the world in reducing numbers of "out of school" children.[9] And in the latter years of the 20th century, the number of literate adults worldwide more than doubled from 1970 to 1998 – from 1.5 billion to 3.3 billion (an increase of 85% for men and 74% for women) (United Nations, 2000).[10] Gender inequality remained an issue, however, and illiteracy rates, especially among females, were still too high. More than half (60%) of the world's out-of-school children were girls – a figure that paralleled the two-thirds of adult illiterates who were women. Of great concern were areas of Africa and South Asia where persistent poverty, conflicts and HIV/AIDS had profound consequences for their education systems.

The gulf in average levels of education between developed and developing countries continued to be a concern well into the 21st century. In 2015, Winthrop and McGiveny of the Brookings Institution remarked: "When it's shown as an average number of years in school and levels of achievement, the developing world is about 100 years behind developed countries" (Winthrop & McGiveny, 2015, webpage).

Education concerns reported at the turn of the century were not, however, limited to emerging and developing countries. In England, February 1997 saw the publication of an influential report on literacy – "Implementation of the National Literacy Strategy" (1997), written by a task force established by the Labour Party and chaired by Professor Michael Barber (Literacy Task Force, 1997). Its stated target was that by the year 2002, 80% of 11-year-olds should reach the standard expected for their age in English in the national curriculum tests.[11] Following the Labour Party's victory in the May 1997 election, many of the ideas from the Report were incorporated into the White Paper "Excellence in Schools".[12]

In 1999, following a review of basic adult education in England, a report by Sir Claus Moser stated: "Something like one adult in five in this country is not functionally literate and far more people have problems with numeracy. This is a shocking situation and a sad reflection on past decades of schooling" (Moser, 1999, p. 8). The Report proposed that by 2010, the number of functionally illiterate adults of working age should be halved (p. 10), 95% of 19-year-olds should have adequate levels of literacy and 90% should have adequate levels of numeracy (p. 11).[13] This prompted an English "Skills for Life" Strategy (2001), with a focus on adult basic skills, which remained a government policy priority until 2010. The strategy succeeded in raising consciousness of the problem of poor basic skills through high-profile campaigns and delivered millions of qualifications in literacy and numeracy. However, more than two decades after the publication of the Moser Report, the statistics remain alarmingly similar, with estimates of around 9 million adults having poor basic skills (one in five adults with low literacy or numeracy). In 2018, the number of adults participating in basic literacy and numeracy learning had dropped by about 40% (from 1,083,000 in 2011–12 to 664,200 in 2017–18) (Stevenson, 2019, webpage). According to the Learning & Work Institute, it will take twenty years on current trends for all adults in England who need help with basic skills to get it (Evans, 2021). In 2019, Learning & Work identified five initiatives the government would need to accelerate: more investment; more outreach; better awareness of poor basic skills; better basic skills screening; and more involvement of employers.

The situation in the USA was no less bleak. Around the middle of the 1990s, significant global attention was beginning to focus on international assessment comparisons of student achievement. The United States was particularly keen to draw lessons from both comparative data from international benchmark assessments and the education policies of the countries surveyed. The first results of the Third International Mathematics and Science Study (TIMSS) were published in November 1996 and revealed that US eighth graders scored slightly below the international average in mathematics. The second TIMSS report comparing fourth-grade students in mathematics became available in June 1997. Outcomes showed that US fourth-grade students were slightly above average across the participating countries. A final report, which made comparisons between students at the end of their high school years, was published in 1998. The mathematics achievement of US twelfth graders was among the lowest of the participating nations.

During 1999–2002, "more than three dozen congressional statements, debates, and bills cited TIMSS results to justify passing specific education bills, or to call for reforms in education to keep the United States internationally competitive" (Mullis et al., 2016, 'Use and Impact of TIMSS' webpage). Despite similarly disappointing rankings of the United States in successive comparative reports by the OECD on its Programme for International Student Assessment (PISA) in the early 2000s, Tom Loveless – the well-known education researcher and author of the Brown Centre Report on American Education from 2000 to 2017, observed: "We once were terrible and now we're mediocre" (webpage in Robelen, 2011; see also Friedman & Mandelbaum, 2011).[14]

On the other hand, there were examples of developed national educational jurisdictions that appeared to demonstrate improvement and high performance at the turn of the 21st century. Both Finland and Singapore (with different systems) attracted attention in the early 2000s for their apparent success in international tests, although of the two, it was Singapore that sustained their high performance well into the 21st century.[15] In the case of Finland, there was a flurry of commentary on links between their historic and current practices and their performance in international tests (see Kupiainen et al., 2009; Lavonen & Laaksonen, 2009 on the one hand; and Oates, 2017, and Sahlgren, 2015, on the other).

Lifelong learning

"Lifelong learning" is not a new concept: historians tell us of developments in the 19th century to tackle adult literacy and teach immigrants to the USA. In the UK, the early years of the 20th century saw the "Extension Movement", in which ancient universities – notably Oxford and Cambridge – reached beyond their walls to engage workers. Organisations involved (not always in harmony with each other) included the "Workers Education Association", which was set up in 1903 with a mission "to bring adult education within reach of everyone who needs it, fighting inequality and promoting social justice",[16] the National Council of Labour Colleges (NCLC) and Ruskin College, Oxford. Generations of workers attended evening classes and correspondence courses to gain qualifications and increase their learning, sometimes to university level and beyond, making up for opportunities not available to them when they were younger. There was a strong link with the Trades Union Movement, and alumni of these institutions included successive generations of politicians in the British Labour Party in the 20th century.

Moving to higher education, in the UK, the Open University gained its Royal Charter in 1969 with a mission "to be open to people, places, methods and ideas". Initially making use of television and radio – the "University of the Air" – it morphed in the world of the internet to be the "University of the Cloud",[17] but its purpose remains in the tradition of the 20th-century movements to give opportunities to the disadvantaged to develop their potential to the full:

> We promote educational opportunity and social justice by providing high-quality university education to all who wish to realise their ambitions and fulfil their potential.[18]

These developments, which have continued into the 21st century, are based on the objective of providing opportunities for personal fulfilment, rather than explicitly meeting the needs of employers or the economy, although the first objective may support the second.

The emphasis on personal fulfilment also found expression in the 1970s and 1980s in developments by universities across the world to provide learning opportunities for older people who had retired from the workforce. "Universities of the Third Age" sprang up in France in 1973 and in the UK in 1982 as part of an "education movement providing opportunities for older adults to enjoy a range of activities associated with well-being in later life" (Swindell & Thompson, 1995, p. 429). By definition this movement did not have economic objectives, focusing rather on individual well-being, as well as speaking out against "ageism" in society. As we shall discuss in Chapter 3, the emphasis on well-being as an objective of education – for all ages – has found fertile ground in early 21st-century thinking.

These are examples of 19th- and 20th-century movements that continued into the 21st century, championing lifelong learning – or learning in adult life – based on concepts of social justice, individual rights and well-being. They can be distinguished from arguments based on the needs of a "knowledge economy". At the beginning of the 21st century, lifelong learning was increasingly depicted as a catalyst for competitiveness and employability and a support for democracy (Mayor, Director General of UNESCO, 1999). The argument was that it was crucial to foster a learning culture in which learners possessed the knowledge, skills and competencies necessary to compete in a global economy as well as exercising the rights and responsibilities of citizenship (see Egan-Simon, 2021).

Yet another linked, but distinct, idea that found increased traction in the 21st century, was that workers would repeatedly have to learn new skills throughout their working lives. From the early 2020s, the changing nature of work, both in the type of tasks undertaken and in the way that activities were organised, was already starting to challenge the three long-standing features that had characterised the traditional "linear" model of career: expertise, duration and rewards (Bersin, 2016, p. 65). It was evident that the idea of a single, long-term career, only ever requiring an unchanging skill set, with a fixed point of retirement, was becoming increasingly obsolete. By the 2020s, there were different models of what would replace a single progressive career and what kinds of expertise would be needed. But some trends were already clear. Many workers would regularly have to (re)learn how to use technology that was always changing and developing, and the job roles required to use the new tools would change too. Bersin (2016) argued that the need for particular technical skills waxed and waned, but that there was a common thread of an increased need for analytical skills to use the products of technological processes. He applied a "surfing" model to developing and using skills for work:

> I suggest that each of us should think about our career as a series of waves from post-education to pre-retirement: We'll catch a wave and ride it until

it crests, and then, as it calms on the beach, we paddle out and catch the next one. In each new wave, we gain new skills and new experiences.

(Bersin, 2016, pp. 68–69)

In the quarter-century, work patterns are still uncertain, long-term financial security is by no means the norm and workers of all ages are requiring resilience, adaptability and self-managing skills to enable them to "surf", as Bersin envisaged – if, indeed, such "surfing" remains the order of the day.

In these different manifestations, demand for "lifelong learning" has been a notable feature of the first quarter of the new century. However, the supply of lifelong learning opportunities and equitable access to them have been different matters. The OECD (2021) reported that in 2016, more than 50% of adults did not participate in adult learning, with the Covid-19 pandemic reducing future prospects of doing so. Adult participation beyond the formal school years was low. Many employers still bemoaned a "skills gap" when looking for recruits (Bollington, 2015). In the UK, the National Census in 2021 reported that "In 2021, almost one in five [adults] (18.2%, 8.8 million) reported having no qualifications".[19]

The late 20th century saw two reports for UNESCO that championed lifelong learning. "Learning to Be: The World of Education Today and Tomorrow" (also known as the Faure Report, 1972) argued for a "learning society" in which:

> We should no longer assiduously acquire knowledge once for all, but learn how to build up a continually evolving body of knowledge all through life – "learn to be".[20]

This was echoed some twenty years later by the Delors Report ("Learning: The Treasure Within", 1996).

Under the chairmanship of Delors, the International Commission on Education for the 21st century proposed four pillars as the foundations of education: learning to know, learning to do, learning to live together and learning to be (the latter having been the dominant theme of the Faure Report). Although the influence of these reports on national education policies is difficult to evaluate and may not have been very great, the underlying message that "The idea of lifelong education is the keystone of the learning society" (Faure et al., 1972, p. 181) resounded well into the decades which followed.[21]

"21st century skills"

The years before and after the turn of the century saw an industry of compiling lists of so-called 21st century skills. Those familiar with Bloom's taxonomies of learning objectives in the cognitive domain in the 1950s (Bloom et al., 1956), followed by similar hierarchies in the affective and psychomotor domains, may have wondered what was specifically "21st century" about these lists. Indeed, a revised version of Bloom's cognitive hierarchy appeared at the turn of the century (Anderson & Krathwohl, 2001).

The competing lists of "21st century skills" often claimed to be justified by changes in the knowledge economy and in society, which were seen to make national and individual success reliant on the acquisition of the skills (Ananiadou & Claro, 2009; Voogt & Roblin, 2010, 2012). The lists usually comprise a broad set of knowledge, skills, work habits, character traits and learning dispositions, going beyond the Bloom domains and linked to the demands of contemporary workplaces. Andreas Schleicher (Director for Education and Skills, OECD) observed that education was "also about ways of working, including communication and collaboration, as well as the tools they require, such as the capacity to recognise and exploit the potential of new technologies, or indeed, to avert their risks" (Schleicher, 2011, p. 42). This thinking prompted fresh guidance on implications for curriculum and assessment (e.g. Trilling & Fadel, 2009).

Knowledge, skills and competency

The 21st-century skills movement became (and continues to be) a focus of intense scrutiny and sustained commentary, although there has never been consensus on the exact definition of 21st-century skills or the implications for teaching and assessment, and as the century has progressed the discussions may be perceived as rather dated. However, using the label of "skills" in this way to denote such a wide range of characteristics fed into philosophical, ideological and political debates about the place of "knowledge" and "skills" in educational objectives. We shall explore the thinking behind these arguments in Chapter 5 and ask whether they are based on a false dichotomy between knowledge and skills, but here we note the positions taken at the turn of the century and beyond.

In one corner were critical voices questioning the adequacy of traditional, knowledge-based educational systems for preparing learners for the labour market and life in contemporary society (e.g. Mulder, 2012; Priestley & Sinnema, 2014). In the opposing corner were defenders of traditional subject knowledge as an objective of education (e.g. Hirsch, 2016; Kitchen, 2014). E.D. Hirsch Jr. wrote critically of curriculum movements in France and the USA away from discrete academic subjects into "vague evocations of vague general skills".[22]

Straddling the knowledge/skills dichotomy was the language of "competence" and "competencies". Mulder et al. (2007) argued that competence was concerned with the positioning of learners to be ready to 'function effectively in society' (p. 68). The "New Skills Agenda for Europe" (2020)[23] reiterated the necessity to invest in education and lifelong learning to equip citizens with a wider range of competences needed for personal fulfilment and social inclusion. These were described as "a combination of knowledge, skills and attitudes appropriate to the context" (European Commission Education & Culture, 2007, p. 3). The OECD highlighted the cross-disciplinary nature of competence when it identified three "transversal" categories: acting autonomously, interacting in socially heterogeneous groups and using tools interactively (Rychen & Salganik, 2003).

Generation Z and Generation Alpha

The all-pervasive diffusion of information technology and the development of the informational society were affording new opportunities for education and presenting new challenges. In developed countries, two generations of students – "Generation Z" and "Generation Alpha" – grew up in the 21st century surrounded by digital communication technology as a norm in their home and school environments (Gallardo-Echenique et al., 2015). Born between 1995 and 2009, Generation Z students had been "shaped" in the 21st century and were predicted to make up 27% of the workforce by 2025.[24]

Generation Alpha was the first generation to have grown up with the ubiquitous influence of the internet and other modern technologies, free of even the residue of the previous generation's analogue behaviours. They were likely to see in the 22nd century in significant numbers. As the first "digital natives", they began to assume an entire new layer of independence gained from owning or having access to personal devices from an early age (UNESCO, 2011). As such, they manifested three behavioural features that characterised digital natives: accessing new knowledge, networking and developing collective intelligence (a form of intelligence that cannot be reached at the individual level) (UNESCO, 2011, pp. 4–7).

The term "digital native" (Prensky, 2001) sometimes prompted assumptions that 21st-century children could use information technology instinctively and did not need to learn how to do so. However, the International Computer and Information Literacy Study (ICILS)[25] and reports by the multinational research organisation "EU Kids Online"[26] found that exposure to technology – like exposure to words and spoken language – did not equate with ability to use it.

Generation Alpha – which is expected to reach close to 2 billion by 2025 (Williams, 2015) – was to form the basis for a new kind of future employee. Potentially working alongside up to five generations, their approach to work and problem-solving was expected to differ greatly from that of their predecessors. Generation Alpha children would also demonstrate international awareness and might have experienced life in several different locations by the time they reached their teens as a result of their "millennial" parents having changed their jobs more often than their predecessors. Clearly, the 21st-century learner was becoming increasingly practised with technology and comfortable with global and intercultural communication.

Generation Alpha learners were learning to think and understand their world differently from those who had not been as unrelentingly exposed to modern digital technology. Today's older generation (the digital immigrants),[27] for example, had been "socialized" (Prensky, 2001, p. 2) differently from their children and were now in the process of learning a new "language". This meant that in the classroom, Alpha learners spoke a different language from their teachers, prompting Prensky (2020) to call for a transformation in the way children were taught so that they might learn in a language they understood. As learners were becoming increasingly ensconced in a world of rich technological innovation, there was an ever-greater need for teachers to acquire enhanced technological skills so that they might have "a strong understanding of how students are learning in the 21st century" (Finger & Jamieson-Proctor, 2009, p. 78). This would avoid "an education of students constricted by adults that is an anachronism in the modern world" (Cumming & Wyatt-Smith, 2009, p. 5). There are clear implications for the role, medium and language of assessment, to which we shall turn in the next section.

However, it would be wrong to move on from this broad characterisation of the new generations without pointing out that a quarter of the way through the 21st century, there remain, including in developed countries, groups of children and adults who have little or no access to the internet in their homes. This "digital divide" led to crucial inequalities of learning during the Covid-19 pandemic, when most schools were closed.[28] A report by the Pew Research Center in 2020 found that in the USA "[o]verall, roughly one-in-five parents with homebound schoolchildren say it is very or somewhat likely their children will not be able to complete their schoolwork because they do not have access to a computer at home (21%)".[29] Similarly, talk of the "global awareness" of the new generation jars with the limited horizons of many children and adults in poverty. A Forbes Report in 2019 found that 11% of Americans had never travelled beyond the state where they were born.[30]

The Fourth Industrial Revolution

The first quarter of the 21st century witnessed seismic advancements in technological phenomena, including digital data systems, "deep" and transformative technologies,[31] computational intelligence and smart automation. The technological landscape was moving at such speed that the leading economist Klaus Schwab, founder and Executive Chairman of the WEF, coined the phrase "Fourth Industrial Revolution" (Schwab, 2016; McGinnis, 2020).

The Fourth Industrial Revolution (also known as Industry 4.0) announced a succession of social, political, cultural and economic upheavals that were expected to continue to unfold over the remainder of the century, resulting in global systemic change across numerous domains, fields and areas of life.

Fundamentally different from the three revolutions that preceded it,[32] Industry 4.0 heralds a wide range of interrelated breakthroughs. These are reflected in nanotechnology (which manipulates and modifies the molecular structure of materials to change their intrinsic properties in order to create "smart" objects), renewable energies, gene sequencing, quantum computing (a branch of computer science based on the principles of the superposition of matter and quantum entanglement) and blockchain (a feature of cryptocurrency architecture). Automation technology has already spawned a raft of technologies that have achieved recognition and status of their own, including robotics (in which machines possess certain anthropomorphic characteristics), neurotechnology (in which an electronic device can interact with the brain to monitor or modulate neural activity) and AI (the ability of a digital computer or computer-controlled robot to undertake tasks more usually associated with the intellectual capabilities and processes characteristic of human beings). Unparalleled strides in how each of these, and other, technologies can be employed, their fusion (redefining and obscuring the boundary between the digital and natural worlds), and their interaction across the physical, digital and biological domains have reinforced how radically different Industry 4.0 is proving to be from previous industrial revolutions.

The onslaught of these innovations is truly remarkable. In 2020, new technologies accounted for around 10% of all innovation. The European Patent Office (2020) estimated that by the end of 2023, there would be 29 billion connected devices globally. The impact on the global economy and the need for workers to upskill and reskill was proving to be momentous, with a projected disruption and insecurity among workers at nearly all skill levels. Twenty years into the new century, "gigging", in which temporary positions are common and organisations hire independent workers for short-term commitments, had increased to the extent that the size of the world's gig[33] economy was expected to exceed approximately $455 billion in gross volume by the end of 2023 (Graham, 2019).[34]

The information deluge

One of the most dramatic developments in the first quarter of the 21st century (an outcrop of Industry 4.0) affecting educational assessment has been the "information revolution" – the "radical changes wrought by computer technology on the storage of and access to information since the mid-1980s" (Oxford Reference, 2023). The resulting deluge of available information continues to transform societies, global economies, markets and industry structures; products and services (and their flow); consumer segmentation, values and behaviour; as well as labour markets (Drucker, 1999; Nye, 2003). While the value of information in the knowledge economy is undeniable,[35] some have asked whether the impact of data proliferation is always positive. The common complaint of "information overload" has also been challenged on the grounds that what the economy needs has "less to do with quantity of information in production or circulation at any time than with the qualities by which knowledge is presented" (Serrat, 2014, slide 10) (see also Jennings, 2023; Quach et al., 2022). Moreover, the gathering, assembling, processing and analysis of data can expose or give rise to inequalities reflecting differing levels of access and ability to undertake analysis. A potential outcome is the creation of "digital divides" between those with the technical and financial ability to utilise available technology and to access and interpret data meaningfully and those who do not.

The concepts of "knowledge economy" and "knowledge economy worker" are founded on the premise that information and knowledge are at the core of economic growth and development. This has obvious and important implications for education, as the ability to generate, interpret and use information efficiently becomes a critical capability for learners. It follows that assessment should reflect these changes too, although there is always a risk of an increasing disjunct between the way students learn and how they are assessed, especially where tests and assessments written on paper are used to monitor learning.

However, learners are now beginning to engage with digital formative assessments that provide immediate feedback, and it is increasingly commonplace for students to submit work online that is assessed remotely. Advances in the evolution of digitally mediated ways to assess student progress authentically in context, some using AI, hold promise for further automation of grading and the provision of personal learning solutions to students. Technical advances in the capture of process data make possible the deployment of learning analytics at scale in schools, higher education institutions and other learning settings.

Within 21st-century information economies, it has become much cheaper and easier to capture, save and analyse vast amounts of education data and information about the individual learner. Traceable and measurable online activity (Martin & Sherin, 2013) can offer more detailed information about student learning and how it can be enhanced (Wong, 2017). Digitised assessment data can provide specific, significant volumes of data about learner performance and evidence of learning in progressively more innovative ways. Information is becoming increasingly smaller in focus and larger in volume. That may prompt new challenges,[36] but the information revolution is now able to facilitate real-time data analysis in schools through sophisticated devices used by educators, teachers and students. In Chapter 5, we consider at greater length how the development of these technical options has affected our thinking about assessment.

Arguably, the 21st century has ushered in the intelligent education era, though the extent to which that potential is being – or will be – realised in practice may vary. One key possible benefit of digitised data in the classroom, for example, is the potential to create a personalised learning environment (Major et al., 2021). That should facilitate and optimise learning based on learner requirements (Maseleno et al., 2018; Pane et al., 2015). There is also the potential to promote socially interactive learning (Pardo et al., 2019) and embolden teachers to break out of a passive instructional mode and make their lessons more interactive (Twyman, 2018). Learners, too, can be empowered to use tools and online programs to enrich and develop their knowledge, attain new skills needed for the knowledge economy (Mulder et al., 2007) and, increasingly, equip them to progress in education and into employment (European Commission Education & Culture, 2007).

Developments in assessment

"Assessment for learning" (AfL)

At the turn of the century and beyond, there was heightened interest in several countries in Assessment for Learning (Black & Wiliam, 1998a, 1998b). The distinction between "assessment for learning" and "assessment of learning" became commonplace, with most educationists championing the former and advocating formative uses of assessment outcomes (Schildkamp et al., 2020).[37] Formative assessment was beginning to achieve increasing influence on both education policy and practice.[38]

The first priority of AfL was to promote and support learning. Students were encouraged to become more involved in the learning process and, from this, gain confidence in what they were expected to learn and to what level. Some aspects of the AfL movement went a little further with the student entering a partnership with the teacher as co-constructor of knowledge and assessment (see, e.g. the work of Jill Willis and Val Klenowski).[39] AfL first appeared as a feature of English classroom practice in the late 1980s, albeit under the guise of "formative assessment" (Boyle & Charles, 2010, p. 285) and was subsequently formalised in England in 2003 through its inclusion within the government's "Excellence and enjoyment: a strategy for primary schools" (Boyle & Charles, 2010, p. 285; DfES, 2003).

In England, the highly influential "Assessment Reform Group" (ARG) – a group of educational assessment researchers assembled under the auspices of the British Educational Research Association – worked over the turn of the century with the aim that policy on educational assessment should take more account of relevant research evidence in the burgeoning field of AfL.[40] The ARG was at the forefront of challenging thinking and practice in all aspects of assessment, including assessment for learning, through the commissioned Black and Wiliam work "Inside the Black Box" (1998b), and the follow-up "Assessment for Learning: Beyond the Black Box" (Broadfoot et al., 1999). Preferring the term "assessment for learning" as opposed to "formative assessment" (a term the ARG claimed was open to a variety of interpretations), the Reform Group defined AfL as:

> the process of seeking and interpreting evidence for use by learners and their teachers to decide where the learners are in their learning, where they need to go and how best to get there.
> *(Broadfoot et al., 2002, pp. 2–3)*[41]

The ARG claimed that AfL processes could support the development of students' self-regulation, a fundamental factor in promoting independent learning (Assessment Reform Group, 2002). The "Assessment for Learning Strategy" (Fautley & Savage, 2008)[42] aimed to "support schools [to] develop their assessment and to enhance learning and improve the rate at which pupils progress" (p. 3). Since its rise to international prominence, and despite near-continuing attention, the progress of AfL, as embedded classroom practice in England, has been slow. Its supporters credit this to the disproportionately large share of attention given to various developments in summative assessments (Black & Wiliam, 1998a) and a lack of sustained support for teacher professional development (Anders et al., 2022).

There is an ever-growing body of critique of AfL, including calls for further theoretical development of the concept of formative assessment (Yorke, 2003); questioning the desired and actual impact of AfL upon learning and how it is differentiated from other types of assessment (Baird et al., 2014); and questions about the extent of the efficacy of AfL. Research on the efficacy of feedback, questioning, self and peer assessment shows that there is great variability imposed by context. More fundamental questions have included how AfL is defined, how its demands can be supported and the varying contexts in which it operates (Bennett, 2011). AfL has also been questioned in cases where student answers cannot be relied on (Fletcher-Wood, 2017). Even more fundamentally, Didau has questioned the basic premise of formative assessment – that performance in the classroom is indicative of learning (Didau, 2014),[43] and Brown has asked whether AfL can legitimately be treated as assessment (Brown, 2019). Two decades into the 21st century, the jury is still out on AfL. In England, Coe reported that "there has been no (or at best limited) effect on learning outcomes nationally" (Coe, 2013, p. 10). Clearly, the promised benefits of AfL have yet to materialise fully, particularly in terms of implementation and teacher ownership (Fautley & Savage, 2008; Stewart, 2012).

Impact of the cognitive sciences on educational assessment

In the earlier years of the 20th century, the relationship between assessment and cognitive psychology had a bumpy ride, with controversies around intelligence testing and the use of assessment for selection. However, looking forward to the 21st century, assessment researchers seemed receptive to take on board developments in cognitive psychology. Also, around the turn of the century, the relevance of cognitive psychology to the field of educational assessment seemed both appropriate and anticipated as a focus for promising assessment research. Advances in understanding of cognitive processes were heralded as "promising to reinvigorate intelligence and ability testing" (Embretson & Gorin, 2001, p. 343), and it was envisioned that the future potential of cognitive psychology was to be "fully realized through item design" (ibid., p. 343).

In the early 2000s, there was mounting pressure to make assessments more revealing about the cognitive processes they measured (US Department of Education, 2004). In 2004, the OECD Directorate of Education carried out a detailed study of student performance in mathematics (based on the 2003 PISA assessment). Their report emphasised mastery of processes, the understanding of concepts and the ability to function in various situations within each assessment area as well as cognitive, affective and attitudinal aspects of test-taker performance. A survey of PISA students elicited responses about their approach to learning, which included the "Cognitive strategies that require information processing" (OECD, 2004, p. 116).[44] The competencies required for "mathematisation" in the PISA assessment, such as memorisation/rehearsal strategies, elaboration strategies and control strategies, encompassed cognitive activities and demands (OECD, 2004, p. 40).

The turn of the century also witnessed an emerging science of assessment design with an emphasis on explaining how theories of cognition and learning relate to assessment and pedagogy (Embretson & Gorin, 2001; Pellegrino et al., 1999; Pellegrino et al., 2001; Mislevy et al., 2002).

As the new century progressed, the developing discipline of neuroscience (the study of the structure and function of the human brain and nervous system) was also being linked to areas of education research and practice (Dhawan, 2014; Kirby & Smith, 2021). Despite challenges in integrating the two fields, there were calls to bridge the divide between neuroscience and educational assessment practice, especially given the links educational psychology had with strong cognitive constructs such as attention, retrieval, metacognition and memory (Guli, 2005; Bruer, 2006; Craig et al., 2020). However, to date, educational neuroscience has arguably had little impact on educational practice (Mason, 2009).

Alongside these developments there has been a revival of interest in cognitive ability and intelligence testing, informed by developments in understanding of cognitive processes, such as sustained attention, response inhibition, speed of information processing, cognitive flexibility, multiple simultaneous attention, working memory, category formation and pattern recognition. Cognitive Diagnostic Assessments (CDAs) have provided guidance in recognising potential areas of intervention for students grappling with their learning. By directly targeting cognitive skills, CDAs have sought to ensure that all relevant cognitive skills are accounted for during item and test design and development; that the justifications underpinning the design of tasks are transparently documented; and, that assessment scores lead to meaningful and valid interpretations about students' cognitive skills and abilities. We shall explore these ideas further in Chapter 5, but their increasing prominence in the development of assessment is worth noting here.

The promise of a pre-employment cognitive test was that it predicted future job performance, especially when assessment tasks resembled those encountered in the future workplace. Schmidt (2002) offered a compelling case for the link between general cognitive ability and job performance, arguing that cognitive ability and intelligence testing were reliable and valid predictors of employment success in a wide variety of occupations. However, such assessments were thought to be discriminatory if they adversely affected certain protected groups, such as those defined by gender, race, age, ethnicity or national origin. Other ethical, legal and privacy issues around personnel assessment and selection also became more prominent at this time (Lowman, 2013).

Technology and educational assessment

It was very evident at the turn of the century that developments in technology had the potential to be a key to innovative assessment in the 21st century. Not necessarily, according to the OECD (2016), which asserted that "Innovation in education is not synonymous with the introduction of digital technology" (p. 32). Key assessment organisations, consigned to the inevitable union of assessment and technology, were focusing on the "smart" and responsible implementation of technology. This all begged the question as to what digital technologies could offer educational assessment. Should digital technology lead curriculum, pedagogy and assessment, or was that putting the cart before the horse? What differences were required in assessment when knowledge and performance could be represented digitally? And how might the assessment and testing industry use technology more effectively? It seemed that it would merely be a matter of time before digital technologies would drive fundamental changes in the design and content of assessment (Bennett, 2002; Shute & Becker, 2010), offer an alternative means for supporting learning (Säljö, 2010) and prompt efforts to reconfigure existing teaching, learning and assessment practices (Shute et al., 2013; Thornton, 2012).

The early 2000s witnessed a glut of prophetic voices proclaiming the "inevitable and inexorable" (Bennett, 2002, p. 2) concoction of technology with assessment. In the United States, Pellegrino (1999) envisioned how the US educational assessment landscape might appear in 2099. He anticipated that "technology-assisted dynamic learning environments would be available for numerous domains of knowledge, skill and understanding, with assessment featuring as an essential constituent of the overall environmental architecture and design" (p. 18). Bennett (2002) claimed that technological advances would force fundamental changes in the format and content of assessment, arguing that no matter how great the challenges, they should not impede the continuing exploration of technology and assessment. In the UK, Ken Boston, the Chief Executive of the Qualifications and Curriculum Authority,[45] called for a five-year strategic blueprint for the national delivery of electronic assessment and announced that "By 2009, e-assessment shall be normal, if not the norm, for thousands of children each year". He continued to argue for thoughtful, serious consideration of how digital technologies might expedite improved assessment systems (Boston, 2007).

Among the perceived benefits of digital technologies was the use of multiple forms of representation to enable learners to characterise their learning in ways of their choice; the development of new ways of assessing performance in different subjects for summative purposes; the development of ways to operationalise and capture learning skills, competences and dispositions that were less resistant to traditional assessment methods; and the development of ways of capturing peer interaction, group performance and collaboration. Technology was also seen to have a crucial role in the implementation of learning analytics and education data mining (Timmis et al., 2016).

Translation of standard, paper-based, testing practices to digital assessments taken online was becoming progressively more familiar: the computer was replacing pen and paper as the instrument for completing the test. However, "translation" methods were thought to introduce different demands with consequent threats to validity: Would the use of technology to replicate how a learner would work on paper, for example, be fair, reliable, and valid? Could technology be utilised to have a positive impact on teaching and learning? Would digital assessment reconceptualise traditional notions of comparability?

These questions promoted critics to ask whether it was right to expect (technologically supported) assessments of the future to be comparable to (pen-and-paper) assessments of the past. As the first part of this chapter has illustrated, thinking about what was to be assessed was itself changing, bringing a need to assess new, complex and "hard-to-measure" competencies (Stecher & Hamilton, 2014) such as the test-taker's mental problem-solving processes (Bennett, 2013). Under the auspices of the Gordon Commission on the "Future of Assessment in Education", Bennett proposed thirteen claims for how educational assessment might keep pace with a rapidly, dramatically changing world and, in particular, what educational assessment had to do if it was to remain relevant and contribute proactively to individual and institutional achievement (Bennett, 2013). However, Bennett's argument also implied that the use of technology without the guarantee of a strong benefit ought to be avoided (p. 19).

To enlarge our understanding of the panorama of educational assessment practice, a review of the literature on developments in technology-enhanced assessment at primary, secondary, further education and higher education levels in the UK and internationally was conducted in 2012 (Oldfield et al., 2012). The review had two purposes: to understand the potential that digital technology offered in improving assessment and to advance the debate about how it could facilitate such reforms. The investigation sought to seek answers to the three most commonly asked questions at the time: What do digital technologies offer for educational assessment? How might assessment be different when knowledge and performance can be represented digitally? And where is the "cutting edge" in such developments at present? Review recommendations included the cultivation of new assessment practices exploiting the role that feedback plays in assessment and the development of new assessment tools that give learners more control over their own learning. The Review also asked for attention to be paid to contexts that had added relevance for assessment using digital technologies, including learners' lives, and social, cultural, educational and technical backgrounds, and the ever-changing role of educational provision.

Digital data and computational capacity increased hugely across the late 20th and early 21st centuries as large-scale and ongoing assessment practices moved progressively into the digital space. "Big Data" were key to large-scale educational assessments and innovations in learning (Shilo et al., 2020). Big data promised to alleviate the difficulties associated with storing huge amounts of data (particularly through the development of data lakes); afforded an extensive display of formats – from structured, numeric data in traditional databases (such as test scores and grades) to unstructured text documents, emails, videos, audios and log files – and offered unprecedented speed with data being streamed for analysis in almost real time (Raikes, 2019; Baig et al., 2020). Wyatt-Smith et al. (2019) chronicled the evolution of digital learning assessments and digitally mediated ways to evaluate learner progress authentically in context. We say more in Chapter 5 about the impact of big data on thinking about assessment.

Despite the rapid development of digital assessments and big data, Wyatt-Smith et al. (2019) noted that their potential remained "aspirational". It was evident early in the new century that the influence of digital technologies on educational assessment was "shallow" (OECD, 2016, p. 3).[46] Educational assessment appeared markedly slow in embracing innovation or significant change (Perrotta & Wright, 2010). While assessors acknowledged the varied and potentially creative opportunities for innovation from technology-supported assessment, there was an aversion to the risks such a seismic shift in assessment would create (Claxton, 2007, Mogey, 2011; Whitelock & Watt, 2008). Broadfoot et al. (2013) expressed some of the prevailing scepticism by suggesting that "technology alone cannot transform assessment practices" (p. 3).

Ethical questions in response to the development and use of technology-enhanced assessment practice were also beginning to rear their head,[47] and we shall return to some of these in Chapter 7. There were also questions about the effect of technology on the professional identity and core skills of teachers (Wyatt-Smith et al., 2019).

We have already referred to the inequities raised by the "digital divide". These promoted the question of whether technology-enhanced assessment would increase or decrease the gap between advantaged and disadvantaged learners. The new arena of "data ethics" began to impinge on educators, policy makers and test developers, with new questions about the proliferation of digitised assessment data, particularly issues relating to collection, use and protection of huge personalised data sets (including data about children), ownership and control of information (see Timmis et al., 2016).

Artificial intelligence

Though not entirely new as a concept and still in its early development,[48] impressive progress has already been made in artificial intelligence (AI) in recent years, and it is now the world's fastest-growing deep technology (HM Government, 2022). AI refers to "any cognitive process exhibited by a non-human entity" (Anirudh, 2022). In other words, machines that are programmed to simulate or imitate human intelligence and intelligent human behaviours are machines that exhibit AI (Raphael, 1976). Notably AI has *generative* powers – to create new material – true or false, moral or immoral – using what it has learned. This is different in kind from the analytic use of technology to process large amounts of data.

AI is demonstrating enormous potential to reform the rules of industries and organisations, drive significant economic growth and transform all sectors of life (HM Government, 2021). Such is the computational potency of AI that it affords opportunities for machines to model, and even improve upon, the capabilities of the human mind. AI facilitates computers to undertake a variety of advanced functions, including perceiving, learning, synthesising, problem-solving, making recommendations, conversing in natural language, visual perception, speech recognition, decision-making and inferring information demonstrated by machines based on vast and robust datasets with high-performance computers on a scale beyond what humans can analyse. AI systems work by merging large amounts of data with intuitive, iterative processing algorithms, allowing the software to learn automatically from patterns, correlations, or features in the data that they analyse. Following each iteration of data processing, an AI system tests and evaluates its own performance and develops additional capabilities. Thus, a customer service "chatbot" that has been programmed with examples of text has the capability to learn to generate realistic exchanges with humans.

Artificial intelligence and education

AI has the potential capacity to tackle some of the greatest challenges in education, including transforming teaching and learning practices, as well as hastening progress towards the United Nations "Sustainable Development Goal 4" ("Ensure inclusive and equitable quality education and promote lifelong learning opportunities").

However, adoption of AI within the education sector (as with other similar technologies) has been slower than in other industries like banking, entertainment, recreation and healthcare (Ionnou, 2018). This has been particularly true for developing countries. Lynch (2019) lists barriers to adopting digital learning. These include lack of key infrastructure (including access to reliable electricity), national disparities in spending per student and disparities in the status of education. More generally, professional development and training for educators in new technology can be expensive, is often time-consuming and demanding, and can necessitate changes in how learning is both understood and delivered. Nevertheless, AI in education was expected to be worth $6 billion by 2024 (Fengchun et al., 2018). However, for AI to contribute to achieving Sustainable Development Goals "system-wide policy adjustments and calls for robust ethical oversight as well as in-depth engagement with practitioners and researchers globally" were seen to be a necessity (Fengchun et al., 2018, p. 1).

Artificial intelligence and assessment

While the development of AI within the domain of testing and assessments has not been hurried, the opposite can be said about the rapid increases in the 2020s in awareness of AI by students and teachers. Across the assessment world, there has been a strange mix of panic about the dangers of AI and partially explored optimism about its opportunities.

AI has been seen as having the potential to automate, either fully or partially, parts of traditional assessment practice, create assessment tasks, identify appropriate peers to mark work and automatically mark student work (Adesope et al., 2017). AI has the capacity to offload tasks from humans, thereby reducing workload across the education sector and freeing up teachers' time, allowing them to focus on delivering high quality teaching and assessment (Department of Education, 2023). Considerable interest has also been generated over the potential for AI-related educational assessment to enrich test validity and efficacy (Glanville, 2023). The visionaries talk of the potential use for assessment of "Large Language Models" (LLMs): a type of AI algorithm that consists of a neural network with many parameters trained on extensive data sets (using self-supervised learning or semi-supervised learning) in order to comprehend, summarise, generate and predict new content.

However, both insiders (assessment professionals) and outsiders (teachers, students, parents, politicians) in the world of educational assessment remain very cautious about all this. Speaking of digital technologies, Richardson and Clesham wrote in 2021: "We continue to not trust them in high-stakes assessments" (p. 4). Echoing a similar sentiment, Aloisi (2023) outlines the detrimental effect that AI and Machine Learning Systems could have on the validity of national examinations in secondary education and how lower validity would adversely affect public and stakeholder trust in the examination system.

According to Richardson and Clesham (2021), the tenor of evolving conversations that seek to endorse AI technologies might best focus on how AI can be used to better support practice rather than whether it should be used at all. In any event, effective implementation of AI in educational assessment will require that educational programmes and assessment practices be adapted and transformed so that teachers and their students can use AI tools ethically, effectively, transparently and responsibly (Glanville, 2023).

The ethical dilemmas and moral problems that AI present to the principles of academic and educational integrity[49] are gaining considerable attention in the educational assessment community, particularly in the higher education sector. There is little doubt that academic integrity is tainted when students engage in malpractice. Progressively, more sophisticated AI natural language processing tools are capable of adeptly completing tasks currently within the orbit of professional roles, and university staff are considering how the increased use of these tools will change their assessment practices.

Cotton et al. (2023) discuss a range of strategies that higher education institutions can implement to ensure that AI tools are used ethically and responsibly, including developing policies and procedures, providing training and support, and using a variety of methods to detect and prevent cheating and forms of plagiarism.[50] Measures taken by public, school and university authorities across the world range from outright bans on the use of some AI functions to more nuanced guidance.

"Chatbots"

At the time of writing, around half a dozen branded products are openly available, providing immediate access to generative AI. Perhaps the most famous is "ChatGPT" which has experienced rapid growth and extensive adoption. These "chatbots" (computer programmes designed to simulate human conversation to solve customer queries) can generate highly organised, interconnected, human-like responses to questions or prompts posed to it. Their rapid escalation has kindled interest in their potential to support new approaches to assessment and evaluation, but this has largely been subordinated to a chorus of concerns, particularly after the release of ChatGPT in November 2022. Its ability to produce credible, high-quality responses to assignments, create essays and write computer code with minimal human input, all in a matter of moments, raised questions about how to ensure that work submitted for assessments was the student's own – and even about what, in the world of AI, is meant by "original work".

There is little doubt that chatbots have considerably enhanced students' access to information, enabling them to locate answers to questions in a speedy fashion (Yin et al., 2021). ChatGPT and similar products can make teaching easier and reduce teacher workload. They can generate lesson plans for teachers and produce a wealth and variety of pedagogic resources.[51] Heaven (2023) argues that after the initial panic accompanying the introduction of ChatGPT, teachers and other educators are now re-evaluating its use in the classroom: "Advanced chatbots could be used as powerful classroom aids that make lessons more interactive, teach students media literacy, generate personalized lesson plans, save teachers time on admin, and more"[52] (webpage). Phillip Dawson (Centre for Research in Assessment and Digital Learning [CRADLE], Deakin University) is an assessment research scholar at the forefront of issues arising from the emergence of ChatGPT and a specialist in feedback and cheating ("AIgerism", or AI-assisted plagiarism) in higher education. He has considered generative AI in the context of future-authentic assessment and argues that the principal assessment challenge twenty-five years into the new century will be how to design assessment that continues to enable educators to construct a true representation of where students are in their learning, even if they use ChatGPT (Dawson, 2023).

Because chatbots have the capability to create an essay on a vast range of selected topics on request, with the platform producing clear, highly organised answers to complex questions or topics, many higher education institutions have reported that their students have attempted to palm off AI-generated work as their own. A central concern, therefore, among those working in education is the potential impact of ChatGPT on the authenticity and credibility of assessments. This is exemplified in headlines such as "ChatGPT passes MBA exam given by a Wharton professor" (NBC, 23 January 2023);[53] "ChatGPT: Why AI should be banned from assessment and regulated" (Schools Week, May, 2023);[54] and "Lecturers urged to review assessments in UK amid concerns over new AI tool" (The Guardian, 13 January 2023).[55] Headlines such as these have become all too commonplace.

The *Guardian* article cited here prompted Weale (2023) to report that in one case, "staff in the computer science department at University College London recently decided to change an assessment. Previously students were offered a choice between an essay-based or skills-based assessment as part of final coursework, but the essay option has been removed".

Chatbots have sparked trepidation about the potential for hard-to-detect plagiarism and raised questions about the validity of the essay format as a future form of assessment. In response, in the UK, the Joint Council for Qualifications (JCQ)[56] has produced guidance for teachers and assessors in schools for protecting the integrity of qualifications, where AI has been used to obtain information and content that might be used in work produced for assessments that lead towards UK qualifications. Any use of AI that means students have not independently demonstrated their own attainment is likely to be considered malpractice. The JCQ permits the use of AI tools, however, "when the conditions of the assessment permit the use of the internet and where the student is able to demonstrate that the final submission is the product of their own independent work and independent thinking" (2023, p. 3). The International Baccalaureate Organization seeks to work with schools in order to support their students in the ethical use of AI-enabled tools as part of successful academic work and in accordance with its principles and practice of academic integrity (Glanville, 2023).

In England, universities are required by the Office for Students (a statutory regulatory body) to ensure that assessments are valid, reliable and "designed in a way that minimises the opportunities for academic misconduct and facilitates the detection of such misconduct where it does occur" (2022, p. 120). The very real potential for malpractice has prompted some universities to ban its use. For example, several universities in the prestigious "Russell Group" have explicitly banned students from using ChatGPT. Other universities, however – including other Russell Group universities – have sought to see AI as a positive educational resource and have seen a blanket ban on access to chatbots as neither feasible nor practicable, especially against the backdrop of an impending, all-pervasive release of a myriad array of AI-enhanced technologies. These universities have published staff guidance on the appropriate use of generative AI and advice for using AI tools for revision, checking answers or refining an essay. University teaching and research staff are assuming responsibility to instruct students on how best to use AI tools and resources in a constructive but ethical manner, both in the context of university study and working life beyond graduation (e.g. Russell Group principles on the use of generative AI tools in education;[57] Times Higher Education, 2023;[58] University College London[59]).

A primary rationale for higher education guidance has been to adapt, where possible, existing practices to utilise the undoubted benefits of AI more fully. The European University Association's Learning and Teaching

Steering Committee has shared key AI considerations for European universities (2023),[60] as in the UK has the Quality Assurance Agency for Higher Education (QAA, 2023). The QAA urges universities to "communicate early with students and discuss the technology with them; design assessments around co-creation, iteration, and critical thinking skills". They discourage reliance on "unverified and ineffective" detection tools (Bagshaw et al., 2023).[61]

It may be that the anxious response to, and concerns around, ChatGPT and similar products are "more about academic culture than about the tool itself" (Mihai, 2023, webpage).[62] Accordingly, efforts are being made to create appropriate AI teaching, learning and assessment cultures. Mills and Goodlad (2023), for example, offer language models, text generators and AI tools to help protect academic integrity and student learning, as well as enriching teaching and assessment communities. They argue that teachers need to help students develop a critical awareness of generative machine models, together with an understanding of their risks and limitations. D'Agostino (2023) has also compiled a useful resource consisting of advice from a tranche of academics on how to harness AI potential and obviate the risks of AI technology.

The rise of AI and language model tools like ChatGPT has triggered interest in using these technologies to support, develop and even reconfigure educational assessment and evaluation (e.g. Fatkullina et al., 2015) although this is proving divisive. There are moral risks from the use of generative AI in assessment: generative intelligence will use what it has "learned", true or false, imagined or real, prejudiced or unprejudiced. In this chapter's account of developments, we note that in the early 2020s, there is no consensus as yet on whether or how the risks of bias in assessment supported by AI can be managed.

Swiecki et al. (2022) argue that the challenge of AI-assisted assessment and its applications offers insights into how traditional assessment practices can be reconfigured in more meaningful ways. The authors argue that the traditional assessment paradigm, while largely successful and important for understanding and enhancing student learning, is not without its issues (e.g. onerous to design and implement; snapshot of performance; unadapted to specific knowledge skills and backgrounds of test-takers, inauthentic; and, antiquated, assessing skills that humans routinely use machines to perform). While AI approaches have the potential to address these issues, at least in part, they are not a "panacea" (p. 8), introducing new challenges when designing and implementing assessments.

Conclusion

This chapter has offered an overview of some of the main developments up to and during the early 21st century, which have implications for our stocktake of educational assessment a quarter of a century on. We have described some of the key developments in education, assessment and AI. They all raise questions for assessment.

Each of the educational developments and objectives we have described poses questions concerning how progress in them can be assessed. How are basic literacy and numeracy best taught and assessed? How can 21st century skills such as collaboration and working in teams be assessed, given that assessment has normally been assumed to be focused on individuals? How can affective traits and emotional skills be assessed? And should they be? What is assessment for? How can it support teaching and learning of the kind that is required in the new century? Should assessments use the language of Generations Z and Alpha and be made using the digital technology that they have grown up with? And will technology make human assessors redundant?

The developments in assessment described here, including the "assessment for learning" movement, and different views about the role of technology in assessment, may come to be seen as key steps forward in the development of assessment practice as the century progresses, or may soon be dated and forgotten. We have noted how cautious the world of assessment is about change, particularly in high-stakes assessments and tests that can open or close doors for students' futures. Is this caution justified as rightful prudence in the interests of students, or is it a drag-anchor holding back educational progress?

This chapter concludes with an overview of recent – and rapid – developments in AI. These raise key questions for assessment. Should assessment designers and developers seek to resist the impact of AI by creating defences against AI in assessment? Or should they rethink assessment in ways that use AI? Older readers will remember the days of alarm in the assessment world about the use of calculators and the complicated rules to limit their use. These concerns seem quaint to us now. But we feel the challenge of AI becoming a major presence at the end of the first quarter of the new century.

Notes

1 Although some questioned the inevitability of globalisation, and the scope for alternative choices (e.g. Maguire, 2002).
2 https://ec.europa.eu/commission/presscorner/detail/en/SPEECH_03_47
3 Subject to continuing debate in some cultures and religious traditions about the extent of the schooling of girls.
4 Department for Education, 2019, accessed at https://assets.publishing.service.gov.uk/government/uploads/system/uploads/attachment_data/file/843542/Publication_HEIPR1718.pdf
5 The Education for All Forum was an inter-agency body established in 1990 by the United Nations Development Programme (UNDP), the United Nations Educational, Scientific and Cultural Organization (UNESCO), the United Nations Population Fund (UNFPA), the United Nations Children's Fund (UNICEF) and the World Bank.
6 The Jomtien Declaration included the expansion of early years provision; universal primary education by 2000; improvement in learning achievement to a defined

standard; reduction of the adult illiteracy rate to one-half its 1990 level by 2000; expansion of provisions for basic education and training in other essential skills required by youth and adults; and increased acquisition by individuals and families of the knowledge, skills and values required for better living and sound and sustainable development.
7 UNESCO. https://assets.publishing.service.gov.uk/government/uploads/system/uploads/attachment_data/file/843542/Publication_HEIPR1718.pdf – "Education for All 2000–2015: Achievements and Challenges" (2015).
8 See Benavot et al. (2015) for a brief overview of global progress in achieving the six "Education for All" goals and international aid for "Education for All"' policies.
9 Vayachuta et al. (2016) define the term "out-of-school" children and youth as "the population between the ages of 3–25 years who do not attend schools or who have studied in schools but dropped out before completing their compulsory or basic education" (p. 1).
10 United Nations (2000). World Education Forum in Dakar, Senegal, 26–28 April to Boost Drive for Education For All. 20000411. Press Release SOC/4543. 11 April 2000. https://press.un.org/en/2000/20000411.soc4543.doc.html.
11 In England, as in many countries, the national curriculum lists the content that should be taught between the reception year at primary school and the end of compulsory schooling. The statutory force of these requirements varies from country to country. In England, progress is tested at the end of "key stages", and current test requirements are described at Standards and Testing Agency – GOV.UK (www.gov.uk).
12 Cm 3681, July 1997, London, HMSO.
13 The Moser Report (1999) had its clearest bearing on the further education sector, where, as a consequence of Moser's recommendations, all teachers of adult basic skills were subsequently required to possess a specialist teaching qualification, and teachers of all other subjects in further education were required to demonstrate mastery of core skills, including language, literacy, numeracy and information communication technology, before they could gain their teaching qualification.
14 Timssandpirls.bc.edu/times2015/encyclopedia/countries/united-states/use-and-impact-of-timss/
15 See Oates (2017, pp. 30–31) for the key features characterising educational improvement in Singapore.
16 www.wea.org.uk/about-us?gad=1&gclid=Cj0KCQjw4NujBhC5ARIsAF4Iv6f_8jPm6WaEHF1DAcO5HUN9sLa5amTrWxPvZZXpFqXCA06klMVutVAaAs-UiEALw_wcB
17 https://about.open.ac.uk/strategy-and-policies/history-ou
18 https://about.open.ac.uk/policies-and-reports/mission
19 www.ons.gov.uk/peoplepopulationandcommunity/educationandchildcare/bulletins/educationenglandandwales/census2021
20 Excerpt from a letter of Edgar Faure to Rene Maheu, Director-General of UNESCO, about the presentation of the report Commission. Learning to be: The World of Education Today and Tomorrow, 18 May 1972, vi.
21 See Elfert (2019) for a comprehensive analysis of why UNESCO's utopian vision of lifelong learning was perceived as an "unfailure".
22 Hirsch (2016): quoting at the front of his book "Why knowledge matters" from the French writer Marc Le Bris (*Et vos enfants ne sauront pas lire . . . ni compter* (2004)).
23 https://ec.europa.eu/social/main.jsp?catId=1223&langId=en
24 https://mccrindle.com.au/insights/blogarchive/gen-z-and-gen-alpha-infographic-update/

25 www.iea.nl/studies/iea/icils
26 www.eukidsonline.ch/files/Eu-kids-online-2020-international-report.pdf
27 "Digital immigrants are considered individuals who were born prior to the influx of technology, specifically computer use, the Internet, and smartphones" (Riegel & Mete, 2017, p. 50).
28 See Coleman (2021) for a discussion of the digital divide in the UK post-pandemic.
29 www.pewresearch.org/internet/2020/04/30/53-of-americans-say-the-internet-has-been-essential-during-the-covid-19-outbreak/
30 www.forbes.com/sites/lealane/2019/05/02/percentage-of-americans-who-never-traveled-beyond-the-state-where-they-were-born-a-surprise/?sh=719d20cb2898
31 Deep technologies are grounded in important scientific advances and engineering innovations but require a longer period of gestation and/or extensive capital investment prior to commercial application. Transformative technologies have the potential to impact across many sectors of the economy (as opposed to a single sector).
32 The First Industrial Revolution (around 1765) followed the proto-industrialisation period and was characterised by mechanisation, steam and water-powered factories and mechanical production equipment. The Second Industrial Revolution (around 1870) witnessed the division of labour and the application of science to mass production and manufacturing. The Third Industrial Revolution (around 1969) presaged the rise of electronics, telecommunications and the application of computerisation/digitisation, all of which gave rise to an era of high-level automation.
33 The "gig" economy is a free labour market system in which temporary positions (occupied by independent contractors and freelancers rather than full-time permanent employees) are commonplace. "Gig" is slang for a job that lasts a predetermined period of time.
34 Fourth Industrial Revolution: How is the Fourth Industrial Revolution changing our economy? 26 November 2019. www.weforum.org/agenda/2019/11/the-fourth-industrial-revolution-is-redefining-the-economy-as-we-know-it/
35 At the turn of the 21st century, knowledge-based industries accounted for more than half of OECD GDP and have since continued to grow rapidly (OECD, 2001).
36 The requirement for collecting enormous quantities of information is increasingly being scrutinised and the reliability of its analysis has been disputed (see, e.g. Leckie & Goldstein, 2011).
37 'Assessment of learning' is carried out for the purposes of grading and reporting (Broadfoot et al., 1999). See Bennett (2009) for a discussion of how the idea of equating assessment for learning with formative assessment and assessment of learning with summative assessment is both unhelpful and too simplistic.
38 The term formative assessment has perhaps the longest history in the educational assessment literature and is usually attributed to Scriven (1967). In their 1998 review, Black & Wiliam declared that that formative assessment "does not have a tightly defined and widely accepted meaning" (p. 7). Black, P., & Wiliam, D. (1998). Assessment and classroom learning. *Assessment in Education: Principles, Policy & Practice*, 5(1), 7–14.
39 Willis, J., & Klenowski, V. (2018). Classroom assessment practices and teacher learning: An Australian perspective. In *Teacher learning with classroom assessment* (pp. 19–37). Springer.
40 www.nuffieldfoundation.org/project/the-assessment-reform-group.
41 These definitional debates continue today, but according to Black and Wiliam (2009, 2018), the difference is that AfL refers to assessment processes that intend to support learning, while formative assessment is associated with the use of assessment information to make decisions about learning.

42 A joint project between the Department for Children, Schools and Families (DCSF), the National Strategies and the Qualifications and Curriculum Authority (QCA), together with the Chartered Institute of Educational Assessors,
43 It is important to note that there is a significant difference between performance and learning: see the work of Nicholas C. Soderstrom and Robert A. Bjork (2015). They argue that the observation and measurement of performance are invariably an unreliable index of whether the relatively long-term changes that constitute learning have taken place.
44 "Learning strategies are the plans students select to achieve their goals: the ability to do so distinguishes competent learners who can regulate their learning" (OECD, 2004, p. 116).
45 The Qualifications and Curriculum Authority (QCA) was an Executive Non-Departmental Public Body of the Department for Education in England.
46 OECD (2016) was a background report to the second Global Education Industry Summit, held in Jerusalem on 26–27 September 2016. The report covered the available evidence on innovation in education, the impact of digital technologies on teaching and learning and the role of digital skills and the education industries in the process of innovation, using data from OECD surveys.
47 For example, Lowman (2013) raised the issue of using unproctored or proctored internet testing (p. 107).
48 The term "Artificial Intelligence" was coined in the 1950s. See Turing (1950).
49 The International Centre for Academic Integrity defines academic integrity as "a commitment, even in the face of adversity, to six fundamental values: honesty, trust, fairness, respect, responsibility, and courage. From these values flow principles of behaviour that enable academic communities to translate ideals into action. The Fundamental Values of Academic Integrity describes these core values in detail and provides examples of how to put them into practice on campuses, in classrooms, and in daily life". https://academicintegrity.org/about/values
50 Cotton et al. (2023).
51 See the Question & Answer session between Dr Vaughan Connolly and Dr Steve Watson (Faculty of Education, University of Cambridge) in ChatGPT (We need to talk). Published 5 April 2023. https://www.cam.ac.uk/stories/ChatGPT-and-education
52 www.technologyreview.com/2023/04/06/1071059/chatgpt-change-not-destroy-education-openai/
53 https://www.nbcnews.com/tech/tech-news/chatgpt-passes-mba-exam-wharton-professor-rcna67036
54 ChatGPT. Why AI should be banned from assessment and regulated". Daisy Christodoulou. Schools Week Wednesday, 10 May. https://schoolsweek.co.uk/chatgpt-why-ai-should-be-banned-from-assessment-and-regulated/
55 Lecturers were urged to review assessments in the UK amid concerns over a new AI tool. Sally Weale. *The Guardian*. Friday, 13 May 2023. www.theguardian.com/technology/2023/jan/13/end-of-the-essay-uk-lecturers-assessments-chatgpt-concerns-ai
56 The Joint Council for Qualifications is a membership organisation comprising the eight largest providers of qualifications in the UK. Current member providers include AQA, CCEA, City & Guilds, Edexcel, NCFE, OCR, SQA and WJEC.
57 https://russellgroup.ac.uk/media/6137/rg_ai_principles-final.pdf
58 www.timeshighereducation.com/news/get-out-plagiarism-rut-and-teach-students-how-use-ai
59 www.ucl.ac.uk/teaching-learning/generative-ai-hub/using-ai-tools-assessment
60 Artificial intelligence tools and their responsible use in higher education learning and teaching. 14 February 2023. https://eua.eu/resources/publications/1059:artific

ial-intelligence-tools-and-their-responsible-use-in-higher-education-learning-and-teaching.html
61 QAA Briefs on Artificial Intelligence Threat to Academic Integrity. 30 January 2023. www.qaa.ac.uk/news-events/news/qaa-briefs-members-on-artificial-intelligence-threat-to-academic-integrity
62 https://educationalist.substack.com/p/lets-get-off-the-fear-carousel

References

Adesope, O. O., Trevisan, D. A., & Sundararajan, N. (2017). Rethinking the use of tests: A meta-analysis of practice testing. *Review of Educational Research*, 87, 659–701. http://doi.org/10.3102/0034654316689306

Aloisi, C. (2023). The future of standardised assessment: Validity and trust in algorithms for assessment and scoring. *European Journal of Education*, 58(1), 98–110. https://onlinelibrary.wiley.com/doi/abs/10.1111/ejed.12542

Ananiadou, K., & Claro, M. (2009). 21st century skills and competences for new millennium learners in OECD countries. *OECD Education Working Papers, No. 41*. OECD Publishing.

Anders, J., Foliano, F., Bursnall, M., Dorsett, R., Hudson, N., Runge, J., & Speckesser, S. (2022). The effect of embedding formative assessment on pupil attainment. *Journal of Research on Educational Effectiveness*, 15(4), 748–779. https://doi.org/10.1080/19345747.2021.2018746

Anderson, L. W., & Krathwohl, D. R. (2001). *A taxonomy for learning, teaching and assessing: A revision of Bloom's taxonomy of educational objectives: Complete edition*. Longman.

Anirudh, V. K. (2022, February 10). *What are the types of artificial intelligence: Narrow, general, and super AI explained*. www.spiceworks.com/tech/artificial-intelligence/articles/types-of-ai/

Assessment Reform Group. (2002). *Assessment for learning: 10 principles*. Author.

Bagshaw, J., Knight, C., & Kernohan, D. (2023, February 20). ChatGPT, assessment and cheating – have we tried trusting students? Do AI advancements highlight problems with assessment itself? *Wonke*. https://wonkhe.com/blogs/chatgpt-assessment-and-cheating-have-we-tried-trusting-students/

Baig, I. M., Shuib, L., & Yadegaridehkordi, E. (2020). Big data in education: A state of the art, limitations, and future research directions. *International Journal of Educational Technology in Higher Education*, 17(1), 44. https://doi.org/10.1186/s41239-020-00223-0

Baird, J. A., Hopfenbeck, T. N., Newton, P. E., Stobart, G., & Steen-Utheim, A. T. (2014). State of the field review: Assessment and learning. *Oxford University Centre for Educational Assessment Report OUCEA/14/2*. Norwegian Knowledge Centre for Education (case number 13/4697).

Barber, M. (2001, December 7). Pupils will never have had it so good. *Times Educational Supplement*, p. 20

Benavot, A., Antoninis, M., Bella, N., Delprato, M., Härmä, J., Jere, C., Joshi, P., Koseleci, N., Longlands, H., McWilliam, A., & Zubairi, A. (2015). Education for all 2000–2015: Review and perspectives. *Zeitschrift für internationale Bildungsforschung und Entwicklungspädagogik [Journal of International Education Research and Development Education]*, 38(1), 10–15.

Bennett, R. E. (2002). Inexorable and inevitable: The continuing story of technology and assessment. *The Journal of Technology, Learning and Assessment*, 1(1). https://ejournals.bc.edu/index.php/jtla/article/view/1667

Bennett, R. E. (2011). Formative assessment: A critical review. *Assessment in Education: Principles, Policy & Practice*, 18(1), 5–25. https://doi.org/10.1080/0969594X.2010.513678.

Bennett, R. E. (2013). Preparing for the future: What educational assessment must do. *Published by the Gordon commission on the future of assessment in education.* www.gordoncommission.org/publications_reports/assessment_ paradigms.html

Bennett, W., & Wilezol, D. (2013). *Is college worth it?* Thomas Nelson.

Bersin, J. (2016, October 4). *HR technology in 2017: Disruption ahead. Insights on corporate talent, learning, and HR technology.* Update November 4, 2016. https://joshbersin.com/2016/10/hr-technology-in-2017-disruption-ahead/

Black, P., & Wiliam, D. (1998a). Assessment and classroom learning. *Assessment in Education: Principles, Policy & Practice*, 5(1), 7–74.

Black, P., & Wiliam, D. (1998b). *Inside the black box: Raising standards through classroom assessment.* King's College London School of Education.

Black, P., & Wiliam, D. (2009). Developing the theory of formative assessment. *Educational Assessment, Evaluation and Accountability*, 21(1), 5–31. https://doi.org/10.1007/s11092-008 9068-5

Black, P., & Wiliam, D. (2018). Classroom assessment and pedagogy. *Assessment in Education: Principles, Policy & Practice*, 25(6), 551–575. https://doi.org/10.1080/0969594X.2018.1441807

Bloom, B. S., Engelhart, M. D., Furst, E. J., Hill, W. H., & Krathwohl, D. R. (1956). *Taxonomy of educational objectives: The classification of educational goals. Handbook I: Cognitive domain.* David McKay Company.

Bollington, A. (2015). *Business brief: Why isn't everyone lifelong learning?* OECD Yearbook. www.oecd.org/education/lifelong-learning.ht

Boston, K. (2007). Tipping points in education and skills. *Speech to QCA Annual Review*, London

Boyle, W. F., & Charles, M. (2010). Leading learning through assessment for learning? *School Leadership & Management*, 30(3), 285–300. http://doi.org/10.1080/13632434.2010.485184

Broadfoot, P. M., Daugherty, R., Gardner, J., Gipps, C., Harlen, W., James, M., & Stobart, G. (1999). *Assessment for learning: Beyond the black box.* Nuffield Foundation and University of Cambridge. www.nuffieldfoundation.org/sites/default/files/files/beyond_blackbox.pdf

Broadfoot, P. M., Daugherty, R., Gardner, J., Harlen, W., James, M., & Stobart, G. (2002). *Assessment for learning: 10 principles.* Assessment Reform Group. Nuffield Foundation and University of Cambridge. http://assessmentreformgroup.files.wordpress.com/2012/01/10principles_english.pdf

Broadfoot, P. M., Timmis, S. E., Payton, S., Oldfield, A., & Sutherland, R. J. (2013). *Rethinking assessment 2012/2013 series of discussion papers: Six discussion papers published by University of Bristol.* www.bris.ac.uk/education/research/sites/tea/publications/index.html

Brown, G. T. L. (2019). Is assessment for learning really assessment? *Frontiers in Education*, 4, Article 64. http://doi.org/10.3389/feduc.2019.00064

Bruer, J. T. (2006). Points of view: On the implications of neuroscience research for the science of teaching and learning: Are there any? *CBE Life Sciences Education*, 5, 104–110. http://doi.org/10.1187/cbe.06-03-0153

Claxton, G. (2007). Expanding young people's capacity to learn. *British Journal of Educational Studies*, 55(2), 115–134.

Coe, R. (2013). *Improving education: A triumph of hope over experience.* Centre for Evaluation and Monitoring, Durham University.

Coleman, V. (2021). Digital divide in UK education during COVID-19 pandemic: Literature review. *Cambridge Assessment Research Report.* Cambridge Assessment.

Cotton, D. R. E., Cotton, P. A., & Shipway, J. R. (2023). Chatting and cheating: Ensuring academic integrity in the era of ChatGPT. *Innovations in Education and Teaching International*, 1(12). http://doi.org/10.1080/14703297.2023.2190148

Craig, H., Wilcox, G., Makarenko, E., & MacMaster, F. P. (2020). Continued educational belief in pre- and in-service teachers: A call for de-implementation action for school psychologists. *Canadian Journal of School Psychology*. http://doi.org/10.1177/0829573520979605

Cumming, J. J., & Wyatt-Smith, C. (2009). Framing assessment today for the future: Issues and challenges. In C. Wyatt-Smith & J. J. Cumming (Eds.), *Educational assessment in the 21st century*. Springer. https://doi.org/10.1007/978-1-4020-9964-9_1

D'Agostino, S. (2023, January 11). ChatGPT advice academics can use now. *Inside Higher Ed (IHE). Faculty Issues*. www.insidehighered.com/news/2023/01/12/academic-experts-offer-advice-chatgpt

Dawson, P. (2023, June 8). Don't fear the robot: Future-authentic assessment and generative artificial intelligence. *Virtual Presentation*. University of Calgary, Werklund School of Education. www.upei.ca/notice/2023/05/don-t-fear-robot-future-authentic-assessment-and-generative-artificial-intelligence

Delors, J. (1996). Learning: The treasure within. *Report to UNESCO of the international commission on education for the twenty-first century* (pp. 99–100). UNESCO Publishing.

Department of Education (DoE). (2023, March 29). Generative artificial intelligence in education. *Departmental Statement*. www.gov.uk/government/publications/generative-artificial-intelligence-in-education

Department for Education and Skills (DfES). (2003). *Excellence and enjoyment: A strategy for primary schools*. DfES.

Dhawan, V. (2014). Education and neuroscience. *Research Matters: A Cambridge Assessment Publication, 17*, 46–55.

Didau, D. (2014, March 12). Why AfL might be wrong, and what to do about it. *David Didau Website*. https://learningspy.co.uk/myths/afl-might-wrong/

Drucker, P. F. (1999, October). Beyond the information revolution. *The Atlantic*. www.theatlantic.com/magazine/archive/1999/10/beyond-the-information-revolution/304658/

Egan-Simon, D. (2021). Moving in the wrong direction: A critical history of citizenship education in England from the early twentieth century to the present day. *Educational Futures, 12*(1).

Elfert, M. (2019). Revisiting the faure report and the delors report: Why was UNESCO's Utopian vision of lifelong learning an "unfailure"? Chapter 2. In *Power and possibility. Adult education in a diverse and complex world* (pp. 17–26). Brill Sense. http://doi.org/10.1163/9789004413320_002

Embretson, S., & Gorin, J. (2001, Winter). Improving construct validity with cognitive psychological principles. *Journal of Educational Measurement, 83*(4), 343–368.

European Commission. (2003, November 11). *Education and training: the success of the Lisbon strategy hinges on urgent reforms*. IP/03/1520. Brussels.

European Commission Education & Culture. (2007). *Key competencies for lifelong learning – A European framework*. European Communities. www.erasmusplus.org.uk/file/272/download

European Patent Office. (2020, December 9). *Fourth industrial revolution*. www.epo.org/news-events/in-focus/ict/fourth-industrial-revolution.html

Evans, S. (2021, October 15). New skills for life alliance to tackle England's adult basic skills deficit. *FE Week*. https://feweek.co.uk/new-skills-for-life-alliance-to-tackle-englands-adult-basic-skills-deficit/

Fatkullina, F., Morozkina, E., & Suleimanova, A. (2015). Modern higher education: Problems and perspectives. *Procedia – Social and Behavioral Sciences, 214*, 571–577. https://doi.org/10.1016/j.sbspro.2015.11.762

Faure, E., Herrera, F., Kaddoura, A. R., Lpes, H., Petrovsky, A. V., Rahnema, M., & Ward, F. C. (1972). *Learning to be: The world of education today and tomorrow*. UNESCO. Retrieved October 17, 2022, from https://unesdoc.unesco.org/ark:/48223/pf0000001801/PDF/001801eng.pdf.multi

Fautley, M., & Savage, J. (2008). *Assessment for learning and teaching in secondary schools*. Learning Matters.

Fengchun, M., Wayne, H., Huang, R., & Zhang, H. (2018). *AI and education: Guidance for policy-makers*. UNESCO Education 2030. https://unesdoc.unesco.org/ark:/48223/pf0000376709

Finger, G., & Jamieson-Proctor, R. (2009). Assessment issues and new technologies: ePortfolio possibilities. In C. Wyatt-Smith & J. J. Cumming (Eds.), *Educational assessment in the 21st century*. Springer. https://doi.org/10.1007/978-1-4020-9964-9_4

Fletcher-Wood, H. (2017. March 26). Is formative assessment fatally flawed? Confusing learning & performance. *Improving Teaching*. https://improvingteaching.co.uk/2017/03/26/formative-assessment-flawed-confusing-learning-performace

Friedman, T. L., & Mandelbaum, M. (2011). *That used to be us: How America fell behind in the world it invented and how we can come back*. Farrar, Straus and Giroux.

Gallardo-Echenique, E., Marques-Molas, L., Bullen, M., & Strijbos, J. (2015). Let's talk about digital learners in the digital era. *The international review of research in open and distributed learning*. www.irrodl.org/index.php/irrodl/article/view/2196/3337

Glanville, M. (2023, February 27). *Artificial Intelligence in IB assessment and education: A crisis or an opportunity?* https://blogs.ibo.org/2023/02/27/artificial-intelligence-ai-in-ib-assessment-and-education-a-crisis-or-an-opportunity/

Graham, M. (2019, November 1). How to build a fairer gig economy in 4 steps. *World Economic Forum*. www.weforum.org/agenda/2019/11/gig-economy-in-4-steps/

Guli, L. A. (2005). Evidence-based parent consultation with school-related outcomes. *School Psychology Quarterly*, 20, 455–472. http://doi.org/10.1521/scpq.2005.20.4.455

Heaven, W. D. (2023, April 6). ChatGPT is going to change education, not destroy it. *MIT Technology Review*. www.technologyreview.com/2023/04/06/1071059/chatgpt-change-not-destroy-education-openai/

Hirsch, E. D. (2016). *Why knowledge matters: Rescuing our children for failed educational theories*. Harvard Educational Press.

HM Government. (2021, September). *National AI strategy*. Presented to Parliament by the Secretary of State for Digital, Culture, Media and Sport by Command of Her Majesty. Command Paper 525. Published by the Office for Artificial Intelligence. ISBN 978-1-5286-2894-5.

HM Government. (2022). *National AI strategy*. Presented to Parliament by the Secretary of State for Digital, Culture, Media and Sport by Command of Her Majesty. Command Paper 525. Updated 18 December 2022. Published by the Office for Artificial Intelligence.

Ionnou, A. (2018). A model of gameful design for learning using interactive tabletops: Enactment and evaluation in the socio-emotional education classroom. *Educational Technology Research and Development*, 67(2), 277–302.

Jennings, J. (2023, July 21). Information overload: Unravelling the Paradox of investment knowledge. *Forbes*. www.forbes.com/sites/johnjennings/2023/07/21/information-overload-unraveling-the-paradox-of-investment-knowledge/

Joint Council for Qualifications (JCQ). (2023). AI use in assessments: Protecting the integrity of qualifications. *Guidance for Teachers & Assessors*. www.jcq.org.uk/wp-content/uploads/2023/04/JCQ-AI-Use-in-Assessments-Protecting-the-Integrity-of-Qualifications.pdf

Kirby, A., & Smith, T. (2021). *Neurodiversity at work* (1st ed.). Kogan Page. www.perlego.com/book/2800960/neurodiversity-at-work-pdf

Kitchen, W. H. (2014). *Authority and the teacher*. Bloomsbury.
Kupiainen, S., Hautamäki, J., & Karjalainen, T. (2009). *The Finnish education system and PISA*. Ministry of Education. www.pisa2006.helsinki.fi/files/The_Finnish_education_system_and_PISA.pdf
Lavonen, J., & Laaksonen, S. (2009). Context of teaching and learning school science in Finland: Reflections on PISA 2006 results. *Journal of Research in Science Teaching*, 46(8), 922–944. http://doi.org/10.1002/tea.20339
Leckie, G., & Goldstein, H. (2011). Understanding uncertainty in school league tables. *Fiscal Studies*, 32(2), 207–224. http://doi.org/10.1111/j.1475-5890.2011.00133.x
Levy, F., & Murnane, R. J. (2004). *The new division of labor: How computers are creating the next job market*. Princeton University Press.
Literacy Task Force. (1997). *The implementation of the national literacy strategy*. Department for Education and Employment.
Lowman, R. (2013). Ethical issues related to personnel assessment and selection. Chapter 6. In *New directions in assessing performance potential of individuals and groups: Workshop summary*. National Academies of Sciences, Engineering, and Medicine (pp. 101–107). The National Academies Press. https://doi.org/10.17226/18427
Lynch, D. E. (2003). *Education in a knowledge economy*. Article for Edited Collection EdCA, CQU 25/. Research Perspectives on Education, pp. 13–20.
Lynch, M. (2019, July16). Why are some countries slow to adopt digital learning? *The TECH Advocate*.
Machin, S., & McNally, S. (2007). *Tertiary education systems and labour markets*. OECD. Accessed at Tertiary Education Systems and Labour Markets (oecd.org).
Maguire, M. (2002). Globalisation, education policy and the teacher. *International Studies in Sociology of Education*, 12(3), 261–276. http://doi.org/10.1080/09620210200200093
Major, L., Francis, G. A., & Tsapali, M. (2021). The effectiveness of technology-supported personalised learning in low- and middle-income countries: A meta-analysis. *British Journal of Educational Technology*, 52(5), 1935–1964.
Manyika, J., Lund, S., Chui, M., Bughin, J., Woetzel, J., Batra, P., Ko, R., & Sanghvi, S. (2017, December). Jobs lost, jobs gained: Workforce transitions in a time of automation. *McKinsey Global Institute*. https://epic.org/wp-content/uploads/foia/epic-v-ai-commission/EPIC-19-09-11-NSCAI-FOIA-20200529-5th-Production-pt4-Outside-Reports-Resource.pdf
Martin, T., & Sherin, B. (2013). Learning analytics and computational techniques for detecting and evaluating patterns in learning: An introduction to the special issue. *Journal of the Learning Sciences*, 22(4), 511–520. https://doi.org/10.1080/10508406.2013.840466
Maseleno, A., Sabani, N., Huda, M., Ahmad, R., Jasmi, K. A., & Basiron, B. (2018). Demystifying learning analytics in personalised learning. *International Journal of Engineering & Technology*, 7(3), 1124–1129.
Mason, L. (2009). Bridging neuroscience and education: A two-way path is possible. *Cortex*, 45, 548–549. http://doi.org/10.1016/j.cortex.2008.06.003
Mayhew, M. G., Ashkanasy, N. M., Bramble, T., & Gardner, J. (2007). A study of the antecedents and consequences of psychological ownership in organizational settings. *The Journal of Social Psychology*, 147(5), 477–500. https://doi.org/10.3200/SOCP.147.5.477-500
Mayor, F. (1999). *Higher education in the 21st century: Vision and action*, October 5–9, 1998. UNESCO.ED.98/CONF.202/CLD.49.
McGinnis, D. (2020, October 27). What is the fourth industrial revolution? *The 360 Blog from Salesforce*.
Mihai, A. (2023, January 23). Let's get off the fear carousel! *The Educationalist*. https://educationalist.substack.com/p/lets-get-off-the-fear-carousel

Mills, A., & Goodlad, L. M. E. (2023). Adapting college writing for the age of large language models such as ChatGPT: Some next steps for educators. *Critical AI (Updated 4/17/2023 to Include New Links)*. https://criticalai.org/2023/01/17/critical-ai-adapting-college-writing-for-the-age-of-large-language-models-such-as-chatgpt-some-next-steps-for-educators/

Mislevy, R. J., Steinberg, L. S., & Almond, R. G. (2002). Design and analysis in task-based language assessment. *Language Testing*, 19, 477–496.

Mogey, N. (2011). What is it that is really acting as a barrier to widespread use of summative e-assessment in UK higher education? *International Journal of e-Assessment*, 1(1).

Moser, C. (1999). Improving literacy and numeracy: A fresh start – the report of the working group in the United Kingdom. *Moser Report*. Department of Education and Employment.

Mulder, M. (2012). Competence-based education and training. *The Journal of Agricultural Education and Extension*, 18(3), 305–314.

Mulder, M., Weigel, T., & Collins, K. (2007). The concept of competence in the development of vocational education and training in selected EU member states: A critical analysis. *Journal of Vocational Education and Training*, 59(1), 67–88. http://doi.org/10.1080/13636820601145630

Mullis, I. V. S., Martin, M. O., Goh, S., & Cotter, K. (Eds.). (2016). *TIMSS 2015 encyclopedia: Education policy and curriculum in mathematics and science*. Retrieved from Boston College, TIMSS & PIRLS International Study Center website: http://timssandpirls.bc.edu/timss2015/encyclopedia/

NCEE (1983). *National Commission on Excellence in Education (NCEE) a nation at risk: The imperative for educational reform*. NCEE.

Nye, J. S. (2003, March). The information revolution. Chapter 2. In *The Paradox of American power: Why the world's only superpower can't go it alone* (pp. 41–76). Oxford Academic Books. https://doi.org/10.1093/0195161106.003.0002

Oates, T. (2017, September). *A Cambridge approach to improving education: Using international insights to manage complexity*. University of Cambridge Local Examaintions Syndicate. https://www.cambridgeassessment.org.uk/Images/cambridge-approach-to-improving-education.pdf

OECD. (2001). *Competencies for the knowledge economy*. Chapter 4. https://one.oecd.org/document/DEELSA/ED/CERI/CD(2000)12/PART4/REV2/en/pdf

OECD. (2004). *Learning for tomorrow's world: First results from PISA 2003*. Author.

OECD. (2016). *Innovating education and educating for innovation: The power of digital technologies and skills*. OECD Publishing. http://doi.org/10.1787/9789264265097-en

OECD. (2021). *United Kingdom country note – Skills outlook 2021: Learning for life*. OECD. www.oecd.org/unitedkingdom/Skills-Outlook-UnitedKingdom.pdf

Office for Students. (2022, November 24). *Securing student success: Regulatory framework for higher education in England*. Presented to Parliament pursuant to section 75 of the Higher Education and Research Act 2017. OfS 2022.69. ISBN 978-1-5286-3792-3.

Oldfield, A., Broadfoot, P., Sutherland, R., & Timmis, S. (2012). *Assessment in a digital age: A research review*. STELLAR. University of Bristol.

Oxford English Dictionary. (2023). www.oed.com/

Pane, J. F., Steiner, E. D., Baird, M. D., & Hamilton, L. S. (2015, November). Continued progress: Promising evidence on personalized learning. *Report for the RAND Corporation*. Reports no. R-136-BMGF. RAND Corporation.

Pardo, A., Jovanovic, J., Dawson, S., Gašević, D., & Mirriahi, N. (2019). Using learning analytics to scale the provision of personalised feedback. *British Journal of Educational Technology*, 50(1), 128–138.

Patrinos, H. A. (2016). The skills that matter in the race between education and technology. *Prepared for the 2016 Brookings Institution Blum Roundtable.* https://www.researchgate.net/publication/339956474_The_skills_that_matter_in_the_race_between_education_and_technology

Pellegrino, J. W. (1999, November 17). *The evolution of educational assessment: Considering the past and imagining the future.* The Sixth Annual William H. Angoff Memorial Lecture presented at Educational Testing Service.

Pellegrino, J. W., Baxter, G. P., & Glaser, R. (1999). Addressing the "two disciplines" problem: Linking theories of cognition and learning with assessment and instructional practice. In A. Iran-Nejad & P. D. Pearson (Eds.), *Review of research in education* (vol. 24, pp. 307–353). American Educational Research Association.

Pellegrino, J. W., Chudowski, N., & Glaser, R. (Eds.). (2001). *Knowing what students know: The science and design of educational assessment.* National Academy Press.

Perrotta, C., & Wright, M. (2010). *New assessment scenarios. A Futurelab report.* www.futurelab.org.uk/resources/new-assessment-scenarios

Prensky, M. (2001, October). Digital natives, digital immigrants. *On the Horizon,* MCB University Press, 9(5).

Prensky, M. (2020, August 18). Why "education" can't be fixed. *Medium.* https://marcprensky.medium.com/why-education-cant-be-fixed-6fd264d6fb6b

Priestley, M., & Sinnema, C. (2014). Downgraded curriculum? An analysis of knowledge in new curricula in Scotland and New Zealand. *Curriculum Journal,* 25(1), 50–75.

QAA Briefs on Artificial Intelligence Threat to Academic Integrity. (2023, January 30). https://www.qaa.ac.uk/news-events/news/qaa-briefs-members-on-artificial-intelligence-threat-to-academic-integrity

Quach, S., Thaichon, P., Martin, K. D., Scott, W., & Palmatier, R. W. (2022). Digital technologies: Tensions in privacy and data. *Journal of the Academy of Marketing Science,* 50, 1299–1323. https://doi.org/10.1007/s11747-022-00845-y

Raikes, N. (2019). Data, data everywhere? Opportunities and challenges in a data-rich world. *Research Matters: A Cambridge Assessment Publication,* 27, 16–19.

Raphael, B. (1976). *The thinking computer.* W.H. Freeman.

Richardson, M., & Clesham, R. (2021). Rise of the machines? The evolving role of AI technologies in high-stakes assessment. *London Review of Education,* 19(1), 9, 1–13. https://doi.org/10.14324/LRE.19.1.09

Riegel, C., & Mete, R. E. (2017). Educational technologies for K-12 learners: What digital natives and digital immigrants can teach one another. *Educational Planning,* 24, 49–58.

Robelen, E. W. (2011, February 7). Report aims to DEBUNK "myth" about days of U.S. achievement. *Education Week.* www.edweek.org/leadership/report-amims-to-debunk-myth-about-glory-days-of-u-s-achievemnt/2011/02

Rychen, D. S., & Salganik, L. H. (2003). *Key competencies for a successful life and well-functioning society.* Hogrefe & Huber Publisher.

Sahlgren, G. H. (2015). *Real finnish lessons: The true story of an education superpower.* Centre for Policy Studies.

Säljö, R. (2010). Digital tools and challenges to institutional traditions of learning: Technologies, social memory and the performative nature of learning. *Journal of Computer Assisted Learning,* 26, 53–64.

Schildkamp, K., van der Kleij, F. M., Heitink, M. C., Kippers, W. B., & Veldkamp, B. P. (2020). Formative assessment: A systematic review of critical teacher prerequisites for classroom practice. *International Journal of Educational Research,* 103, 101602. https://doi.org/10.1016/j.ijer.2020.101602.

Schleicher, A. (2010). *The case for 21st-century learning*. Retrieved February 11, 2013, from www.oecd.org/document/2/0,3746,en_21571361_44315115_46846594_1_1_1_1,00.html

Schleicher, A. (2011, January). *Organisation for economic cooperation and development*. The OECD Observer, Suppl. OECD Yearbook 2011. Paris Issue. 282/283.

Schleicher, A. (2019). *Presentation at the forum on transforming education*. Global Peace Convention.

Schmidt, F. L. (2002). The role of general cognitive ability and job performance: Why there cannot be a debate. *Human Performance*, 15(1–2), 187–210. http://doi.org/10.1080/08959285.2002.9668091

Schwab, K. (2016, January 14). The fourth industrial revolution: What it means, how to respond. *World Economic Forum*. https://www.weforum.org/agenda/2016/01/the-fourth-industrial-revolution-what-it-means-and-how-to-respond/

Serrat, O. (2014, April 20). Information overload in the attention economy. *Asian Development Board*. www.researchgate.net/publication/275155424_Information_Overload_in_the_Attention_Economy

Shilo, S., Rossman, H., & Segal, E. (2020). Axes of a revolution: Challenges and promises of big data in healthcare. *Nature Medicine*, 26, 29–38.

Shute, V. J., & Becker, B. J. (2010). Prelude: Assessment for the 21st century. In V. J. Shute & B. J. Becker (Eds.), *Innovative assessment for the 21st century: Supporting educational needs* (pp. 1–11). Springer Science + Business Media. https://doi.org/10.1007/978-1-4419-6530-1_1

Shute, V. J., Ventura, M., & Kim, Y. J. (2013). Assessment and learning of informal physics in Newton's Playground. *The Journal of Educational Research*, 106(6), 423–430. http://doi.org/10.1080/00220671.2013.832970

Soderstrom, N. C., & Bjork, R. A. (2015). Learning versus performance: An integrative review. *Perspectives on Psychological Science*, 10(2), 176–199. http://doi.org/10.1177/1745691615569000

Stecher, B. M. & Hamilton, L. S. (2014). *Measuring hard-to-measure student competencies: A research and development plan*. RAND Corporation. https://www.rand.org/pubs/research_reports/RR863.html. Also available in print form

Stevenson, A. (2019, November 8). Moser 20 years on: Why improving literacy and numeracy still matters. *NCFE*. www.fenews.co.uk/exclusive/moser-20-years-on-why-improving-literacy-and-numeracy-still-matters/

Stewart, W. (2012). Think you've implemented assessment for learning? *Times Educational Supplement*. Retrieved February 3, 2023, from ww.tes.com/news/tes-archive/tes-publication/think-youve-implemented-assessment-learning

Swiecki, Z., Khosravi, H., Chen, G., Maldonado, R. M., Lodge, J. M., Milligan, S., Selwyn, N., & Gašević, D. (2022). Assessment in the age of artificial intelligence. *Computers and Education: Artificial Intelligence*, 3, 100075.

Swindell, R., & Thompson, J. (1995, September). An international perspective of the university of the third age. *Accessed at U3A historical paper*. worldu3a.org.

Thornton, K. (2012). Editorial. *Studies in Self-Access Learning Journal*, 3(1), 2–5.

Timmis, S., Broadfoot, P., Sutherland, R., & Oldfield, A. (2016). Rethinking assessment in a digital age: Opportunities, challenges and risks. *British Educational Research Journal*, 42(3), 454–476.

Trilling, B., & Fadel, C. (2009). *21st century skills – Learning for life in our times*. Jossey-Bass.

Turing, A. M. (1950). Computing machinery and Intelligence. *Mind*, 49, 443–460.

Twyman, J. S. (2018). Digital technologies in support of personalised learning. *Report, center on innovations in learning university*. Temple University.

UNESCO. (1990, March 5–9). World declaration on education for all and framework for action to meet basic learning needs. *World conference on education for all meeting basic learning needs. Jomiten, Thailand.* UNESCO Publishing.

UNESCO. (2000a). World education report 2000. *The right to education: towards education for all throughout life.* United Nations (UNESCO Publishing). https://unesdoc.unesco.org/ark:/48223/pf0000119720

UNESCO. (2000b). *Global synthesis of UNESCO education for all assessment 2000.* UNESCO.

UNESCO. (2011, September). Digital natives: How do they learn? How to teach them? *IITE Policy Brief.* UNESCO Institute for Information Technologies in Education. UNESCO Institute.

UNESCO. (2015). Education for all 2000–2015: Achievements and challenges. *12th edition of the EFA global monitoring report.* United Nations Educational, Scientific and Cultural Organization. UNESCO Publishing.

UNESCO Institute for Information Technologies in Education. (2011, May). Digital literacy in education. *Policy Brief.* https://iite.unesco.org/pics/publications/en/files/3214688.pdf

UNITED NATIONS. (2000). World education forum in Dakar, Senegal, 26–28 April to boost drive for education for all. *Press Release SOC/4543.* www.un.org/press/en/2000/20000411.soc4543.doc.html

U.S. Department of Education, National Center for Education Statistics. (2004). *Stronger accountability: Testing for results: Helping families, schools, and communities understand and improve student achievement.* www.ed.gov/nclb/accountability/ayp/testingforresults.html

Vayachuta, P., Ratana-Ubol, A., & Soopanyo, W. (2016). The study of "out-of-school" children and youth situations for developing a lifelong education model for "out-of-school" children and youth. *SHS Web of Conferences, 26,* 01015. ERPA 2015. http://doi.org/10.1051/shsconf/20162601015

Voogt, J., & Roblin, N. P. (2010). *21st century skills (discussion paper).* University of Twente.

Voogt, J., & Roblin, N. P. (2012). A comparative analysis of international frameworks for 21st century competences: Implications for national curriculum policies. *Journal of Curriculum Studies, 44*(3), 299–321. http://doi.org/10.1080/00220272.2012.668938

Weale, S. (2023, January 23 Friday). Lecturers urged to review assessments in UK amid concerns over new AI tool: ChatGPT is capable of producing high-quality essays with minimal human input. *The Guardian.* www.theguardian.com/technology/2023/jan/13/end-of-the-essay-uk-lecturers-assessments-chatgpt-concerns-ai

Whitelock, D., & Watt, S. (2008). Reframing e-assessment: Adopting new media and adapting old frameworks. *Learning, Media and Technology, 33*(3), 151–154.

Willetts, D. (2017). *A university education.* Oxford University Press.

Williams, A. (2015, September 19). Meet alpha: The next "next" generation. Fashion. *The New York Times.* Retrieved September 7, 2019. https://www.nytimes.com/2015/09/19/fashion/meet-alpha-the-next-next-generation.html

Willis, J., & Klenowski, V. (2018). Classroom assessment practices and teacher learning: An Australian perspective. In *Teacher learning with classroom assessment* (pp. 19–37). Springer.

Winthrop, R., & McGivney, E. (2015, June). Why wait 100 years? Bridging the gap in global education. *The Brookings Institution.* www.brookings.edu/reserach/why-wait-100-years-bridging-the-gap-in-golbal-education

Wong, B. T. M. (2017). Learning analytics in higher education: An analysis of case studies. *Asian Association of Open Universities Journal, 12*(1), 21–40. https://doi.org/10.1108/AAOUJ-01-2

World Bank. (2019). *World development report 2019: The changing nature of work*. World Bank. https://doi.org/10.1596/978-1-4648-1328-3

Wyatt-Smith, C., Lingard, B., & Heck, E. (2019). Digital learning assessments and big data: Implications for teacher professionalism. *Education research and foresight working paper 25*. UNESCO.

Yin, J., Goh, T.-T., Yang, B., & Xiaobin, Y. (2021). Conversation technology with micro-learning: The impact of chatbot-based learning on students' learning motivation and performance. *Journal of Educational Computing Research*, 59(1), 154–177. https://doi.org/10.1177/0735633120952067

Yorke, M. (2003). Formative assessment in higher education: Moves towards theory and the enhancement of pedagogic practice. *Higher Education*, 45(4), 477–501.

3
NEW PRIORITIES AND AN UNEXPECTED SHOCK

Introduction

In this chapter, we discuss three 21st-century developments that are important for our stocktake of educational assessment in the second quarter of the 21st century. The first two are issues that are not new but have come to the fore in the early 21st century, both in educational thought and more widely. The first of these is concern about climate change. The second is the importance given to well-being, both as an objective and as a concern if it appears to be lacking. We have classified these two sets of issues as "new priorities". The third development described in this chapter – the "unexpected shock" – is the onslaught of a global pandemic. We are only beginning to understand the impact of Covid-19 on teaching, learning and the content and practicalities of educational assessment. What is clear is that the pandemic has created a fissure in long-term thinking about education and assessment: it is not possible to chart continuous straight-line development through the first quarter of the century. In this changing context and in light of the new priorities, educational assessment has itself changed and will need to continue to change.

Climate change – a new priority

The devastating effects of climate change are being experienced across the planet. Interestingly, however, its impact on education has not received similar global attention and scrutiny (Delgado, 2022). Natural changes like the greenhouse effect were first identified in the early 19th century, for example, by the French physicist Joseph Fourier. Towards the end of the 19th century,

DOI:10.4324/9781003346166-3

scientists began to link human emissions of greenhouse gases to the climate, arguing that industrial-age coal burning would enhance the natural greenhouse effect. In 1896, a landmark paper by Swedish scientist Svante Arrhenius first predicted that changes in atmospheric carbon dioxide levels could substantially modify the surface temperature through the greenhouse effect. Climate change became an official concern among scientists towards the end of the 1950s, although the term was introduced by US scientist Wallace Broecker some twenty years later. The scientific community began to unite in favour of action on climate change in the 1980s.[1]

Climate change very quickly aggravated environmental and social anxiety across the planet, as well as affecting all organisations, institutions and areas of life directly or indirectly. Education systems have been required to respond urgently to climate change (UNICEF, 2019). According to the United Nations, education has become a critical agent in addressing the issue of climate change.[2]

In many countries, the frequency, intensity and duration of climate-related extreme weather events, including damaging winds, flash floods, fires, tropical cyclones, rising sea levels and droughts have brought about significant disruption to schools, especially in the poorest communities. Drought and increasing temperatures have led to meagre harvests and a dearth of food, with a damaging impact on educational attainment. Severe weather conditions reduce the obtainability of safe drinking water, increase the prevalence of weather-connected diseases such as malaria and diarrhoea, and endanger sanitation. All of these can lead to absenteeism and likely withdrawal of children from school. Quite apart from the primary impacts, climate change can have secondary impacts on education, resulting from the measures that households take in response to climate change, such as migration and dispersing families.

The havoc of climate change is being felt around the world. Research demonstrates that climate vulnerability has hindered learning progress and is damaging to learning outcomes (Education Development Trust, 2022). Catherine Porter (2021), Director of the Young Lives Foundation (and Professor of Economics, Lancaster University, England),[3] spotlights a largely unheeded impact of climate change on education. The Young Lives' longitudinal research project – a study of poverty and inequality among young people (from their early years, through adolescence, and into young adulthood) – has been following the lives of 12,000 children in Ethiopia, India (Andhra Pradesh and Telangana), Peru and Vietnam since 2001. The research discloses how childhood exposure to extreme weather conditions has had an unequal effect on children's development, with the worst effects on the poorest and most vulnerable children (Porter, 2021). For example:

> Children living in the very poorest households have been significantly more affected [by extreme weather events]. In Ethiopia, a startling 81%

of children in [the] poorest households experienced at least one extreme weather event, compared to only 22% in the least poor households.

(Porter, 2021, webpage)

Girls and young women are particularly vulnerable as they tend to bear the added responsibilities of household work in times of climatic crisis, thereby increasing the real possibility of failing to complete their schooling. Porter (2021) argues that climate-related shocks (e.g. weather events destroying crops) in the prenatal period and the first few years of the lives of children have negative long-term consequences on the development of their bodies, malnutrition being a real danger. Their cognitive maturation may also be affected, evidenced by poor vocabulary and low levels of basic mathematics, especially in children whose parents received little or no education. Randell and Gray (2019) have argued that in parts of the tropics, exposure to severe temperatures or rainfall in very early life is related to fewer years of schooling in later childhood.

East Asia and the Pacific regions are particularly susceptible to climate change. Half of the population is directly affected every year by floods, droughts and storms (UNISDR, 2019). The rapid mobilisation of populations from rural to urban areas in recent years threatens to intensify climate risks. UNICEF (2019) has projected a shift in the growth of population towards coastal areas, where the influences of severe weather conditions (including sea level rise) are at their greatest. A report published by the World Meteorological Organisation (2022)[4] and based on data between 1998 and 2020 indicated that in Latin America and the Caribbean, more than 312,000 lives had been lost and 277 million people had been affected by climate change with inevitable impacts on education. As the climate crisis continues, Latin America and the Caribbean will be one of the hardest-hit regions.

Climate change threatens to undermine the achievement of progress towards quality education enshrined in UN 2030 Global Sustainable Development Goal 4, particularly in areas of the world at greatest risk of destruction or upheaval because of climate change. UNESCO (2010) was committed to eradicating poverty and improving living conditions through attainment of the MDGs. However, it has become increasingly challenging to achieve the MDGs while simultaneously reducing reliance on carbon, encouraging climate resilience and safeguarding balanced economic development (Newman & Smith, 2021).

Thus, the increasing impact of climate change is evident. In addition, education is increasingly identified as one means of combatting it. Emerging evidence (Education Development Trust, 2022) demonstrates that education can be a significant means to enable people to adjust to climatic shocks, analyse risks and entrench sustainable practices in their daily lives. Enlarging environmental mindfulness and education on climate change can contribute to successful adaptation and mitigation (UNICEF, 2019). Exploring the link between education and climate change, the International Institute for Applied Systems Analysis

(2020) demonstrated that increasing the level of educational attainment within a population correlates with a significant reduction in vulnerability.

The worldwide community has understood the significance of education in confronting climate change. The UN Framework Convention on Climate Change, the Paris Agreement and the associated Action for Climate Empowerment agenda have called on governments to educate, galvanise and engage all stakeholders on policies and actions relating to climate change.[5] Global education systems must necessarily appropriate the knowledge, skills, means and funding to first avert, then manage risks associated with climate change. The need for approaches to education that prepare and embolden people of all ages to tackle unexpected environmental, economic and political outcomes and empower them with the knowledge, skills, values and attitudes needed has been radically underlined. Education is called on to equip learners to make informed decisions in the face of these challenges.

Climate change education

How can education contribute to the fight against climate change? One way is through the taught curriculum. According to the United Nations, the impact of global warming and how to adapt to climate change can and should be taught in classrooms. Increasing overall climate and environmental "literacy" among young people is an initiative gaining traction and support internationally (e.g. UNESCO, 2020). Prominent among the 17 Sustainable Development Goals (SDGs) promoted by the United Nations in 2012, number 13 is Climate Action.

Building on the UN Decade on Education for Sustainable Development (ESD) (2005–2014) and the Global Action Programme on ESD (2015–2019), a new framework, "ESD for 2030", was adopted by the 206th UNESCO Executive Board and the 40th UNESCO General Conference and acknowledged by the 74th UN General Assembly. "ESD for 2030" develops the Global Action Programme that sought to realign and reinforce education and learning to contribute to all activities that encourage sustainable development. "ESD for 2030" places a stronger focus on education's major contribution to the attainment of the SDGs. It calls on nations to deliver appropriate education that puts responsibility for the future at the centre (UNESCO, 2020, p. iii). Research undertaken by Cordero et al. (2020) claims to demonstrate that even if only 16% of high school students in high- and middle-income countries were to receive climate change education, there would be a reduction of almost 19 gigatons of carbon dioxide by 2050.

A study produced by Earth Warriors – an environmental curriculum provider – analysed data from a WHO-UNICEF-Lancet report (Clark et al., 2020) and concluded that no country in the world performs well on both environmental education and wellness of children. Moreover, no country performs well on all three measures of child flourishing, sustainability and equity. The report also found that Italy was the only country to include both climate change and sustainable development in its national curriculum – a development announced in a Reuters interview by Education Minister Lorenzo Fioramonti, to be in place by 2019.

Kwauk and Winthrop (2021) of the Brookings Institute argue that when education facilitates students and learners to cultivate a deep personal association with potential climate change solutions, it not only has a positive impact on their daily actions and decision-making that lessens their general lifetime carbon footprint but also enlarges their personal agency and empowerment. Increasingly, experts in the field of climate change are emphasising the significance of educating children and young people on environmental issues and nurturing a culture of caring for the climate.

Kwauk and Winthrop (2021) claim that in the United States, 80% of parents and in the UK, 77% of adults, support teaching climate change in school. However, they suggest that teachers in the UK and more widely across Europe say they are currently ill-equipped to teach climate change issues and would require more training and materials. Resources are becoming increasingly available and popular. For example, the World Wide Fund for Nature (formerly the World Wildlife Fund) has produced introductory climate change resources designed to introduce the topic of climate change to students aged 7–11. Secondary school students and primary school students with an existing knowledge of climate change are able to explore the effects of climate change through a series of school curriculum-linked programmes and activities. Provocative research has suggested that children can have a strong influence on their parents' views (Lawson et al., 2019).

In England in 2021, the then Education Secretary Nadhim Zahawi stated that all children should be taught about the importance of conserving and protecting the planet (Department for Education, 2022). Consequently, in England, issues relevant to climate change are now included on the national curriculum for Key Stages 3 (11–14 years) and 4 (14–16 years) (see Kulakiewicz et al., 2021). The Curriculum for Excellence[6] in Scotland includes a number of ways in which students are expected to learn about climate change between ages 3 and 15. Under the theme of "Learning for Sustainability", climate change is addressed through combining experiences and outcomes across curriculum areas in a variety of contexts.

By 2023, the UK government expected teachers in England to provide "world-leading climate change education" through a "model science curriculum" (Civinini, 2021). The curriculum would teach children about nature and their impact on the world around them. The Royal Society of Chemistry (RSC) has appealed for the scientific basis for climate change, and the indisputable role of human behaviours and interventions, to be made essentially clear in the school curriculum. This was supported strongly by Professor Charlton-Perez,

Professor of Meteorology at Reading University, who was a leading academic supporting the "Climate Education Action Plan" launched at COP26.[7]

There are those who have questioned whether changes to the designed curriculum for teaching in English schools have gone far enough. For example, the word "climate" occurs twice in the science curriculum for Key Stage 4 (KS4) for 15- and 16-year-olds – requiring teachers to explain the "potential effects" of greenhouse gases, plus "evidence and uncertainties" for human-caused climate change. It occurs once at KS3 (12–14 years), but not at all at KS2 (8–11 years) or KS1 (5–7 years). In geography, there are three mentions in the KS3 curriculum, including the requirement to teach "the change in climate from Ice Age to the present" and "how human and physical processes interact to influence and change landscapes, environments, and the climate".

Dr Elizabeth Rushton, co-creator of the British Educational Research Association (BERA) "Manifesto for Education for Environmental Sustainability",[8] contends that education about climate change should not be confined to the remit of the sciences and geography, and that doing so makes it less successful. She argues that sustainability ought to be as pervasive in schools as safeguarding and that there are possibilities in the designed curricula for other subjects too, including the arts and humanities (The Guardian, 2022).

According to Worth (2021), in the United States some teachers are providing misleading, outdated or false information. Worth alleges that the fossil fuel industry is doing all that it can to undermine education about climate change. Despite the fact that approximately 75% of public school science teachers in the United States teach climate change and almost all public school students are likely to receive at least some education about recent global warming. Plutzer et al. (2016) claim that students have been receiving mixed messages from teachers about the causes of global warming. UNESCO (2021) surveyed teachers about their schools' attitudes and approaches to climate change education, and exposed some worrying data (p. 3):

- Nearly half (47%) of the national curriculum frameworks of 100 countries reviewed had no reference to climate change.
- Only 55% of teachers reported that they had received training – either pre-service or in-service – on climate change and sustainable lifestyles, and fewer than 50% reported that their school had an action plan on climate.
- Fewer than 40% were confident in teaching climate change and only about one-third felt able to explain well its effects on their region or locality (in other words, 60% felt uncomfortable teaching the subject).

Whatever the curriculum design, the curriculum experienced by young people may be a different matter. A survey of 500 young people in England reported that 66% felt they did not learn enough about climate change in school and over 50% said they learned the most about climate change from documentaries and social media, compared to just 13% who learned the most from school or college (Gallone & Syed, 2021). And the experienced curriculum extends beyond the lessons taught and beyond the school. A report by the OECD in 2022 entitled "Are Students Ready to Take on Environmental Challenges?" suggested that students' willingness to act to improve the environment (as distinct from understanding the scientific and other issues around climate change) was more influenced by the wider life of the school and the community than by formal instruction:

> To develop students' sense of environmental purpose, which is crucial to their acting on climate change, schools that are the most successful are those that are themselves environmentally active. Schools can encourage students to carry out climate action projects either in the classroom or after regular school hours.
>
> *(OECD, 2022, p. 12)*

For teachers to engage students effectively on climate change, they need confidence in tackling the subject and an understanding of how it links to other parts of the designed and taught curriculum. Standing back from the proliferation of reports we have cited, there appear to be at least four ways in which education – and education providers – can tackle the new priority of climate change. The first, as we have seen, is in the content of subject curricula, not only in science and geography, but also in the arts and humanities. The second is in cross-curricular study (involving more than one subject), aiming to develop learners' abilities to think synoptically and apply learning gained in one context to new situations. Climate change does seem to be a topic well-suited for this approach. The third is through the atmosphere and activities of the school more generally and the ways that school life – and the engagement of schools with the wider community – display environmental awareness. The fourth is in the management and activities of school and college systems, including such things as the design of school buildings and the use of fossil fuels in school transport.

New climate initiatives in the United States (and elsewhere) are revealing the surprising impact K–12 schools are having on the environment and what they can do to be more green (e.g. Bauld, 2021). The K–12 Climate Action Plan 2021, for example, provides readily actionable climate solutions at various levels, including steps that schools can take to become more sustainable. The Plan's mission is to unlock the power of the education sector to be a force towards climate action, solutions and environmental justice to help prepare children and youth to advance a more sustainable, resilient and equitable society.[9]

Fiona Carnie, the Director of Alternatives in Education and author of *Rebuilding Our Schools from the Bottom Up*, claims that as of March 2019,

2,052 demonstrations about climate change had taken place in 123 countries. This number has almost certainly risen steeply since. Mounting numbers of educators and academics are supporting young people to put pressure on governments to take the climate crisis seriously (Carnie, 2022). There is no question that climate change is a clear priority for education as we enter the second quarter of the 21st century.

Impact on educational assessment

Recognition that the link between education and climate change is a powerful one must have implications for educational assessment. That is increasingly acknowledged, with statements that climate change "is poised to be a defining factor in the future of educational assessments" (Sitta et al., 2023, p. 6) and that climate change promises to be an influential driver of the future of teaching, learning and assessment (Newsome et al., 2023; Intergovernmental Panel on Climate Change, 2022).[10] The impact of global warming and how to adapt to climate change, according to the United Nations, can and should be taught. But, beyond such high-level statements, what does this mean for educational assessment? We outline here some answers to that question.

Implications for the constructs of assessment and the tasks set

In accordance with SDG 4 Indicator 4.7.5, Bermingham and Chainey (2022) argue for an assessment transformation that reflects the social and economic impacts of climate change, greenhouse gas pollution and biodiversity collapse.[11] Indicator 4.7.5 reads:

> Percentage of students in lower secondary education showing proficiency in knowledge of environmental science and geoscience.
> *(United Nations, 2015)*[12]

Underlying this indicator is the assumption that as understanding of climate issues grows, countries become more likely to develop foundations for protecting the planet and its environment.

The recommendations for changes to the subject curricula for teaching in schools (as described in the earlier sections of this chapter) can, and arguably should, be reflected in the constructs of subject assessments and tests, whether used for formative or summative purposes. We have referred to the increased prominence of climate change in designed curricula (e.g. the national curriculum for Key Stages 3 and 4 in England and the Curriculum for Excellence in Scotland). Summative assessments linked to these curricula must be designed to ensure that they measure what really matters. For example, for PISA 2025, the OECD proposes a strong emphasis on science (to better equip young people for the world they will live in), which will include:

> "The development of Scientific knowledge and its Misuse", to give students a better appreciation of how knowledge is developed, and help them navigate the incorrect use of knowledge such as in climate change denial or the anti-vaccination movement.
> *(OECD, 2023, p. 3)*

The PISA 2025 Science Framework, developed by a group of international experts led by the OECD and delivered by Oxford University Press (OUP), seeks to assess skills that the OECD argues are crucial for subsequent generations of citizens. Learners, they argue, will need to be able to apply key information about health, environment and the physical world to everyday life, and to navigate demanding global issues such as climate change and evaluate "fake news", in the hope that that scientific literacy can empower learners to create solutions.[13] The Framework will assess students on their ability to use scientific skills to analyse data and evidence, examine how science education can be used to empower action for sustainability and the environment and, it is hoped, shape "science citizens". Fathima Dada, OUP's Managing Director for Education, argues that the PISA 2025 Science Framework "will be a catalyst for an evolution in science education, enabling young people to combat climate change in an age of misinformation" (2024, webpage).[14]

Climate change contexts for the PISA 2025 science assessment include environmental quality and hazards, within personal, local, national and global settings (OECD, 2023, p. 20):

	Personal	*Local/National*	*Global*
Environmental Impacts & Climate Change	Sustainable practices of recycling and reduction of resource use.	Population distribution, waste management, environmental impact. Use of regenerative agriculture.	Environmental sustainability, management of pollution and air quality, loss of soil/biomass. Mass extinction of species. Ocean acidification.
Hazards	Risk assessments of lifestyle choices.	Rapid changes (e.g. earthquakes, severe weather), slow and progressive changes (e.g. coastal erosion, sedimentation), risk assessment. Facial recognition.	Threats posed by climate change, impact of modern communication, energy and its production (e.g. fracking, nuclear, gas).

Context-based climate change assessment not only demonstrates that learners understand the causes of the existential threat to the planet but also incorporates practical actions and creative solutions to the problems caused by global warming. According to Sitta et al. (2023), climate change is one factor (together with the impact of AI and changes in assessment itself) that "could lead to more compassionate humanitarian responses and the need for flexible, . . . assessments" (p. 6).

The scope for environmental impacts and climate change to be studied through cross-curricular projects has gained traction in recent years. Current climate change elements in the secondary school curriculum often focus on scientific facts and, as such, are concentrated in taught science and geography programmes of study. However, the findings of a survey in 2023 by University College London (UCL) ("Teaching climate change and sustainability: A survey of teachers in England"),[15] concluded that teaching climate change and sustainability in more subjects would empower young people (and their communities) to take action on the pertinent issues.

The UCL survey found that teachers from across the curriculum – not just teachers of geography or science – and at all stages, would like to embed climate change more broadly in their teaching. The majority said it was a priority for the topic to feature more strongly on the curriculum, particularly at primary level and in subjects other than geography and science. However, fewer than half (44.9%) said they had received formal professional development related to climate change and sustainability.

In a Policy Report undertaken by the University of Bristol (England), published a year before the UCL Report, the content of UK government plans was compared with views expressed by teachers in England, and with expert international opinion.[16] The study entailed surveying secondary and primary teachers (n = 626) who were attending mandatory staff development events unrelated to climate change. Overall, most of the teachers in the survey, irrespective of their subject area, were already talking about climate change to their students and wanted to see a cross-curricular approach to climate change education that involved at least six subjects delivering it. UK teacher educators are arguing that climate change must be addressed in the curriculum through interdisciplinary frameworks of understanding that include its ethical dimensions (Hawkey et al., 2019).

If it is important for environmental issues to be studied through cross-curricular projects, that importance should be supported and reinforced by assessment systems that include – and reward – such work. One of the authors was told by teachers that there was "no time" for students to embark on work of this kind (even if it led to a qualification) because of the time pressure to deliver the content for subject examinations. Something has to give to enable priorities in assessment to match priorities in the world and students' lives.

In summary, reflecting the importance of climate change in the constructs of assessment and the tasks set has implications both for the focus within individual subjects and for the need to provide assessment opportunities for learners to bring disciplinary thought together to address climate issues.

Assessing attitudes to climate change and/or willingness to be involved in action to address it

Education has the power to motivate learners to take action. Akrofi et al. (2019) argue that boosting student responsiveness through education is vital to nurturing proactive participation to promote climate change actions – a call echoed by the United Nations and UNESCO. In Australia, ACER (2022) also argues strongly for transforming assessment to empower students to take such action.[17] Increasingly, initiatives to promote climate and environmental "literacy" in young people are gaining traction internationally (e.g. UNESCO, 2020).

Relevant literature reveals numerous national and transnational attempts to measure the levels of knowledge, attitudes, perceptions and engagement of young people (including university students) in climate change using questionnaires and surveys (e.g. Leal Filho et al., 2023a; Ejaz et al., 2022; Liu et al., 2022; Arıkan & Günay, 2021). Surveys have collected information on and attempted to assess:

- global warming/climate change-related knowledge;
- attitudes towards climate change mitigation;
- concerns about the seriousness of the threat posed by climate change and its urgency;
- baseline awareness of key climate policies;
- awareness of any climate commitments made by their governments; and
- perceptions of international burden sharing.

More difficult is the question of how to assess students' *feelings* about climate change and/or their willingness to do something about it, whether by engaging in public debate or by changing their own lifestyles. To date, there is no universally agreed approach to measuring and comparing attitudes towards climate change and emotions about it. Despite significant efforts to canvass the views of respondents, it remains difficult to measure what learners feel as distinct from what they know and can do. We suggest that this is an issue that needs to be considered further. This should start with exploring critically what the desired outcomes are – for example, do we regard it as a successful outcome of education if students go on demonstrations? Or is such a suggestion improperly importing partisan sociopolitical views into educational debate? Only then can work begin on how to assess whether these outcomes have been realised and, if so, to what extent.

The agenda of assessment work on climate change is still largely unexplored. It is a new priority for society and education, and it will need to be so for assessment in the next quarter-century.

The modes of assessment and the impact of the assessment industry on the climate

One link between education and climate change is the impact of education provision and consumption on the environment. Given the size of the education estate in all countries and the numbers of people involved, common sense would draw attention to a range of factors: the carbon efficiency of school buildings; the extent to which learners and staff are driven (or drive themselves) to school or college in cars; the use of school transport and the modes of transport used, the exposure of learners to air pollution; the use of paper, etc. The list can go on. And there are clearly similar factors affecting the world of assessment.

Whether tests or assessments are provided by an external organisation, by the state or by educational institutions themselves, the processes involved need to be scrutinised for their environmental impact. For assessments taken on paper, the processes for printing, packaging and transportation of papers before and after the test is taken need to be considered, together with the use of vans and other transport for distribution. Clearly, even in systems relying heavily on paper-based assessments, developments in recent decades to scan papers for marking purposes have reduced the need for papers to be transported to markers. For international assessment organisations, whether in educational or professional contexts, there are questions to be asked about the need for international travel and the impact of the processes for taking tests on the environment in the particular circumstances of the countries where the tests are being taken.

The increase in the use of technology for taking and marking tests and assessments reduces some of the concerns about the use of paper. However, it raises more 21st-century questions about the environmental impact of the instrumentation used by assessment providers and by candidates and their institutions. These questions are relevant whether assessment takes place at home or in the workplace (The British Psychological Society, 2021; Sitta et al., 2023).

The issues we have raised in this section may strike the reader as fairly obvious. Our reason for repeating them here is that they need to be asked more frequently and with more care than appears to be the practice now. This is important for two reasons. First, assessment is a widespread activity within one of the largest sectors of the economy in most countries, so the effects on the environment are not insignificant. Second, we suggest that arrangements for high-stakes tests or examinations may be of heightened significance in their impact on the perceptions and feelings of learners. They will not be impressed if there appears to be a tension between what they are taught in their science class about climate change and the processes used for an assessment of great importance for them.

Well-being – a new priority

There is nothing new in talking about well-being. The Greek philosophers mused on the components of the good life, and their successors continued the debate, joined by economists and psychologists. What is distinctive in the early 21st century, we suggest, is the prominence of well-being both with thought leaders and with the wider public in discussions about education – and about public policy more generally. *Happiness: Lessons from a New Science*, a book by the economist Richard Layard, was published in 2006 and widely read. Its popularity promoted a second edition in 2011, and in the preface to the later edition, Layard wrote:

> The well-being movement . . . is now in full flood. Policy-makers worldwide are questioning whether wealth is a proper measure of welfare. And it has become quite respectable to say that what matters is how people experience life, inside themselves. Not everyone agrees with that, but talking about the happiness and misery which people feel no longer provokes an amused smile. The debate is on, at all levels in our society.
> *(Layard, 2011, p. 13)*

From an educational perspective, John White observed in 2007: "The idea that education should equip people to lead flourishing lives and help others to do so is now becoming salient in policy-making circles" (White, 2007, p. 17). And at a policy level, in 2010, the UK Prime Minister, David Cameron, announced that the Office for National Statistics (ONS) would "devise a new way of measuring wellbeing in Britain". He added: "We'll start measuring our progress as a country, not just by how our economy is growing, but by how our lives are improving; not just by our standard of living, but by our quality of life".[18] The terms of this announcement reflect a 21st century move away from the unquestioned dominance of economic public policy objectives in many discussions.

The ONS now publishes regular reports on well-being, based on responses from a structured sample to four questions:

1. Overall, how satisfied are you with your life nowadays?
2. Overall, to what extent do you feel that the things you do in your life are worthwhile?

3. Overall, how happy did you feel yesterday?
4. On a scale where 0 is "not at all anxious" and 10 is "completely anxious", overall, how anxious did you feel yesterday?[19]

It will be noted that these questions cover a range of language – "satisfied", "worthwhile", "happy" – and the more negative "anxious". The positive language of the first three questions, together with "well-being" itself (the title of the survey) and "quality of life" form a bundle of related ideas that, we suggest, have become increasingly prominent in recent decades. And as we shall see later in this chapter, the experience of the pandemic has been an added prompt for such a focus (e.g. Downie, 2021).

Emphasis on the importance of well-being has been balanced by increasing emphasis on mental health and concern about mental illness – in all its variants, ranging from "anxiety" (the fourth of the ONS survey questions), through distress and depression to the range of classified mental illnesses, suicidal thoughts and suicide itself. Statistical trends can be affected by changes in definition, but there has been a significant increase in reported mental illness across the spectrum in the second decade of the 21st century. That trend was becoming clear before the onset of the pandemic and continued through it and beyond. Based on a survey of adults in 2014, the UK mental health charity MIND reported that "the amount of people [in England] with common mental health problems went up by 20% between 1993 and 2014, in both men and women" (McManus et al., 2016).[20] They also reported increases in suicidal thoughts, suicide attempts and actual suicides.

There has been a similar trend in reported mental illness among young people. In a report on England published in late 2022 (in the context of Covid-19) the Sutton Trust and UCL reported, using different cohort studies for each year cited, that in 2007, 23% of 16–17-year-olds reported "distress". In 2017, 35% of 17–18-year-olds reported distress, and in 2022, the proportion of 16–17-year-olds had risen to 44%.[21] The UK counselling service charity Childline (2019) affords a listening ear to children and young people who have worries or concerns. In their most recent Annual Review (2019), the most talked-about concern was emotional health and well-being, with more than 39% of sessions discussing this as the principal concern. ChildLine highlighted that sessions about anxiety had increased by 55%, from 13,700 between April 2016 and March 2017 to 21,300 between April 2017 and March 2018.

All these trends raise questions about definition and meaning, but they cluster together to illustrate increased prominence in thinking about the importance of well-being and (mental) illness. One of the authors was involved in a (voluntary) survey in a part of the UK of views about education, involving young people, parents, teachers and the wider public. Responses to questions about important features of good education were collated in a "word cloud" in which "mental health" was one of the most-mentioned items.[22] Richard

Layard does seem to be right in saying that "the debate [about well-being and mental health/illness] is on, at all levels in our society" (2011, p. 13).

What do we mean by well-being (and its opposites)? Has understanding of it changed? What are the implications for education (Davis, 2019)? And for educational assessment? Well-being is defined by the *Oxford English Dictionary* as "the state of being comfortable, healthy, or happy" (20 July 2019). That raises questions about the relationship between each of these states (comfort/health/happiness), but a common feature of all three is that they denote more than just the absence of their opposite – discomfort, illness or unhappiness. That point was emphasised back in 1946 by the World Health Organization in the words of their Constitution: "Health is a state of complete physical, mental and social well-being and not merely the absence of disease or infirmity" (webpage).[23] Also, it may be wrong to see well-being as a linear continuum, with unhappiness and ill-health at one end and a high state of well-being at the other. Care workers often speak admiringly of clients who display remarkable contentment despite the most severe health, social or financial problems, or in the face of the grief of bereavement.

What is the link between well-being and happiness? There are three possible ways of understanding "happiness" in this context. The first sense refers to pleasurable feelings experienced by each individual. In that sense, what brings happiness may differ greatly from person to person. Sometimes subjective accounts of happiness focus on long-term good feelings (rather than short-term "highs"), as in Layard's "So by happiness I mean feeling good – enjoying life and wanting the feeling to be maintained. By unhappiness I mean feeling bad and wishing things were different" (Layard, 2011, p. 13).

The second sense has been described by John White as "informed desire fulfilment" (White, 2007, p. 17). This is still largely a subjective view, but it excludes from "happiness" good feelings about something that the person mistakenly thought would have desirable outcomes beyond their immediate impact. In that sense, taking a recreational drug at a party might not be said to make a young person happy (or "really" happy).

However, there is a tradition of thought in which well-being goes beyond pleasurable feelings, however informed about consequences. Downie (2021) cites the 12th-century philosopher Maimonides, who distinguished between "perfection of the body" and "perfection of the soul".[24] But who is to say what constitutes "perfection of the soul"? And are the constituent elements of that perfection the same for everyone? There have been attempts to arrive at a more objective account of well-being, which can be applied to all or most people. John White has reported that "most of the following items appear on list after list:

(1) accomplishing things in one's life which make that life meaningful
(2) being self-directed or autonomous in the conduct of one's life

(3) knowledge and understanding
(4) the enjoyment of beauty
(5) deep personal relationships
(6) moral goodness
(7) sensual pleasures"

(White, 2002, p. 443)

But the justification for including particular items in this list varies among the authors of the lists from which it was drawn. The inclusion of some items – for example, self-direction or autonomy – may derive from a Kantian view of human nature. Some may be culturally determined: for example, as White points out, G.E. Moore's account of well-being in his *Principia Ethica*, written in 1903, resonates with the lifestyle of the Bloomsbury Group, of which Moore was part, in its emphasis on beauty and personal relationships (White, 2002, p. 444).

What is the relevance for education of these differing accounts of well-being? First, it should be noted that an entirely individualistic subjective account of well-being (with well-being potentially meaning something different for each person) would make it very difficult for it to be an objective of a curriculum designed for more than one pupil, beyond dealing with visible signs of unhappiness or distress. Most teachers would echo Layard in hoping that their pupils felt good rather than feeling bad. But in our view, a thought experiment[25] can demonstrate that most educational practitioners would want to go further than an account of well-being confined to pleasurable feelings.

Let us imagine a class of children, many of whom come from poor families, have poor health records (with frequent absences for health reasons) and often show signs of anxiety. The teacher does his or her best to support them, but it's a difficult task. Then the teacher is told that a new pill has been developed that can be administered to the pupils and makes them feel good. It has no side effects, is non-addictive and there is an indefinite supply for everyone in the class. Would administering this to all the pupils be a means to secure well-being?

Leaving aside the improbability of this story, we think that most readers would feel uncomfortable about administering the pleasure pill. They might feel that it was a form of abuse of the pupils, particularly if they had no choice about taking the pill. Some might feel it was a sinister way for the authorities offering the pill to bypass their responsibility to address causes of the social and economic hardship experienced by the pupils. But arguably the discomfort that many would feel with this imaginary case indicates that the well-being that has assumed such a high profile in 21st-century thought and which featured so prominently in the recent Northern Ireland survey (2023)[26] of "good education" is more than simply stimulating pleasurable feelings in young people (which the pill would do). Even in a pluralistic society featuring different cultures and different justifications for moral views (we say more about the latter in Chapter 6), educationists in the mid-21st century will need to explore more fully the views of well-being expressed in society and by writers and thinkers. Fresh thinking is required to populate the concept for the mid-century and think through the implications for education.

Turning to the opposite of well-being: (mental) illness, anxiety, distress and feeling bad, in many countries there has been a rising expectation that education will play a large part in addressing those. Roles that might in the past have been seen as more appropriate for parents, the church or leaders of the local community have tended to gravitate towards the school. In addition, rising instances of reported mental illness among children of school age, combined with financial limitations on mental health services, can leave teachers being seen as having a multiplicity of roles in promoting the well-being – or dealing with its opposite – of all their pupils. This can provoke the exasperated reaction that teachers are expected to be social workers and dieticians – and, by implication, to solve all the problems of society. Anecdotally, we have found this irritation felt more by teachers of older pupils than by those of young children, with the latter more likely to see their educational objectives in terms of the development of the whole child rather than the imparting of subject knowledge or the preparation of students for examinations.

As well as being seen as an objective of education, the concept of well-being has been applied to the educational environment and the life experience of young people attending school or college (see, e.g. Sitta et al., 2023). The OECD 2018 PISA survey included optional questions on well-being, and they reported that:

> Across OECD countries, about two in three students reported that they are satisfied with their lives, a percentage that shrank by five percentage points between 2015 and 2018. More than 85% of students reported sometimes or always feeling happy, cheerful, or joyful; but about 6% of students reported always feeling sad.
>
> *(Schleicher, 2019, p. 47)*

The countries with the highest "well-being" scores were not the same as those with the highest scores in the tests of maths, science and reading, and the three factors that the young people reported most frequently as making them sad were the way they looked, their relationship with their parents and their relationship with school life.

Schleicher (2019) also reported on experiences of bullying (including cyberbullying). There was an increase between 2015 and 2018 in reported experiences of bullying, and in the later year, "more than one in five students reported being bullied at school at least a few times a month" (p. 2). This experience was correlated with lower academic performance and lower perceived well-being:

> Students who reported being frequently bullied scored 21 points lower in reading than students who did not report so, after accounting for socio-economic status. Frequently bullied students reported feeling sad, scared and less satisfied with their lives.
> *(op. cit., p. 51. See also Dake et al., 2003)*

As readers of *Tom Brown's Schooldays* will know, there is nothing new about bullying in educational environments, and the increased number of reports of bullying can in no way be taken to imply that there was necessarily less bullying in earlier times, as distinct from fewer reports. However, concern about bullying, together with the availability of different instruments for bullies to use, including social media, is a distinctive part of the increased 21st-century focus on well-being and its opposite.

The European Commission includes on its website in the European Education Area a section on "well-being at school",[27] which it describes as "a state in which pupils are able to develop their potential, learn and play creatively". They unpack this description by giving examples of what this means for each pupil:

- "feeling safe, valued and respected
- being actively and meaningfully engaged in academic and social activities
- having positive self-esteem, self-efficacy and a sense of autonomy
- having positive and supportive relationships with teachers and peers
- feeling a sense of belonging to their classroom and school
- feeling happy and satisfied with their lives at school".

(webpage)[28]

These items apply to the pupil's experience of living in the school, the pupil's feelings and their experiences both inside and outside the taught curriculum.

Thus, the implications for education of the concept of well-being affect the objectives of education and the experiences of young people at school and at home. And our observations on the meaning of "well-being" over and above pleasurable feelings should not hide the obvious point that some enjoyment and pleasure should have an important part in the educational experience of young people. In the famous words of Thomas Hughes in *Tom Brown's Schooldays*, written in 1857, "Life isn't all beer and skittles; but beer and skittles, or something better of the same sort, must form a good part of every Englishman's education".

What is the relevance of the increased focus on well-being to educational assessment? We shall identify two related assessment issues. The first is a dilemma: how to assess well-being in an educational environment. To our surprise, very little has been written about this in the literature of educational assessment (despite the ever-growing literature about test anxiety).[29] This contrasts with developments in medicine and social care to categorise and develop indicators to measure the well-being of elderly people[30] or the checklists used by health visitors when assessing the development of babies and toddlers. The "Warwick-Edinburgh Mental Wellbeing Scale"[31] offers a framework for assessing the mental well-being of the general population. Where are the educational assessment professionals and researchers involved in this work?

The most obvious method for assessing the well-being of an individual is to ask them how they feel. This is the method used by the OECD in its PISA questions related to happiness, and the ONS uses the same approach in its survey of well-being. This does seem the most practicable option for assessing feelings – who, one might ask, would know better about them than the person having them? However, the answers can be culturally determined by the extent to which young people are encouraged – or expected – to talk about their feelings. Just as medical diagnosis can combine reports by patients with observations of their behaviour and test results, arguably it might be possible to identify behaviour and actions associated with different levels of well-being and include observations and answers to questions (other than "how well do you feel?") in an assessment. The outcomes could be used for evaluating education provision, identifying causes of unhappiness and dealing with them, as well as successes in supporting well-being among students. If promoting well-being is a characteristic of good education, we should be able to evaluate it through assessment. It is also important to consider indicators of well-being (or its opposite) among education providers – teachers and non-teaching staff in a school or college.

The second implication for assessment is that assessment itself can be a source of well-being – or its opposite. A report issued by the OECD in 2017, using data from PISA in 2015, included the finding that "around 64% of girls and 47% of boys reported that they feel very anxious even if they are well prepared for a test. Schoolwork-related anxiety is negatively related to performance at school and to students' satisfaction with their life".[32] If well-being is one of the objectives for the educational experience of young people, and if assessment is part of that experience, then it is necessary to consider the impact that participation in assessment can have on the well-being of the young people.

There are also questions about the impact of pupil assessments on the well-being of teachers and other staff in schools or colleges. Arguably, any anxiety felt by teachers may come from empathy with their pupils, but also from worry that the assessment outcomes will be used to evaluate them as teachers or the school as a whole. In England, there has been a debate on the place that examination results should have in the evaluation of schools by the national inspectorate (OFSTED).[33] This has been discussed in the context of concern about the anxiety felt by school heads and others about the grade assigned to schools following an inspection.[34]

Taking an informed view of this issue requires a sense of proportionality and respect for evidence. Proportionality involves taking a balanced view of the ups and downs of life and the need for students to be able to handle occasional important or special events. However, systems that involve successions of tests (prepared for by even more mock tests) for two or three years of a young person's life may raise legitimate questions about the impact on their well-being, over and above any educational concerns about the effect on teaching and learning of "teaching to the test(s)" (see, e.g. Zakharov et al., 2014; Jennings & Bearak, 2006; Lazear, 2006; Bond, 2005; Crocker, 2003; Popham, 2001).

Respect for evidence requires efforts to test widely shared views about assessment against evidence as far as is possible. The prominence of well-being in educational and public debate makes that need particularly important for views shared on social media and elsewhere about assessment and well-being. An example of such work is a recent report by John Jerrim (2021) on work related to the claim that the tests taken in England at the end of primary school ("Key Stage 2") caused stress to pupils and teachers. Jerrim compared data on children in England and children in other parts of the UK that did not have these tests and found "[n]o evidence . . . that the Key Stage 2 tests in England [are] associated with lower levels of happiness, enjoyment of school, self-esteem or children's mental wellbeing" (p. 507). Jerrim does not have the last word on this, and no doubt his report will prompt further work. But it is important that research for evidence relevant to well-being is carried out and publicly reported.

When consideration is being given to the number and method of assessments, the effect on well-being is one of the considerations that need to be taken into account. Thus, for example, consideration of moves to increase or decrease the use of modular systems for summative assessments, or to increase or decrease the role of students' own teachers in determining their grades, needs to include in the decision-making any evidence of the effect of the outcomes on students' well-being and reported levels of anxiety. Of course, well-being effects will vary from individual to individual, and there are reported gender differences (see, e.g. European Institute for Gender Equality, 2021; Matud et al., 2019).

There are also concerns about the effect on students' well-being of the build-up to, and experience of, stressful final examinations. (Putwain, 2009; Putwain & Daly, 2014; Putwain & Symes, 2018; Flitcroft & Woods, 2018). It has been argued that being put under this kind of pressure is good preparation for coping with stresses at university or the world of work (Jamieson et al., 2016). But we suggest that those taking this line should look afresh at how universities carry out their assessments nowadays and how performance at work is evaluated by modern employers.

We are not saying that the effect on well-being is necessarily the overriding criterion to be used in decisions about how to assess (we say more about that in Chapter 6), but the increasing focus on well-being in 21st-century thought means that well-being needs to have a seat at the policy table when these decisions are being made.

Finally, we should not overlook the opportunity for assessment to contribute positively to well-being. In 2022, a blog by Jay Surti shared by a UK-based assessment organisation included:

> Encouraging students to view assessments positively – as opportunities to demonstrate their skills and knowledge, and to discover how they are progressing – allows them to develop and improve. This continuous progress is highly motivating and rewarding for students.[35]

Surti was writing primarily about formative assessment as a regular part of classroom practice, but the quoted remarks can be applied more widely and are not inconsistent with the common-sense realisation that important opportunities to show what one knows or can do can promote nerves. Indeed, actors and musicians tell us that nerve-free performances are not the best ones. But such opportunities can also be rewarding when they go well. Assessment professionals are usually disparaging about media reports on national examination results day, which tend to show delighted (attractive) teenage girls hugging each other and jumping for joy at their results. But even the disgruntled educationists cannot deny that the girls are happy about their assessment outcomes.

In this section we have described well-being as a "new priority", meaning that it is high on the agenda for educationists, policymakers, children and their parents, and the wider public. We have explored what is meant by well-being and concluded that in educational contexts there is an objective element in judgements of well-being, over and above reported pleasurable feelings by individuals. The implications of this for education include well-being having a part in curriculum objectives and in the evaluation of the school environment. Turning to assessment, the priority now given to well-being raises the question of how to assess well-being and what effect (positive or negative) assessment may have on the well-being of those involved.

Global pandemic – an unexpected shock[36]

Learning poverty

Data from the Tony Blair Institute for Global Change published in 2022 suggested that just before the pandemic, more than half of all 10-year-olds, across the world, were in "learning poverty" and most of the children so described were at school (Iosad et al., 2022, p. 3). According to a report published in the same year by the World Bank, UNESCO, UNICEF, the UK government's Foreign, Commonwealth and Development Office (FCDO), USAID and the Bill & Melinda Gates Foundation, the learning crisis had deepened following the pandemic; the latest projections estimated that the number of people living in learning poverty had risen to 70% (World Bank et al., 2022).

A child in learning poverty – a concept introduced by the World Bank (2019)[37] – is someone who lacks minimum proficiency in mathematics and literacy and is unable to read or understand a simple narrative. In the absence of these functional competencies, it is difficult for children to progress to or succeed in secondary school education. Without foundational learning, young people will fail to acquire the human capital necessary to drive their future careers beyond school or the skills required to facilitate their place as engaged citizens in a knowledge economy (The World Bank, UNESCO & UNICEF, 2021). In a 2022 update, the World Bank, UNESCO and UNICEF voiced a major concern that "The very high levels of learning poverty, both before COVID-19 and now, violate children's right to education" (World Bank et al., 2022, p. 10).

In contrast with the slower-burning "new priorities" described elsewhere in this chapter, the impact of the global pandemic on education was swift, far-reaching and uncompromising:

[T]he COVID-19 pandemic has created the largest disruption of education systems in history, affecting nearly 1.6 billion learners in more than 190 countries and all continents.

(United Nations, 2020, p. 2)

Alice Barnard, the Chief Executive of the (UK-based) Edge Foundation, ominously remarked that

The impact of the coronavirus will be one of the defining features of a whole generation of British children. The lockdown has had a severe impact on every family and on every aspect of education in this country.

(Edge Foundation, 2020, p. 1)

This observation, of course, is as applicable to all countries as it is to the UK.

Covid-19 has exacerbated pre-existing education and learning gaps, revealed systemic weaknesses hindering authentic social mobility and further highlighted inequality of opportunity for access, participation and progression in education (OECD, 2021). Learning losses, for example, have been predicted to broaden beyond the Covid 19-affected generation, thereby obliterating years of progress, particularly affecting girls' and young women's educational access and retention (United Nations, 2020). Students from poor and underprivileged backgrounds have encountered greater challenges adjusting to the vicissitudes imposed by the pandemic. School closures have tended to be longer in countries with lower learning outcomes (Giannini et al., 2022). Furthermore, deprived and disadvantaged children have been less likely to have access to satisfactory tools for remote learning, adequate space for home study or the encouragement of the family. Problems with each and all of these contribute to learners falling behind. Ensuring equity across learners throughout the pandemic was especially challenging, as poorer students were most likely to suffer as a consequence of distance learning and were in greater danger of disengaging with education across continued periods when schools were closed. And some of those with adequate access to remote learning technology suffered from student screen fatigue and adaptation stress (OECD, 2021).

The enormity of the disruption has yet to be fully comprehended. "The State of the Global Education Crisis: A Path to Recovery" (2021) – a joint World Bank, UNESCO and UNICEF Report, presented the findings of a study of the state of global education, following sustained school closures that affected nearly all the world's students, and made recommendations for recovery. Data in the Report showed significant losses in mathematics and reading in high-, middle-, and low-income countries that disproportionately affected the most marginalised students (UNESCO, 2021). A report by Hodgen et al. (2020) also explored the impact of remote mathematics teaching brought about by around fifteen weeks of school closures in England during Covid-19. Their findings were based on a survey of 49 Year 7 pupils (11–12-year-olds) and interviews with a subgroup. While mathematical learning experiences were more limited and restricted for all pupils in comparison to their usual lessons (very limited opportunities for feedback, interaction with teachers, for pupils to engage in metacognitive tasks or to express their mathematical ideas orally), the study reported inequities in pupil participation: pupils from more disadvantaged backgrounds were more likely to spend less time on, and have less access to, remote learning (Hodgen et al., 2020, p. 21).

In Chapter 2 we discussed the increased salience for the 21st century of the concept of "lifelong learning". In 2021, the OECD reported that more than 50% of adults did not participate in adult learning in 2016, with the Covid-19 pandemic having the effect of reducing future prospects of doing so (OECD, 2021, p. 25).

Education as a response to crises

In 2019, the UN General Assembly recognised Education for Sustainable Development (ESD) as a model for reconceptualising learning to achieve the

Sustainable Development Goals (SDGs). ESD was seen as crucial to preparing the world for future crises. Covid-19, which hit an unprepared world only a year after the UN Assembly met, has threatened progress towards the 17 SDGs in the 2030 Agenda as well as the nationally determined contributions under the Paris Agreement.[38] It has been argued that a future UN objective should be to design more resilient education systems that are both receptive and adaptive to future crises (Van der Graaf et al., 2021, p. 3).

Unanticipated threats such as the pandemic have demonstrated a need for individuals and societies to be able to respond appropriately and quickly. The competences seen as necessary for the advancement of sustainable development have included comprehending complexity, agreeing compromises, foreseeing differing scenarios, acting quickly on limited information and collaborating and negotiating in order to arrive at the most fitting solutions. This formidable list of competences has a lot in common with the international programmes for ESD that were in place when the pandemic started. However, the educational impact of the pandemic, particularly on disadvantaged learners, has meant that many remain less likely to participate in education, achieve, find appropriate employment or pursue lifelong learning. It does seem that the competences required by individuals and society to deal with future shocks are still beyond the grasp of many.

The effects of school closure across different countries and groups of learners are, as yet, poorly understood. School closures throughout the pandemic tended to be more prolonged in countries with lower learning outcomes (OECD, 2021, p. 11). Moreover, the attainment gap between students from more and less disadvantaged backgrounds enlarged substantially as a result of Covid-19 (e.g. Education Endowment Foundation, 2020; Müller & Goldenberg, 2021).

Assessment and the pandemic

One of the most immediate implications of the pandemic for assessment was that many countries had to consider whether to continue with national tests and examinations, and if so, how to do so when schools were closed. Problems included taking account of learning opportunities lost by candidates and providing fair and appropriate mechanisms for the assessments to take place. This was a particular problem for countries where national examinations mainly took the form of paper-based written examinations taken in school examination halls. The International Association for Educational Assessment (IAEA) published an interesting survey of the arrangements made for national assessments in 2020 in countries across the world.[39] These ranged from continuing as usual to postponing examinations, cancelling them or adopting different arrangements for awarding marks or grades. In the paragraphs that follow, we use as a case study the experience in the UK, which opted for the last mentioned of these approaches, at the eventual cost of widespread public disquiet. Many other countries took different approaches, but the bumpy ride in the UK raised questions that have rightly attracted wider discussion.

In 2020 and 2021, governments in all the UK countries concluded that the main summer series of examinations would have to be cancelled because of the coronavirus pandemic but that grades should still be awarded to enable students to progress. Instead of examinations, students received grades based on the judgement of teachers or lecturers. They were being asked to assess their students' performance and to estimate how their students would have fared if the examinations had taken place. They had to base their grade decisions on a range of evidence of students' performance related to the subject content they had been taught. But the final decision rested with the school or college, not the external examining organisation. This approach immediately raised issues of fairness (Shaw & Nisbet, 2021). For a grade determined by a school or college to be "relationally" fair (like cases being treated alike), the standards applied should be consistent with those applied by other schools – and by other teachers in the same school (Nisbet & Shaw, 2020). For a grade to be "fair-by-desert" (a fair examination grade should match the quality of the student's work), it should show accurately what the student knows and can do based on the subject content the student has been taught.

Could grades awarded by schools and colleges, using information provided by teachers, be fair in these senses? There would appear to be a reasonable case for fairness-by-desert, for surely teachers know their students better than anyone else does? Arguably, they are best positioned to make judgements based on the wide range of evidence that students will have provided, including tests taken in the classroom as well as work on projects and practical work. However, in the event, problems arose from the fact that most teachers had not been trained to make these kinds of synoptic assessment judgements. In the first year of the pandemic, there was no evidence-base of work already done to inform the judgement, and even in the second Covid-19 year, the guidance and sample materials that were issued came rather late in the day.

There are always likely to be some inconsistencies between the grades awarded by schools, and thus a shortfall against the highest standards of relational fairness. In the event of Covid-19, the grading policies of individual schools and colleges were shown to examination boards, but they were not all the same. Schools were able to choose from a range of types of evidence, and they did not all make the same choices. The Priestley Review, an independent review commissioned by the Scottish government (Priestley et al., 2020), reported on the attitudes of young people to the changing situation regarding the summer examinations in 2020. The Review suggested that varied approaches to estimating grades in Scotland detracted from their reliability. Teachers' estimates were clearly "subject to variation (in the types of evidence available, the processes followed for internal moderation and the support given by local authorities)" (Priestley et al., 2020, p. 12). Some subject teachers knew their students better than others. Also, it was likely that grades determined for students in small school classes studying quite unusual subjects would reflect a richer vein of evidence than those available for teachers of large classes in a college.

In 2020, the initial plans were to award "calculated grades" using a statistical approach that, as the regulators were instructed by the government, should keep results "broadly in line" with previous years. In many cases, these grades were lower than the estimates by candidates' schools, and this led to accusations of unfairness from students, their parents and teachers. After an enormous row and a subsequent U-turn, students were awarded the higher of the calculated grades or the grade proposed by their school or college.[40]

The grades awarded in 2020 and 2021 were markedly higher, overall, than they had been in 2019 (Roberts & Danechi, 2022). The issue of grade inflation is a long-standing one and is not unique to assessments in schools or unique to the Covid-19 years.[41] For many years, the proportion of students achieving higher grades in school examinations in the UK has crept up and this has led to howls of "dumbing down" of standards. Students who have worked hard and done well have been subjected to insensitive comments like "'A' grades are two a penny nowadays". And the external examination boards, the regulators and the government have been between a rock and a hard place: if the results are lower than expected, that reflects poor teaching; if they are higher, that demonstrates grade inflation and lower standards.

The same discussion has taken place about high classes of honours degrees awarded by British universities. The proportion of students achieving a "first" rose from 8% in 1996–97 to 26% in 2016–17 (Richmond, 2018, p. 4), with the universities looking over their right shoulder at the requirement to award a significant number of "good degrees" and over their left at the requirement to maintain standards for degree awards.

The absence of examinations during 2020 and 2021 certainly led the hearts of politicians and regulators to grow fonder towards them, and across the UK, the announced intention was to return to examinations in 2022 because they were considered the best and fairest way to assess students. The Education Secretary told Parliament in July 2021 that "the best form of assessment is always examination" (Hansard, 2021). And in 2020, Ofqual, the examinations regulator in England, stated that "exams are the fairest way to assess what students know and can do", adding that, "despite every effort and good intention, other forms of assessment are likely to be more inequitable" (Ofqual, 2020).

In summer 2022, the General Certificate of Secondary Education (GCSE), Advanced Subsidiary (AS) and Advanced (A) Level examinations were reinstated. For England, Ofqual had announced that grading in 2022 would again be more generous than it was pre-pandemic, but that grades were expected to fall at a midpoint between those in 2019 and 2021. This was indeed the case. The plan for the future was for grades to revert to a more normal distribution. As such, 2022 was described as a "transition year" (Roberts & Danechi, 2022).

Does grade inflation matter? There are good reasons for trying to limit the inflation of examination grading standards, just as there are to control inflation in the economy. A perception that high grades have become easier to obtain can affect public confidence in the whole system. It can be unfair to high-achieving students if the system lacks a way of showing how excellent they are. One of the uses of examination grades – to discriminate between applicants for competitive university courses – may be more difficult if more students present the same (high) grades. And it is difficult for employers to use information based on students' grades if the meaning of those grades is constantly changing.

In England, changes to A-levels and GCSEs in the second decade of the 21st century have been in the direction of putting as much weight as possible on examinations taken at the end of the course, ending modular structures (where parts of a qualification are taken at different times) and minimising the use of what became known – disapprovingly – as "non-examination assessment", such as projects and course work.[42] Almost all the eggs were put in the one basket of traditional end-of-course examinations, because these were regarded as the best and fairest way to assess students. That caused a crisis when the one basket became unavailable.

Examinations in the UK are among the most tightly controlled and closely quality-assured in the world. The external examination boards have elaborate systems for designing, vetting, marking and checking examination papers; identifying and dealing with cheating; adapting examinations to make them accessible to students with disabilities; and carrying out statistical and other analyses to make sure that minority groups of students are not disadvantaged. In England and Wales, all this is checked by a regulator. So, in many technical senses, traditional examinations are fair. As a snapshot of a student's knowledge, understanding and skill, taken on one occasion only and related to tightly defined content, they are reliable and reasonably consistent over time.

But there are downsides. Can a single snapshot do full justice to a student's learning over several years? What if the student has a bad day or the right questions don't come up? And is it fair to test students using only one method – written work in an examination hall at the end of the course? Is that fair to students who could have shown their knowledge or skill more effectively through coursework, practical work or assessment throughout the course?

What are the lessons for assessment from the experience of the pandemic – and from the distinctive experiences of the UK countries retold here?

One possible comment is that the pandemic may have jolted the overly cautious assessment world into accepting that the format of many traditional written examinations is out of date. When examinations are being discussed, almost all UK newspapers and news websites show a stock photo of an examination hall with desks spaced out so that no-one is too near anyone else, and anxious-looking young people sitting at their desk writing vigorously with a pen, talking to no-one. But when will they have to do that ever again? At university? At work? There is no doubt that some young people are good at doing examinations, and they were disappointed when they were cancelled. But if the skill set required for extended pen-and-ink solitary work on a single occasion is not justified in terms of the nature of the subject being assessed or preparation for skills required in the future, is it the "best" form of assessment?

Alternatives to one-off written national examinations include one-off tests taken either at school/college or at home using a computer, and greater use of marks and grades awarded by schools. All of these alternatives have their drawbacks, including risks to security and challenges to reliability and consistency. US high school grades, for example, are notoriously varied (Brookhart et al., 2016). They were also subject to grade inflation during the pandemic (Sanchez & Moore, 2022).[43] Arguably, grades awarded by schools will always lack the consistency of examination grades awarded at the national or state level.

We know from relevant research that when teachers predict grades, their individual judgement needs to be checked by others, and the schemes developed by schools in 2021 provided for that (Everett & Papageourgiou, 2011; Gill & Benton, 2015; Murphy & Wyness, 2020). However, research also demonstrates that forms of assessment that are not like examinations – for example, coursework or holistic judgements made about a student's performance in the classroom – can be subject to bias (unfairness), with the greatest harm to socially disadvantaged students or students with special educational needs (Burgess & Greaves, 2013). A recent study found that students in England from highly educated backgrounds benefited from more generously assessed grades (Anders et al., 2021).

It can be argued that the more generous grades determined by UK schools during the pandemic are a fairer reflection of a student's learning from the totality of a course than their written work on one day at the end of the course, in stressful circumstances. But the grades that are used for GCSEs and A-levels have been developed through traditional examinations and are understood in terms of examination performance. Even after the resumption of examinations, there will be a need for the regulators to consider what to do to avoid grades becoming so inflated in the future that they lose their meaning and the public loses confidence in them.

The Covid-19 experience has forced educators to look for alternatives to traditional terminal examinations, and the alternatives have been far from perfect (Nisbet & Shaw, 2022). It is too soon to know what the long-term effect of the pandemic will be on how assessments are carried out. The immediate response to returning to near-normal when the worst of the pandemic was over may have been to try to revert with a sigh of relief to the good old pre-pandemic days. But the pandemic experience of alternative approaches to assessment may prompt the question of how fair the pre-pandemic approaches were. If they were unfair, it would not be fair to return to them. In our view, in the long term, the fairest approach may be to use a mix of modes of assessment (including coursework and practical work as well as examinations). And surely, we can take the plunge to enable students to present their evidence using a computer, just as they will have to do in their future lives.

Although national and international organisations plan for global emergencies such as pandemics, Covid-19 was unquestionably a shock, and it may become a point of reference in conversation and thought for the rest of the 21st century, distinguishing between "pre-Covid-19" and "post-Covid-19" times. There was an immediate effect on the practicalities and modes of educational assessment, and we have described in some detail the chequered tale of how this was handled in the UK. But the earlier part of this section also has lessons for educational assessment. The pandemic had the effect of holding up a magnifying glass to problems that were evident long before – loss of learning opportunities by some, inequality in access to and benefit from remote learning. There was a sharp check on optimism about international progress in access to – and benefit from – education, and progress towards international educational targets was held back. There will be a need for a regrouping of thinking about how education can overcome the Covid-19-related setbacks, and how good assessment can support the reformed plans.

Conclusion

This chapter has considered three notable developments in the first quarter of the 21st century – two "new priorities" (climate change and well-being) and an "unexpected shock" (the Covid-19 pandemic). Climate change was predictable and long-charted, but the rapidity of its increase in recent decades has made it a priority in educational and policy thinking as the century has progressed. Well-being has been discussed for centuries, but it now occupies a priority space in the concerns and language of thinkers and the wider public in a distinctive way, matched only for concern about the impact of the opposites of well-being, and particularly mental illness.

Both the new priorities have implications for education: their impact on education provision, learners and teachers; and the changes required to the taught and experienced curriculum. We have also identified implications for assessment – what should be assessed and how. In particular, we have noted the need for work on how to assess well-being.

The shock of the Covid-19 pandemic hit education hard across the world. To an extent it magnified and drew attention to problems that had been evident before, including "learning poverty" and inequalities of opportunity to learn and demonstrate learning in assessments. There were also challenges to the accepted methods of assessment in many countries, and the risk-averse world of assessment was forced to innovate in quick time, which was outside its comfort zone.

We have selected these developments for discussion here, but others are discussed in other chapters of this book, and readers will add their own examples. We hope, however, that this chapter will encourage questions about educational assessment to be asked at an early stage in wider policy thinking. For that to be achieved, the assessment world needs to be prepared to change in response to these developments, and assessment theorists and researchers need to help them do so.

Notes

1 The Intergovernmental Panel on Climate Change (IPCC) was formed in 1988 to collate and assess evidence on climate change. In 2013, the IPCC's fifth assessment report reported that scientists were 95% certain that humans were the "dominant cause" of global warming since the 1950s.
2 www.un.org/en/climatechange/climate-solutions/education-key-addressing-climate-change
3 The mission statement of the Young Lives Foundation is to be alongside children and young people in need in ways that: "Enable their voices to be heard and champion their rights and interests – Support them through times of difficulty and distress – Assist them to achieve their potential". https://ylf.org.uk
4 The World Meteorological Organization monitors climatological indicators, including temperature, precipitation, glacial mass balance and sea level rise, in order to observe and predict the climate at both global and regional levels. The trends of these indicators, as well as key extreme weather and climate events and their impacts on factors such as development, food security and migration, are published in the annual State of the Climate reports.
5 "The UN Framework Convention on Climate Change (UNFCCC) Article 6 on education, training and public awareness states that countries shall develop and implement educational and public awareness programmes on climate change and its effects. The Paris Climate Agreement (UNFCCC COP 21, 2015) Article 12 also reiterates the importance of the role of education in enhancing climate actions" (UNICEF, 2019, p. vi).
6 The Curriculum for Excellence aims to enable children and young people in Scotland to gain the knowledge, skills and attributes needed for life in the 21st century.
7 COP26 was the 26th session of the United Nations Climate Change conference held in Glasgow from 31 October to 13 November 2021.
8 National Climate Education Action Plan. Climate in the Classroom. www.reading.ac.uk/planet/-/media/project/uor-main/uor-campaign/climate-for-change/climate-education-summit/climateeducationsummit-actionplan.pdf
9 www.k12climateaction.org
10 See the Summary for Policymakers of the key findings of the Working Group II contribution to the Sixth Assessment Report (AR6) of the IPCC.

11 www.globalpartnership.org/blog/critical-role-assessment-creating-climate-smart-education-system.
12 According to UNESCO, Indicator 4.7.5 "serves to identify [a] country's students' capacity to take informed decisions and responsible actions for environmental integrity, economic viability and a just society, for present and future generations, while respecting cultural diversity. It is about lifelong learning and is an integral part of quality education". https://uis.unesco.org/en/glossary-term/percentage-students-lower-secondary-showing-proficiency-knowledge-environmental
13 www.theeducatoronline.com/k12/news/new-oecd-framework-takes-aim-at-complex-global-challenges/282798
14 https://sciencecitizens.oup.com/what-does-the-pisa-2025-science-framework-tell-us-about-the-future-of-science-education/
15 A report published by the University College London (UCL) Centre for Climate Change & Sustainability Education on 13 July 2023. A total of 870 teachers and head teachers across England responded to the survey, with the demographics being representative of the workforce in state-funded schools. Teachers taking part worked across all subject areas, although most respondents taught science and geography at either primary or secondary levels. www.ucl.ac.uk/news/2023/jul/teaching-climate-change-more-subjects-would-empower-young-people-take-action
16 www.bristol.ac.uk/policybristol/policy-briefings/climate-change-education/
17 www.globalpartnership.org/blog/critical-role-assessment-creating-climate-smart-education-systems
18 www.gov.uk/government/speeches/pm-speech-on-wellbeing
19 www.ons.gov.uk/peoplepopulationandcommunity/wellbeing/methodologies/personalwellbeingsurveyuserguide
20 https://webarchive.nationalarchives.gov.uk/ukgwa/20180328140249/http://digital.nhs.uk/catalogue/PUB21748
21 https://cosmostudy.uk/publication_pdfs/mental-health-and-wellbeing.pdf
22 Independent Review of Education in Northern Ireland, Interim Report Survey Analysis, p 11. Accessed at Survey Analysis – Published 12.10.22.pdf (independentreviewofeducation.org.uk)
23 www.who.int/about/accountability/governance/constitution
24 Downie (2021), p 164, quoting from Maimonides in Pines, S (trans.) Chicago University Press, Chicago, IL, 1963.
25 In developing this, we have borrowed from a similar device developed by Robin Downie for his medical ethics students at Glasgow University.
26 www.independentreviewofeducation.org.uk/final-report
27 https://education.ec.europa.eu
28 https://education.ec.europa.eu/education-levels/school-education/well-being-at-school
29 See Howard (2020) for a review of the academic literature relating to the causes, symptoms and effects of assessment-related anxiety.
30 For example, the index developed by Age UK is available at www.ageuk.org.uk/globalassets/age-uk/documents/reports-and-publications/reports-and-briefings/health-wellbeing/wb_index_indicators_with_understanding_society_definitions.pdf.
31 See https://warwick.ac.uk/fac/sci/med/research/platform/wemwbs/. Use of the scale is dependent on registration.
32 www.oecd.org/pisa/PISA-in-Focus-No-71-Are-students-happy.pdf, p. 2
33 See The *Guardian* 21 August 2018, "Should schools be judged by their exam results?" www.theguardian.com/education/2018/aug/21/should-schools-be-judged-by-exam-results-ofsted.

34 In March 2023 in England, a highly respected head teacher took her own life, reportedly prompted by anxiety over the report expected from the school inspectorate (OFSTED) (see, e.g. www.bbc.co.uk/news/uk-england-berkshire-65021154).
35 "Wellbeing for Students: How can we make Assessments a positive experience?" 30 November, 2022 by Jay Surti. Accessed at https://blog.cambridgeinternational.org/wellbeing-for-students
36 It is possibly not entirely true to say that the global pandemic was unexpected. At least in the UK, such an eventuality had been anticipated, and recommendations for preparation were made but largely not followed through.
37 www.worldbank.org/en/news/press-release/2019/10/17/new-target-cut-learning-poverty-by-at-least-half-by-2030
38 The Paris Agreement – the first universal, legally binding, global climate change agreement, approved at the Paris Climate Conference (COP21) in December 2015 – established a global framework to avoid dangerous climate change by restricting global warming to below-prescribed limits and strengthening countries' ability to address the impacts of climate change.
39 See https://iaea.info/international-approaches-to-exams-given-the-pandemic/
40 The infamous "algorithm" (Stewart, 2020) used in England to calculate grades combined rank orders from teachers with information on the historical performances of schools and the prior attainment of candidates. www.theguardian.com/politics/2020/aug/26/boris-johnson-blames-mutant-algorithm-for-exams-fiasco.
41 Concerns about grade inflation go back as far as 1894 in the United States, as referenced in Kohn (2002). See Smithers (2014) for a history of grade inflation in UK Advanced Levels.
42 See, for example, www.oxfordaqa.com/exams-admin/non-exam-assessment/.
43 The average high school grade point average (GPA) – the sum of all course grades for individual students throughout their high school career divided by the total number of credits – increased by 0.19 grade points, from 3.17 in 2010 to 3.36 in 2021, with the greatest grade inflation occurring between 2018 and 2021.

References

Akrofi, M. M., Antwi, S. H., & Gumbo, J. R. (2019). Students in climate action: A study of some influential factors and implications of knowledge gaps in Africa. *Environments*, 6(12), 1–15. https://doi.org/10.3390/environments6020012

Anders, J., Macmillan, L., Sturgis, P., & Wyness, G. (2021, June 8). The "graduate parent" advantage in teacher assessed grades. *UCL centre for education policy and equalising opportunities (CEPEO)*. https://blogs.ucl.ac.uk/cepeo/2021/06/08/thegraduate-parentadvantageinteacherassessedgrades/

Arıkan, G., & Gunay, D. (2021). Public attitudes towards climate change: A cross-country analysis. *The British Journal of Politics and International Relations*, 23(1), 158–174. https://doi.org/10.1177/1369148120951013

Bauld, A. (2021, November 1). Usable knowledge 2021 why schools need to look at their own Carbon footprint. *Usable Knowledge*. Harvard Graduate School of Education. www.gse.harvard.edu/news/uk/21/11/why-schools-need-look-their-own-carbon-footprint

Bermingham, D., & Chainey, J. (2022, December 13). The critical role of assessment in creating climate-smart education systems. *GPE Transforming Education*. https://www.globalpartnership.org/blog/critical-role-assessment-creating-climate-smart-education-systems

Bond, L. (2005). *Teaching to the test*. The Carnegie Foundation to the Advancement of Teaching. www.carnegiefoundation.org/perspectives/teaching-test

The British Psychological Society. (2021). *How today's psychometric tests can help you recruit and retain the right talent*. https://pminsight.cipd.co.uk/how-todays-psychometric-tests-can-help-you-recruitand-retain-the-right-talent

Brookhart, S. M., Guskey, T. R., Bowers, A. J., McMillan, J. H., Smith, J. K., Smith, L. F., & Welsh, M. E. (2016). A century of grading research: Meaning and value in the most common educational measure. *Review of Educational Research*, 86(4), 803–848.

Burgess, S., & Greaves, E. (2013). Test scores, subjective assessment, and stereotyping of ethnic minorities. *Journal of Labor Economics*, 31(3), 535–576. https://doi.org/10.1086/669340

Carnie, F. (2022). *Ten things schools can do to address the climate crisis*. Schools Week, March 18, 2019. https://schoolsweek.co.uk/ten-things-schools-can-do-to-address-the-climate-crisis/

Childline. (2019). Annual review. *Childline NSPCC*. https://learning.nspcc.org.uk/media/1898/childline-annual-review-2018-19.pdf

Civinini, C. (2021, December 10). Climate change and the curriculum: What needs to change? *Times Educational Supplement (TES) Magazine*. www.tes.com/magazine/teaching-learning/secondary/climate-change-and-curriculum-what-needs-change

Clark, H., Coll-Seck, A. M., Banerjee, A., Peterson, S., Dalglish, S. L., Ameratunga, S., Balabanova, D., Bhan, M. K., Bhutta, Z. A., Borrazzo, J., Claeson, M., Doherty, T., El-Jardali, F., George, A. S., Gichaga, A., Gram, L., Hipgrave, D. B., Kwamie, A., Meng, Q., . . . & Costello, A. (2020, February 22). A future for the world's children? A *Who–Unicef–Lancet Commission* (Lancet 2020, Vol. 395, pp. 605–58). Online publication. https://doi.org/10.1016/S0140-6736(19)32540-1

Cordero, E. C., Centeno, D., & Todd, A. M. (2020, February 4). *The role of climate change education on individual lifetime carbon emissions*. https://doi.org/10.1371/journal.pone.0206266

Crocker, L. (2003). Teaching for the test: Validity, fairness, and moral action. *Educational Measurements: Issues and Practices*, 22(3), 5–11.

Dake, J. A., Price, J. H., & Telljohann, S. K. (2003). The nature and extent of bullying at school. *Journal of School Health*, 73(5), 174.

Davis, T. (2019, January 2). What is well-being? Definition, types, and well-being skills: Want to grow your well-being? Here are the skills you need. *Psychology Today*. www.psychologytoday.com/gb/blog/click-here-happiness/201901/what-is-well-being-definition-types-and-well-being-skills

Delgado, P. (2022, June 30). Climate change is a threat to education. *Institute for the Future of Education*. Technology de Monterrey. https://observatory.tec.mx/edu-news/climate-change-impact-on-education

Department for Education. (2022, April 21). Sustainability and climate change strategy. *Policy Paper*. www.gov.uk/government/publications/sustainability-and-climate-change-strategy

Downie, R. (2021). *Quality of life: A post-pandemic view of medicine*. Imprint Academic.

Edge Foundation. (2020). *The impact of Covid-19 on education: Evidence on the early impacts of lockdown*. Edge Foundation.

Education Development Trust. (2022, June 22). *Connecting education and climate change*. Blog. www.educationdevelopmenttrust.com/our-research-and-insights/commentary/connecting-education-and-climate-change

Education Endowment Foundation. (2020). *Impact of school closures on the attainment gap: Rapid evidence assessment*. Education Endowment Foundation.

Ejaz, W., Mukherjee, M., Fletcher, R., & Kleis Nielsen, R. (2022). *How we follow climate change: Climate news use and attitudes in eight countries*. Oxford Climate Journalism Network. Published by the Reuters Institute for the Study of

Journalism at the University of Oxford with the support of the European Climate Foundation (ECF).

European Institute for Gender Equality. (2021). *Gender equality index 2021: Health*. https://eige.europa.eu/publications-resources/toolkits-guides/gender-equality-index-2021-report/women-report-poorer-mental-well-being-men?

Everett, N., & Papageorgiou, J. (2011, June). Investigating the accuracy of predicted A level= grades as part of 2009 UCAS admission process. *Department for Business Innovation & Skills. Research Paper No.37*. https://docplayer.net/4526070-Investigating-the-accuracy-of-predicted-a-level-grades-as-part-of-2009-ucas-admission-process.html

Flitcroft, D., & Woods, K. (2018). What does research tell high school teachers about student motivation for test performance? *Pastoral Care in Education*, 36(2), 112–125.

Gallone, P., & Syed, R. (2021). *Youth in a changing climate. Groundwork. Changing places. Changing lives*. www.groundwork.org.uk/wp-content/uploads/2021/11/Groundwork-Youth-in-a-Changing-Climate-Report-Final-November-2021.pdf

Giannini, S., Jenksins, R., & Saavedra, J. (2022, January 24). 100 weeks into the pandemic: the importance of keeping schools open and investing in learning recovery programs. *World Bank Blogs*. Published on Education for Global Development. https://blogs.worldbank.org/education/100-weeks-pandemic-importance-keeping-schools-open-and-investing-learning-recovery

Gill, T., & Benton, T. (2015). The accuracy of forecast grades for OCR A levels in June 2014 *Statistics Report Series No. 90*. Research Division Assessment Research and Development Cambridge Assessment. www.cambridgeassessment.org.uk/Images/241261-the-accuracy-of-forecast-grades-for-ocr-a-levels-in-june-2014.pdf

The Guardian. (2022, January 28 Friday). UK pupils failed by schools' teaching of climate crisis, experts say. *National Curriculum*.

Hansard, UK Parliament. (2021). *Covid-19: Education settings. Volume 698: Debated on Tuesday 6 July 2021*. https://hansard.parliament.uk/commons/2021-07-06/debates/0CA3E257-6CDC-46CA-A16F-2B2248A5F372/Covid-19EducationSettings

Hawkey, K., James, J., & Tidmarsh, C. (2019). Using wicked problems to foster interdisciplinary practice among UK trainee teachers. *Journal of Education for Teaching*, 45(4), 446–460. https://doi.org/10.1080/02607476.2019.1639263

Hodgen, J., Taylor, B., Jacques, L., Tereshchenko, A., Kwok, R., & Cockerill, M. (2020). *Remote mathematics teaching during COVID-19: Intentions, practices and equity*. UCL Institute of Education.

Howard, E. (2020). A review of the literature concerning anxiety for educational assessments. *Ofqual Report*. Published by Ofqual. https://assets.publishing.service.gov.uk/media/5e45825340f0b6 / 7bf6eb3ea/A_review_of_the_literature_concerning_anxiety_for_educational_assessment.pdf

Intergovernmental Panel On Climate Change (IPCC). (2023). *Climate change 2022: Impacts, adaptation and vulnerability: Working group II contribution to the sixth assessment report of the intergovernmental panel on climate change*. https://www.ipcc.ch/report/ar6/wg2/

International Institute for Applied Systems Analysis. (2020, April 13). Exploring the link between education and climate change. *ScienceDaily*. www.sciencedaily.com/releases/2020/04/200413120019.htm

Iosad, A., Wright, J., & Esmann, M. (2022, July 28). Time for a world education service: Focused, free and for all. *Tony Blair Institute for Global Change*. https://institute.global/sites/default/files/articles/Time-for-a-World-Education-Service-Focused Free-and-for-All.pdf

Jamieson, J. P., Peters, B. J., Greenwood, E. J., & Altose, A. J. (2016). Reappraising stress arousal improves performance and reduces evaluation anxiety in classroom exam situations. *Social Psychological and Personality Science, 9.* http://doi.org/10.1177/1948550616644656

Jennings, J. L., & Bearak, M. (2006). "Teaching to the test" in the NCLB era: How test predictability affects our understanding of student performance. *Educational Researcher, 43*(8), 381–389. http://doi.org/10.3102/0013189X14554449

Jerrim, J. (2021). National tests and the wellbeing of primary school pupils: New evidence from the UK. *Assessment in Education: Principles, Policy & Practice, 28*(5–6), 507–544.

Kohn, A. (2002). The dangerous myth of grade inflation. *The Chronicle of Higher Education, 49*(11), B7–B9.

Kulakiewicz, A., Long, R., & Roberts, N. (2021). Inclusion of sustainability and climate change in the national curriculum. *House of Commons Library.* https://researchbriefings.files.parliament.uk/documents/CDP-2021-0166/CDP-2021-0166.pdf

Kwauk, C., & Winthrop, R. (2021, March 26 Friday). *Unleashing the creativity of teachers and students to combat climate change: An opportunity for global leadership.* www.brookings.edu/research/unleashing-the-creativity-of-teachers-and-students-to-combat-climate-change-an-opportunity-for-global-leadership/

Lawson, D. F., Stevenson, K. T., Peterson, M. N., Carrier, S. J., Strnad, R. L., & Seekamp, S. (2019). Children can foster climate change concern among their parents. *National Climate Chang, 9,* 458–462. https://doi.org/10.1038/s41558-019-0463-3

Layard, R. (2011/2006). *Happiness: Lessons from a new science* (2nd ed.). Penguin Books.

Lazear, E. P. (2006). Speeding, terrorism, and teaching to the test. *The Quarterly Journal of Economics, 121*(3), 1029–1061. https://doi.org/10.1162/qjec.121.3.1029

Leal Filho, W., Tuladhar, L., Li, C., Balogun, A.-L. B., Kovaleva, M., Abubakar, I. R., Azadi, H., & Donkor, F. K. K. (2023a). Climate change and extremes: Implications on city livability and associated health risks across the globe. *International Journal of Climate Change Strategies and Management, 15*(1), 1–19. https://doi.org/10.1108/IJCCSM-07-2021-0078

Leal Fihlo, W., Yayeh Ayal, D., Wall, T., Shiel, C., Paco, A., Pace, P., Mifsud, M., Lange Salvia, A., Skouloudis, A., Moggi, S., LeVasseur, T., Vinuesa Antonio, G., Azeiteiro, U., Ioannis, N., & Kovaleva, M. (2023b). An assessment of attitudes and perceptions of international university students on climate. *Climate Risk Management, 39.* http://doi.org/10.1016/j.crm.2023.100486

Liu, T., Shryane, N., & Elliot, M. (2022). Attitudes to climate change risk: Classification of and transitions in the UK population between 2012 and 2020. *Humanities & Social Sciences Communications, 9,* 279. https://doi.org/10.1057/s41599-022-01287-1

Matud, M. P., López-Curbelo, M., & Fortes, D. (2019). Gender and psychological well-being. *International Journal of Environmental Research and Public Health, 16*(19), 1–11. www.ncbi.nlm.nih.gov/pmc/articles/PMC6801582/pdf/ijerph-16-03531.pdf

McManus, S., Bebbington, P., Jenkins, R., & Brugha, T. (Eds.). (2016). *Adult psychiatric morbidity survey: Survey of mental health and wellbeing.* England, 2014. ttps://digital.nhs.uk/data-and-information/publications/statistical/adult-psychiatric-morbidity-survey/adult-psychiatric-morbidity-survey-survey-of-mental-health-and-wellbeing-england-2014

Müller, L. M., & Goldenberg, G. (2021). *Education in times of crisis: Teachers' experiences and recommendations for effective distance learning.* Chartered College of Teaching. https://chartered.college/wp-content/uploads/2021/11/MullerGoldenberg_FULL_NOV21.pdf

Murphy, R., & Wyness, G. (2020). Minority report: The impact of predicted grades on university admissions of disadvantaged groups. *Education Economics*, 28(4), 333–350. https://doi.org/10.1080/09645292.2020.1761945

Newman, K., & Smith, L. S. (2021, September 30). Linking global education and the climate crisis: An alternative approach. *Blog*. https://riseprogramme.org/blog/linking-global-education-climate-crisis

Newsome, D., Newsome, K. B., & Miller, S. A. (2023). Teaching, Learning, and Climate Change: Anticipated Impacts and Mitigation Strategies for Educators. *Behaviour and Social Issues*, 32, 494–516. https://doi.org/10.1007/s42822-023-00129-2.

Nisbet, I., & Shaw, S. D. (2020). *Is assessment fair?* SAGE Publishing Ltd.

Nisbet, I., & Shaw, S. D. (2022). Fair high-stakes assessment in the long shadow of Covid-19. *Assessment in Education: Principles, Policy & Practice*, 29(5), 518–533. http://doi.org/10.1080/0969594X.2022.2067834

OECD. (2017). *PISA 2015 results (volume III): Students' well-being*. PISA, OECD Publishing. http://doi.org/10.1787/9789264267510-cn

OECD. (2021). *Education at a glance 2021: OECD indicators*. OECD Publishing. https://doi.org/10.1787/b35a14e5-en

OECD. (2022). *Are students ready to take on environmental challenges?*. PISA, OECD Publishing. https://doi.org/10.1787/8abe655c-en

OECD. (2023). *PISA 2025 science framework (Draft)*. https://pisa-framework.oecd.org/science-2025/assets/docs/PISA_2025_Science_Framework.pdf

Ofqual. (2020). *Ofqual welcomes DfE announcement on 2021 exams* [Press release]. www.gov.uk/government/news/ofqual-welcomes-dfe-announcement-on-2021-exams

Paris agreement to the United Nations framework convention on climate change (December 12, 2015), T.I.A.S. No. 16–1104. https://unfccc.int/process-and-meetings/the-paris-agreement?gad_source=1&gclid=Cj0KCQjw1qO0BhDwARIsANfnkv9S7t1GEs-E8Vba2PGFELwIioHTDsGuHP1hewc6mD9d-rJmoNaQV2YaAgngEALw_wc8

Plutzer, E., Hannah, A. L., Rosenau, J., McCaffrey, M. S., Berbeco, M., & Reid, A. H. (2016). *Mixed messages: How climate is taught in America's schools*. National Center for Science Education. http://ncse.com/files/MixedMessages.pdf

Popham, J. W. (2001). Teaching to the test? *Educational Leadership*, 58(6), 16–20.

Porter, C. (2021, November 8). Education is under threat from climate change – especially for women and girls. *Blog*. www.ox.ac.uk/news/features/education-under-threat-climate-change-especially-women-and-girls

Priestley, M., Shapira, M., Priestley, A., Ritchie, M., & Barnett, C. (2020, September). Rapid review of national qualifications experience 2020. *Final Report*. Faculty of Social Sciences, University of Stirling. www.gov.scot/binaries/content/documents/govscot/publications/independent-report/2020/10/rapid-review-national-qualifications-experience-2020/documents/rapid-review-national-qualifications-experience-2020/rapid-review-national-qualifications-experience-2020/govscot%3Adocument/rapid-review-national-qualifications-experience-2020.pdf

Putwain, D. W. (2009). Assessment and examination stress in Key Stage 4. *British Educational Research Journal*, 35(3), 391–411.

Putwain, D. W., & Daly, A. L. (2014). Test anxiety prevalence and gender differences in a sample of English secondary school students. *Educational Studies*, 40, 554–570.

Putwain, D. W., & Symes, W. (2018). Does increased effort compensate for performance debilitating test anxiety? *School Psychology Quarterly*, 33(3), 482–491. https://doi.org/10.1037/spq0000236

Randell, H., & Gray, C. (2019, April 15). Climate change and educational attainment in the global tropics. *PNAS*, 116(18), 8840–8845. www.pnas.org/doi/epdf/10.1073/pnas.1817480116

Richmond, T. (2018). A degree of uncertainty An investigation into grade inflation in universities. *REFORM*. #*reformHE*. www.tom-richmond.com/wp-content/uploads/2018/06/A%20Degree%20of%20Uncertainty.pdf

Roberts, N., & Danechi, S. (2022). Coronavirus: GCSEs, a levels and equivalents in 2022. *House of Commons Library*. No. 09045. https://researchbriefings.files.parliament.uk/documents/CBP-9045/CBP-9045.pdf

Sanchez, E. I., & Moore, R. (2022, May). Grade inflation continues to grow in the past decade. *ACT Research Report*. www.act.org/content/dam/act/unsecured/documents/2022/R2134-Grade-Inflation-Continues-to-Grow-in-the-Past-Decade-Final-Accessible.pdf

Schleicher, A. (2019). PISA 2018 insights and interpretations. *OECD*. https://issuu.com/pajaropolitico/docs/pisa_2018_insights_and_interpretations_final_pdf

Shaw, S. D., & Nisbet, I. (2021). Attitudes to fair assessment in the light of COVID-19. *Research Matters: A Cambridge Assessment Publication, 31*, 6–21.

Sitta, F. A., Maddox, B., Casebourne, I., Hughes, S., Kuvalja, M., Hannam, J., & Oates, T. (2023). *The futures of assessment: Navigating uncertainties through the lenses of anticipatory thinking*. Cambridge University Press & Assessment. www.cambridgeassessment.org.uk/Images/698413-the-futures-of-assessment-navigating-uncertainties-through-the-lenses-of-anticipatory-thinking.pdf

Smithers, A. (2014). *A-LEVELS 1951–2014*. Centre for Education and Employment Research University of Buckingham August 2014.

Stewart, H. (2020, August 26). Boris Johnson blames "mutant algorithm" for exams fiasco. *The Guardian*. www.theguardian.com/politics/2020/aug/26/boris-johnson-blames-mutant-algorithm-for-exams-fiasco

UNESCO. (2010). Climate change education for sustainable development: The UNESCO climate change initiative. *ED.2010/WS/41, ED.2011/WS/3*. https://unesdoc.unesco.org/ark:/48223/pf0000190101

UNESCO. (2020). Education for sustainable development: A roadmap. *ESDfor2030*. UNESCO.

UNESCO. (2021). Getting every school climate-ready: How countries are integrating climate change issues in education. *Education 2030*. United Nations Educational, Scientific and Cultural Organization.

UNICEF. (2019). It is getting hot. Call for education systems to respond to the climate crisis. *Perspectives from East Asia and the Pacific*. UNICEF East Asia and Pacific Regional Office. www.unicef.org/eap/media/4596/file/It%20is%20getting%20hot:%20Call%20for%20education%20systems%20to%20respond%20to%20the%20climate%20crisis.pdf

UNISDR. (2019). *Global assessment report 2019*. UNISDR.

United Nations. (2015, October 21). Transforming our world: The 2030 Agenda for Sustainable Development. *A/RES/70/1*. Resolution adopted by the General Assembly on 25 September 2015. www.refworld.org/docid/57b6e3e44.html

United Nations. (2020). *Policy brief: Education during COVID-19 and beyond*. www.un.org/sites/un2.un.org/files/sg_policy_brief_covid-19_and_education_august_2020.pdf

Van der Graaf, L., Dunajeva, J., Siarova, H., & Bankauskaite, R. (2021). *Research for CULT committee – education and youth in post-COVID-19 Europe – crisis effects and policy recommendations*. European Parliament, Policy Department for Structural and Cohesion Policies.

White, J. (2002). Education, the market and personal well-being. *British Journal of Educational Studies, 50*(4), 442–456.

White, J. (2007). Wellbeing and education: Issues of culture and authority. *Journal of Philosophy of Education, 41*(1), 17–28.

The World Bank. (2019, October 7). New target: Cut "learning poverty" by at least half by 2030. The World Bank IBRD IDA. *Press Release*. www.worldbank.org/en/news/press-release/2019/10/17/new-target-cut-learning-poverty-by-at-least-half-by-2030

World Bank, the Bill & Melinda Gates Foundation, FCDO, UNESCO, UNICEF, and USAID. (2022, June 23). The state of global learning poverty: 2022 update. *Conference edition*. The World Bank, UNESCO, and UNICEF. www.unicef.org/media/122921/file/State%20of%20Learning%20Poverty%202022.pdf

The World Bank, UNESCO and UNICEF. (2021). *The state of the global education crisis: A path to recovery*. The World Bank, UNESCO, and UNICEF. https://documents1.worldbank.org/curated/en/416991638768297704/pdf/The-State-of-the-Global-Education-Crisis-A-Path-to-Recovery.pdf

World Meteorological Organization. (2022). *WMO provisional state of the global climate 2022*. https://library.wmo.int/viewer/56335/download?file=Provisional_State_of_the_Climate_2022_en.pdf&type=pdf&navigator=1

Worth, K. (2021). *Miseducation. How climate change is Taught in America* (pp. 1–184). Columbia University.

Zakharov, A., Carnoy, M., & Loyalka, P. (2014). Which teaching practices improve student performance on high-stakes exams? Evidence from Russia. *International Journal of Educational Development*. http://doi.org/10.1016/j.ijedudev.2014.01.003

4
CHANGES TO THINKING ABOUT SOCIETY

This is the first of two chapters in which we focus on changes to thinking. Of course, these interact with developments in events and actions – our ideas are influenced by what happens and trends in ideas can prompt us to act differently. But in this chapter, we shall examine some of the many changes to thinking about society in the first quarter of the 21st century that raise questions for educational assessment. In Chapter 5, we turn more specifically to changes to thinking about education and assessment.

If we were attempting a wide picture of developments in ideas since the turn of the century, there are many headings that we shall do no more than mention here, but that are worth bearing in mind when we consider the way forward in assessment. After identifying some of these trends, we shall concentrate here on the challenges offered by developments in "critical thinking" (both in theoretical work and in popular discourse) and then look in more detail at two case studies of particular issues that have been prominent in the first decades of the new century – one from the USA (race-conscious college admissions policies) and one from the UK (decolonising the university curriculum). In each case, we shall ask what the implications are (if any) for educational assessment – a question that is rarely asked.

The first quarter of the new century has seen events that were not anticipated as the bells rang out for the year 2000. These began in 2001 with the "9/11" terrorist attacks against targets in the United States. Almost 3,000 people were killed during those attacks, and, 20 years on, many of us who are old enough can remember where we were when we first heard the news. There was a feeling, not confined to the USA, that life would never be quite the same again.

Another notable development, perhaps related to 9/11 but extending beyond the West, has been a challenge to any assumption that there would be

DOI: 10.4324/9781003346166-4

a continuum of internationalism, with mobile individuals living, studying, working and communicating in ways that made national frontiers seem out of date a century before. John Dewey had written about "how to reconcile national loyalty, or patriotism, with the *superior* devotion to the things which unite men in common ends irrespective of national political boundaries" (Dewey, 1918, p. 114, emphasis added). In the 21st century, while communication between countries has increased, not only in person but through the internet and technological support for international collaboration, there has also been a revival of interest in looking inward and celebrating national values and the values of subgroups within nations, including indigenous populations who were often harshly treated in the centuries before. Despite Donald Trump's celebration of patriotism and rejection of globalism (73rd Session of the UN General Assembly, New York, 2018), the resurgence of interest in national values – and in national and sub-national cultures and languages – is by no means confirmed by the political right.

In Chapter 3, we discussed new priorities (climate change and well-being) and the "unexpected shock" of the global pandemic, with the prolonged "tail" of its after-effects on society. And the 21st century has also seen war in Europe – a first for most generations living in European countries – following the Russian invasion of Ukraine.

In this chapter, we trace some of the ideas that have come to prominence in theoretical, academic and popular discourse. We have given the greatest prominence to issues connected to race. Space has not permitted us to do justice to other important 21st-century themes, such as "identity" and its associated conflicts and disputes (Furedi, 2021).[1] But we shall now turn to a set of theoretical and practical challenges that have increasingly made their presence felt in the new century.

Challenges from theory, ideology and popular discourse (or "Critical Theory", "critical theory", Critical Race Theory, Wokeism and Culture Wars)

Twenty years into the 2000s, any educational practitioner, researcher or observer is faced with a constant barrage of communication and messages, received on their phones or other devices whenever they turn on (which is most of the time). Much of the language used is emotional, some is confrontational, and very little feels "academic". The more familiar source materials of textbooks, academic journals and conference addresses are sharing space with blogs, social media posts and podcasts. Although some of the technology used is new, popular and political interest in education is not, and older readers will recall heated debates in their national popular press and on television and radio about education in the mid-late 20th century. The world of assessment saw bitter debate about eugenics and intelligence testing. In England, educationists, politicians and the wider public took sides in the (unresolved) controversy about comprehensive schooling and continue to do so. In the USA, the educational fallout from the civil rights movement was hugely important, and we discuss one set of 21st-century developments leading from it in the first case study in this chapter.

However, the new century has seen fuel being poured on the fires of educational controversy in a distinctive way. Deep-rooted divisions of ideas and values and challenges from theory and practice in a wide range of areas have come together and have been seen as threatening the inherited cultures and practices of education, including the hallowed specialised domains of assessment practitioners, teachers and researchers. When we were writing this chapter, a brief web search of news items one day found the story of a (Christian) professor of English at a (Christian) university in the USA whose contract had been suspended because of his coverage of race issues in his creative writing class. He said:

> There is a reason why [the university] is threatening me now rather than five years ago or 10 years ago. [The university] is conforming to a toxic political culture, and they are playing a role that is a part of that culture's script: a role that says, "We do not like to have uncomfortable conversations about race".[2]

Let us start with theoretical challenges. "Critical Theory", with capital initials, usually refers to a post-Marxist school of Western European philosophy,[3] proffered in the late 20th century by the "Frankfurt School", including Max Horkheimer (1895–1973). An essential feature of their writings was a view that the social sciences should not seek to be value-free, in the way envisaged by sociologist Weber (1864–1920) and supported by positivists such as Karl Popper (1902–1994). Such efforts, they argued, hid well-entrenched value judgements and protected them from justified criticism. Instead, they said that philosophical arguments should meet three requirements: they should be explanatory, practical and normative.

By the 21st century, "critical theory" (with small initials) came to signal a range of theoretical stances supporting critiques of accepted approaches to areas of public policy and culture, including education. As well as Critical Race Theory, which we shall consider next, these have included some feminist critiques, some post-colonial arguments (exemplified in the second case study in this chapter), critical discourse analysis, critical disability theory, institutional ethnography . . . and no doubt many more.

It is not difficult to see a lineage tracing some modern critical theoretical writings back to the tradition of American pragmatism and to the famous maxim from Charles Sanders Pierce as long ago as 1878:

> Consider the practical effects of the objects of your conception. Then your conception of these effects is the whole of your conception of the object.
> *(Pierce, 1878, paragraph 11)*

The pragmatists developed theories of truth as well as ethical theories in which the effect of a statement or practice in the real world was paramount. The "subjective" pragmatists, including William James (1842–1910) and influencing John Dewey (1859–1952), among others, took particular account of individual situations and the effects on identified people or groups in appraising statements or practices.[4]

Critical Race Theory ("CRT") started as a movement in legal studies in the USA towards the end of the 20th century, although the phrase is now used much more widely. It does seem that the issue that jolted the US legal writers into critical thought was their observation that despite decades of anti-discrimination legislation in the USA and the legal judgements achieved by the civil rights movement, racial injustice and disadvantage were persisting. Did this reflect a deeper malaise than the discriminatory activity precluded by the courts? A publication of "the key writings that formed the movement" describes CRT as a "comprehensive movement in thought and life" that "compels us to confront critically the most explosive issue in American civilisation: the historical centrality and complicity of law in upholding white supremacy (and concomitant hierarchies of gender, class and sexual orientation)" (Crenshaw et al., 1995, p. xi).

A seminal article by Ladson-Billings and Tate in 1995 was entitled "Toward a Critical Race Theory of Education". They argued that race continued to be a determining factor in educational inequity in the USA, and that there was a key link with property rights. The title of a section in their article explicitly attacks a number of concepts dear to many engaged in educational assessment: "Challenging Claims of Neutrality, Objectivity, Color-blindness and Meritocracy" (Ladson-Billings & Tate, 1995, p. 56; see also Ladson-Billings, 1998, and Ladson-Billings, 2006). They referred to the arguments by the legal writer Delgado for "naming one's own reality" because "much of reality is socially constructed" (Ladson-Billings & Tate, 1995, p. 57; see also the exposition of this and related views in Delgado & Stefancic, 2006), and championed the use of stories of individuals to "help overcome ethnocentrism". Later writers have taken up the challenge of applying CRT to education (see, e.g. Gillborn, 2005, 2006).

These writers recognised that Critical Race Theory could be unsettling for traditional thinking about education. Indeed, Ladson-Billings gave her 1998 article the title "Just What Is Critical Race Theory and What Is It Doing in a Nice Field Like Education?". Ladson-Billings and Tate prefaced their 1995 article with an extract from Derrick Bell's polemical "Faces at the Bottom of the Well" (Bell, 1992), which may make reading uncomfortable for readers who see themselves as engaged in educational measurement aiming for validity:

> The presentation of truth in new forms provokes resistance, confounding those committed to accepted measures for determining the quality and validity of statements made and conclusions reached, and making it difficult for them to respond and adjudge what is acceptable.
>
> *(p. 143)*

The key messages of these critical writings about race quickly spread to other fundamental categories that we bring to thinking about society, including gender, religion, poverty and health (see, e.g. Apple, 2019). For these critics, context is all-important. They infer that our institutions and our thinking are structurally unjust or biased and that their and our activities reflect – and seek to reinforce – existing power relationships. Another key theme is *intersectionality*, referring to the complex interrelationship of social categories, challenging any approach that separates these categories for analysis, and drawing attention to what they see as a deeper underpinning of power relationships (Atewologun, 2018).

At first sight, some of the tenets of Critical (Race) Theory may seem highly theoretical and "academic". But in the second decade of the 21st century, these theoretical challenges morphed into ideological and political challenges, notably in the USA, but with echoes in other parts of the world. They also provoked a hostile reaction: in July 2022, the *Economist* reported that forty-two US states "ha[d] introduced bills or taken other actions to limit CRT in classrooms" (Economist, 2022).

Popular support for further action on race and challenge to the adequacy of what had been done in recent decades was strengthened by the reactions to the deaths of two young black men in the USA at the hands of the police – Michael Brown in 2014 and George Floyd in 2020 – which gave a heightened profile to the "Black Lives Matter" movement.[5] There was also a controversial branch of argument based on concepts of "white privilege" and "white fragility" (e.g. DiAngelo, 2019), leading to some unverified accounts (by opponents) of white students being required to stand up in class and apologise for being white. Opponents of CRT have widened their attention to any development that appears to champion the disadvantaged, minorities, and anyone who takes a stand outside the established national culture. An extraordinary example of this from outside the USA is a Facebook entry in January 2021, from Northern Ireland, complaining that the

BBC (the national broadcaster in the UK) was "at its BLM [Black Lives Matter] worst" by broadcasting a Gospel Music competition with black judges and presenters.[6]

The term "Woke", once a (favourable) word in African American slang that denoted being well-informed and aware of injustice in one's surroundings, became reversed into a negative term used as an insult by opponents (Economist, 2021). "Woke" is now used to criticise views ranging much wider than race, and there is a strong link with some branches of Republican politics in the USA, which we shall not explore in depth here.

Within American school education, issues around the curriculum for history and civics have become particularly toxic. In August 2019, the *New York Times* launched their "1619 project and the Racialist Falsification of History", described on their website in the following terms:

> The 1619 Project . . . began in August 2019, the 400th anniversary of the beginning of American slavery. It aims to reframe the country's history by placing the consequences of slavery and the contributions of black Americans at the very center of our national narrative.[7]

Nikole Hannah-Jones – who at the time was a domestic correspondent for the *New York Times* magazine focusing on racial injustice, won the Pulitzer Prize for Commentary in 2020 for her framing essay on "The 1619 Project". In her essay, she argued that "[o]ur democracy's founding ideals were false when they were written. Black Americans have fought to make them true" (p. 14). Her article traced the central role black Americans had played in the nation, including its vast material success and democracy itself, prompting public conversation about the nation's founding and evolution. In his contribution to the 1619 Project for the *New York Times* magazine, sociologist Matthew Desmond commented on the economic role and legacy of slavery: "If you want to understand the brutality of American capitalism, you have to start on the plantation" (2019). Desmond argued that American capitalism has a distinctively cruel character because of its foundation of slavery and that many of the financial ways of working today reflect those practices used for an insidious purpose in the past.

The work of Hannah-Jones, Desmond and others suggests that contemporary inequalities have been fashioned by measured and deliberate political and policy choices. What, on the surface, appears to be an argument about reassessing history is also an argument about ideology – with those defending the legitimacy of the current prevailing social order faced with an account of its historical beginnings that suggests different policy choices could (and would) produce a more equitable society.

Like all the works this period of re-evaluation has produced, the 1619 Project has its detractors. The essays and mini-essays in the 1619 Project have come under strong fire, mostly notably, Hannah-Jones's foregrounding essay and Desmond's essay on the economic role and legacy of slavery. Opponents decried teaching using this material as indoctrinating students to "hate America" by trying to replace references to 1776 – the Declaration of Independence, when the then thirteen American colonies severed their political connections to Great Britain – with references to the date of the arrival of the first slave ships.

It would seem that the details of the 1619 Project factual narrative were not necessarily what some conservatives in America found most unacceptable. Rather, they took issue with the ideological implications of its dominant principle – the larger narrative, "That black Americans, as much as those men cast in alabaster in the nation's capital, are this nation's true 'founding fathers'. And that no people has a greater claim to that flag than us" (Hannah-Jones, 2019).

Subject-based controversy has also ranged to mathematics and in particular the early work of William Tate (1994), and there appears to be a link, however tenuous, with disputes about how to teach reading to small children (otherwise known as the "reading wars") (Pearson, 2004). Tate – an African American social scientist, Fellow and past President of the American Educational Research Association, has argued that traditionally, schools have provided African American students with few opportunities to connect mathematics to their lives and experiences (1994, p. 479). Drawing on the work of Carter Woodson – an American historian, some sixty years earlier, Tate suggests that mathematics pedagogy that is built on a student's life experience provides two mathematics learning environments – within and beyond the school. Unfortunately (in Tate's view), the disciplines that undergird mathematics education – mathematics and psychology – place great stress on objectivity and neutrality. As a consequence, he contends, school mathematics has been implicitly acknowledged as a "colorblind" discipline and very little thought is given to the cultural appropriateness of mathematics pedagogy:

> The prospect of a new beginning for mathematics education rests with the ability of mathematics teachers to provide pedagogy that builds and expands on the thinking and experiences of African American students. Moreover, this pedagogy should focus on preparing these students to function within our democracy.
>
> *(Tate, 1994, p. 484)*[8]

Tate's article "Race, Retrenchment, and the Reform of School Mathematics" (1994) poses questions for education and educational assessment. These include: What role should the reform of school mathematics play in changing this story of incomplete success? What type of pedagogy must African American students negotiate to be successful in school mathematics? What is the effect of the foreign pedagogy on African American students' thinking and achievement in mathematics?

What is the relevance of this debate to the future of education and educational assessment beyond, as well as within, the USA? We start with two preliminary observations: first, some readers may feel that in their country it is less persuasive than in the USA to see race as, in Crenshaw's words, "the most explosive issue in [their] civilisation". However, the approach of the CRT could arguably have analogies in the issues that they see as explosive ones, such as religious or caste-based divisions. Second, the battle between "woke" and "anti-woke" views appear to be based on bundling together ideas, on both sides of the divide, that apparently include technical issues such as the place of phonics in decoding text and the importance of learning multiplication tables in arithmetic. The ideological string tying these bundles of ideas together seems rather fragile: it is conceivable that an educationist who agrees with Tate about mathematics might, for example, agree with the "anti-woke" lobbies about methodologies for teaching infants to read.

Starting with the theoretical approaches of the critical theorists, it does seem to us that they question some of the assumptions and values associated with assessment. Much of the work done by assessment/testing organisations and by assessment researchers is primarily analytic, breaking down the material being assessed into units, making sure that construct-irrelevant contextual differences do not corrupt the scoring and aiming above all for validity and reliability.[9] This is particularly evident in the psychometric "educational measurement" tradition, particularly found in the USA (Brennan, 2006). In contrast, the thinking of the critical theorists is essentially synthetic and raises fundamental questions about the constructs being assessed, the categories used for analysis, the power structures in the organisations that carry out and pay for the assessments and the outcomes of the assessments. Perhaps we should learn from them to think further about the contexts in which evidence for assessment is obtained and the rules made for appraising that evidence and producing an assessment outcome?

A more difficult question is whether assessments of differences – for example, in academic performance – between advantaged and disadvantaged groups are themselves open to criticism as instruments to maintain the power of the advantaged. In many countries, tests are used to measure the "achievement gap" (or "attainment gap") between the levels of performance of different racial groups or of students from different socio-economic backgrounds. The Scottish government has aimed to reduce differences in achievement between rich and poor pupils, although achieving that objective has proved tantalisingly difficult for them (Mowat, 2018). In England, the Office for Students (OfS), which regulates universities, requires universities to set targets for reducing the "significant difference in the proportions of black, Asian and minority ethnic students awarded a good ('first' or '2:1') undergraduate degree when compared to white students".[10] OfS calls this phenomenon the "degree *awarding* gap" (our emphasis), which appears to leave open the possibility that the inequity lies in the classes of degree awarded by the universities rather than in the different levels of performance by the different ethnic groups. Is the assessment leading to the awarding of degrees itself part of the problem?

In the USA, Gloria Ladson-Billings has argued that the focus on the "achievement gap" is misplaced and has diverted attention from the underlying issue of what she called the "educational debt" of non-white Americans, as the result of many years of inequity in schooling. Drawing an analogy with the economic concept of the accumulated National Debt (compared with regular snapshots of "national deficit"), she challenges educationists to consider the underlying debt rather than measuring the gap in achievement at this point in time (Ladson-Billings, 2006). That leaves unanswered difficult questions for assessment practitioners – should they adjust their assessments to bring about more equal outcomes (reducing the "awarding gap"), or would doing so destroy the value of the comparative measures of the gap in drawing attention to differences, perhaps a result of the "debt" referred to by Ladson-Billings, and indicating the need for changes to pedagogy that would support better performance and narrow the gap? In the words attributed to the sociologist Otis Dudley Duncan, "If you want to measure change, don't change the measure" (Duncan, 1968).

At this stage we shall allow some of these questions to hang in the air unanswered as we move on to consider two case studies of particular issues that have been battled with in the early years of the 21st century – the first in the USA and the second in the UK.

Case study 1: race-conscious college admissions policies (USA)

Prominent in the USA in the second half of the 20th century were the "civil rights" movements and campaigns to promote "affirmative action" to combat discrimination on grounds of race or gender. This case study traces thinking in the USA before and during the 21st century about one application of those concepts – consideration of race in college admissions policies. It is a story linking legal cases with educational theory and cultural change, and the legal storyline took what may prove to be a dramatic twist at the time when this book was being written.

This discussion cannot do justice to the history of inequality and segregation in education in the USA and beyond. For our purposes, it is particularly relevant to note the persistence of separateness of different racial groups in access to colleges and universities in the USA, well beyond the mid-20th-century groundbreaking legal case of *Brown* v. *Board of Education*,[11] which declared "separate but equal" policies unconstitutional. John F.

Kennedy's Executive Order in 1961[12] required Federal government organisations to practice "non-discrimination" on grounds of race, colour, religion or national origin in their actions and in awarding contracts. Lyndon B. Johnson followed in 1965 with an Order[13] which added "sex" to the proscribed criteria and provided for "affirmative action" in terms of promoting, advertising and drawing attention to non-discrimination.

Public colleges[14] in the United States were directly affected by these Orders, but all (private as well as public) were aware of the thinking that lay behind them. A distinction is made between "selective" and "non-selective" colleges and between different degrees of selectivity.[15] Within the "selective" group, a further distinction is made between those colleges that select according to grades and/or test scores and those whose admissions policies involve "holistic" review, defined by Liu (2022) as:

> evaluation . . . that relies on a spectrum of criteria that reflect applicants' attitude, knowledge, skills, and competencies. The essential element is the consideration of contextual factors that impact an applicant's qualifications, including the opportunities available to them, their family, their community, and the schools they attended.
>
> (p. 2)

We are concerned here with the policies of selective colleges, which involve holistic review.

The burning question that was carried into the 21st century and continued to flare a quarter of a century on is whether (or how) holistic admissions policies should take account of the race of student applicants. This would normally mean seeking to select more students from ethnic groups who were judged to have had fewer opportunities to get high grades at school. The arguments for doing so include achieving greater diversity in intake than would be achieved by using test scores alone. This is argued to have educational and social benefits, though, as we shall see, the claims of educational benefit are contested. There is also an argument based on fairness at the individual level – to mitigate the effects of (unfair) disadvantage in the student's background. Some have added an argument based on a form of retributive justice – to make up for past discrimination against the ethnic groups represented by student applicants. Ford (2022), for example, writes of "the generations of race-based exclusion and exploitation that make race-conscious hiring and college admissions necessary" (p. 2).

The case against race-conscious admissions is normally based on relational (un)fairness (Nisbet & Shaw, 2020) – that giving preferential treatment to some applicants because of their race means that they are "cutting in line" (American English) or "jumping the queue" (UK English) and may block opportunities for other applicants with higher scores. In the words of Edward

Blum (2022), a campaigner against race-conscious admissions policies in the United States:

> In a multi-racial, multi-ethnic nation like ours, the college admissions bar cannot be raised for some races and ethnic groups but lowered for others. Our nation cannot remedy past discrimination and racial preferences with new discrimination and different racial preferences.[16]

Since the latter years of the 20th century, debates in the USA about race-conscious admissions have gone through two parallel legal channels: Executive Orders at State level and individual cases considered by the courts, including leading cases at the Supreme Court.

A stream of Executive Orders and rulings in the US States started in 1996 in California, where voters backed a Proposition, known popularly thereafter as "Prop 209", barring "preferential treatment based on race". This followed a ruling the previous year by the Regents of the (public) University of California barring preferences based on race in admissions and in hiring and contracting by the University. The first two decades of the 21st century saw similar rulings in nine States – from Florida in 1999 to Idaho in 2020. Attempts to reverse policies through ballots failed in Washington (2019) and California (2020).

In practice, colleges in these states looked for "race-neutral" alternatives, which would still have the effect of boosting enrolment of students from racial minorities. These included outreach programmes with local schools and minority populations. A few colleges dropped selection practices that had benefitted the historical status quo, such as giving preference to children of donors or alumni. However, these actions did not achieve much change. Statistics showing changes in the proportion of "under-represented minorities" in college admissions between the year of the ban in the State concerned and 2020 vary from an increase of 6.3% in the University of Washington to a decrease of 2.2% in the University of Michigan at Ann Arbor (Elias & Perez, 2022).

The second channel has been action in the Courts to challenge race-conscious selection by colleges, normally in the name of white applicants who claimed to have been denied equal opportunities by those policies.

Challenge in the Courts goes back to the 1970s, with cases brought by Marco DeFunis in 1971, who had not been admitted to the Law School of the University of Washington,[17] and by Allan Bakke (1978), who had been rejected by the Medical School of the University of California at Davis in 1973 and 1974.[18] The *DeFunis* case did not produce a ruling on the college's policies; in *Bakke* there was conditional approval of the college's policies, but a ruling that Bakke should be enroled.[19]

These early cases left an important legacy for the 21st century. In particular, there was a clear ruling in *Bakke* that it was unconstitutional to justify admissions policies taking account of race on the grounds that such policies remedied historical injustice to particular ethnic groups. However, there could be a justification for policies seeking to achieve diversity for *educational* reasons. The majority opinion allowed race to be considered among other factors "as long as the intent was not remedying past discrimination, but rather obtaining the educational benefits that flow from an ethnically diverse student body" (*Bakke*, 438 U.S. 265 at 378). As a result of this ruling, which was supported in subsequent judgements, for a long period extending well into the 21st century, discussion about justice (in the sense of righting past wrongs) in college admissions was superseded by educational considerations about the benefits of "diversity" (Ford, 2022).

After a gap of some twenty-five years, the Supreme Court considered two cases that together set the norm that has dominated discussion of this issue in the first quarter of the 21st century. They involved complaints by Barbara Gratz and Patrick Homachar (who had been denied admission as undergraduates to the University of Michigan College of Literature, Science and the Arts) and by Barbara Grutter (who had been denied admission to the University of Michigan's Law School). The Supreme Court considered the two cases together in 2003.[20] They reached a majority verdict on both cases, and the majority opinion set out principles that held the stage for many years to come. We shall label them "the *Grutter* settlement".

Under the *Grutter* settlement, it was accepted that a College could have a "compelling interest" in creating a diverse student body, but admissions policies had to be "narrowly tailored" (the phrase became a mantra) to achieve the educational benefits of diversity. In the *Gratz* case, applicants had been considered under a points system that automatically gave twenty extra points to students from underrepresented minority backgrounds. The majority of judges concluded that this was too much of a blunt instrument and not sufficiently "narrowly tailored" to achieve diversity. Post-*Grutter*, many colleges aimed to craft carefully argued systems for reviewing applications without involving anything as unsubtle as a points system explicitly benefitting racial groups. In 2006, the State of Michigan voted to ban colleges from considering race in evaluating applicants.

The next group of cases were brought on behalf of Abagail Fisher (supported by the "Project on Fair Representation") against the University of Texas. They went twice to the Supreme Court – in 2013 ("Fisher I")[21] and 2016 ("Fisher II").[22] In Texas, the government had legislated in 1997 to apply the "Top Ten Percent Rule", whereby students who graduated in the top 10% of their high school classes in Texas were guaranteed admission to a Texas public university. This was intended to benefit students from schools in poorer areas or with more black students. After *Grutter*, the University of Texas continued to include race in their holistic reviews of admission, even after applying the 10% rule. In Fisher I, the Supreme Court asked the university to carry out a "searching examination" of its policies to ensure that they were "narrowly tailored" to the educational benefits of diversity. In 2014, the US court of appeals ruled that they had done so satisfactorily, but there was a further appeal to the Supreme Court ("Fisher II") in which the majority opinion was that the university "did narrowly tailor its admission policy to serve a compelling government interest [in] creating a diverse student body from which educational benefits flow" (365).

In all these leading cases, the Supreme Court judges failed to agree, and majority judgements were given.

In 2022, with new, more socially conservative, judges appointed to the Supreme Court, it considered oral arguments in a challenge, on behalf of named Asian American students, to the consideration of race in the admissions policies of Harvard (a private institution) and the (public) University of North Carolina. The much-anticipated judgement was given on 29 June 2023.[23] The Supreme Court ruled, by a majority, that the approach to race in the admissions policies of the two universities was incompatible with the Equal Protection Clause of the US Constitution. Although the judgement did not explicitly overrule prior leading cases that had allowed race to be taken into account as a factor promoting diversity, a concurring Judge, Justice Clarence Thomas, wrote that the majority's opinion meant that "*Grutter* is, for all intents and purposes, overruled".

Two aspects of the majority opinion are particularly important. The first is that the judgement distinguished clearly between taking account of the particular circumstances of individuals (which they considered permissible) and giving preferences to groups, such as ethnic groupings, which they judged unconstitutional. In the words of Chief Justice John Roberts, "An applicant must be treated based on his or her experiences as an individual – not on the basis of race".

The second important point to note is that the arguments for diversity as an objective were found by the majority of the judges to be too vague and unmeasurable and to engage in racial stereotyping. In taking this view, they were rejecting the academic arguments presented by several of the leading educational organisations in their *amicus curiae* brief submitted the previous year (see AERA, 2022).

So, it seems that as we enter the second quarter of the 21st century, the *Grutter* settlement has come to an end – as, at least in legal contexts, it has a quarter of a century of arguments based on the concept of "diversity", justified as producing educational benefits. The two dissenting judges were strongly opposed to this outcome and they made the strength of their feelings clear. Justice Sonia Sotomayor, for example, said: "Notwithstanding this Court's actions, however, society's progress toward equality cannot be permanently halted. Diversity is now a fundamental American value, housed in our varied and multicultural American community that only continues to grow. The pursuit of racial diversity will go on".

What happens next is not yet clear. In the words of one commentator:

> The U.S. Supreme Court looked behind the curtain. Then it knocked over the table and chairs. Now, colleges are left with one big mess and a slew of questions that will define a new era for college admissions in a nation riven by racial disparities.
>
> *(Hoover, 2023, webpage)*

The Federal US government has promised guidance to colleges about future lawful admissions policies.[24] Suggestions by writers in the wake of the judgement have included the possibility of taking account of other factors than race, such as family wealth.[25] It is open to question whether the objective of "diversity" will ever be able to be conceptualised sufficiently clearly to meet the majority judges' concerns, and whether the academic received view valuing diversity will survive this setback. The judges' insistence on focusing on individuals rather than wider trends in society would not be accepted by critical theorists or by those who pursue policy goals based on a broader concept of the public good. In the words of the dissenting Justice Sotomayor, "The court's decision leaves the nation's colleges in a challenging position: How to enroll a diverse student body in a land where race continues to matter while using an evaluative process in which, all of a sudden, ... race *can't* matter?".

The moral and educational arguments in this case are potentially relevant beyond and within the USA. Many countries explicitly recognise the educational benefits of diversity. The *amicus curiae* submission to the Supreme Court in 2022 by leading US educational academic bodies included comprehensive literature and research reviews (AERA, 2022), concluding that research backed the *Grutter* settlement – "a compelling governmental interest in diversity, [and] that race-conscious admissions policies are narrowly tailored to the diversity interest" (AERA, 2022, p. 14). Among the claimed educational benefits of diversity are "improvements in [students'] cognitive abilities, critical thinking and self-confidence" (ibid., p. 22).

But readers of this book may expect continued debate on these propositions, particularly in societies where discussion of race remains divisive and emotive.

Attacks on the prominence of "diversity" are not confined to the right wing of ideology or politics. It has also been questioned by the radical left. We have seen that since the *Bakke* judgement in the 1970s, the US courts have ruled out a justification for race-conscious admissions policies based on restorative justice to compensate for unjust discrimination in the past. "Diversity" was a more acceptable substitute, and this prompted challenges on the grounds that the whole "diversity" enterprise was a pale shadow of what ought to have been done explicitly for reasons of social justice. Richard Thompson Ford (2022) writes:

> Diversity is not the same as justice. It is a substitute for justice. Like saccharine instead of sugar in diet soda, diversity serves some of the functions of justice and also takes its place. Diversity has made justice seem redundant. Because it has become a major part of our diet, it's easy to forget the real thing.
>
> (p. 2)

Two more social trends are worth mentioning. The first is that the relation between race and social disadvantage becomes more nuanced in societies with second- and third-generation immigrant populations. That remark in no way belittles the persistence of racial injustice in many countries as we approach the second quarter of the 21st century. But the most recent Supreme Court case has been brought in the name of Asian American students, in contrast with the previous leading cases featuring challenges on behalf of white students. In any holistic review involving race, the categories of racial analysis used need to be reviewed constantly to make sure that they are up to date.

Second, public opinion in the 2020s on race-conscious college admissions appears to have hardened in the USA. We have seen the string of state-level orders barring race-conscious admissions that have been approved by public vote and the failure to get them reversed by public vote. In a survey of freshmen in the USA carried out in 2019, 50.2% supported the proposition that "affirmative action in college admissions should be abolished".[26] And in public opinion research by the Pew Research Centre: 74% thought that "race or ethnicity" should not be a factor in college admissions. In all ethnic categories of respondents, the majority took that view.[27]

What are the implications of this debate for assessment? First, it should be noted that decisions on selection for entry to university or college are themselves educational assessments – making judgements based on evidence in an educational context. The more "holistic" the approach, the more technically complex will be the task of ensuring that the criteria used to select and evaluate the evidence are being applied properly and fairly. In many ways, selection based on examination grades or test scores would be more comfortable for the technical apparatus used by assessors to ensure reliability, validity and fairness. Increasing concern about the fairness of college admission tests in the USA (Marmol, 2016; Newman et al., 2022) led to the alternative path of selection by test score also being shunned, with universities increasingly adapting "test-blind" or "test-neutral" policies. However, in the mid-2020s, there are signs of a return to the use of standardised tests, prompted by concerns about the fairness of alternative sources of evidence.[28] We say more in

Chapter 7 about this important debate. Whatever route is taken, the assessments involved in selection for college or university will be complex and open to challenge in the next quarter-century.

Second, this story is one illustration of the possibility that the criteria for carrying out assessments in educational contexts – or the procedure for carrying them out – may be affected by policy decisions taken on non-educational grounds. In some of the cases we have considered, the colleges had different rules and procedures for considering applications from minority applicants. Those were largely criticised by the courts in the USA, but more generally, within the legal space allowed by the courts governing each country, those carrying out and governing educational assessment need to be able to take account of these policy directions in a way that is transparent and applies the principles consistently and fairly. An example from Ireland is the scope to award additional marks in Leaving Certificate examinations to students who sit them in the language of Irish with the explicit aim of "strengthen[ing] the position of the Irish language in the education system, with the long-term objective of maintaining and reviving it use in everyday life" (Mac Aóghain et al., 2010, p. 25). It is not realistic to expect the world of assessment to be immune from such influences. They set the context in which the principles of good assessment need to be applied.

Third, the arguments about race in the USA have parallels with debates in many countries about how – or whether – assessment for admission to universities should cope with the effects of many kinds of disadvantage on the performances of candidates. For example, the consideration of "personal statements" by UK universities was reviewed in 2023 because, in the words of the University and College Admissions Service (UCAS) in the UK:

> Feedback shows fears that students who do not have access to high quality advice and guidance will not be able to use the statement to shine in the same way that their more advantaged peers can. There are also concerns about the extent to which students understand how providers use personal statements in decision-making.
>
> *(UCAS, 2023, p. 6)*

Finally, 21st-century attacks on the perceived liberal consensus often argue for a return to assessment and decision practices that are taken without knowledge of the candidate's colour, social class, school background or any other characteristic. Thus, historian David Abulafia (2022) writes:

> University admissions have become another site for culture wars in which "white", "male" and "privileged" are terms of disapproval, linked together to justify injustice. Imagined class must not determine admissions. School names should probably be omitted from application forms.[29]

An appeal to remove construct-irrelevant information from assessment decisions may be initially attractive to assessment theorists and practitioners. But the second case study in this chapter suggests that this too is increasingly contested in the 21st century.

Case study 2: decolonising the university curriculum (UK)

The concept of "decolonisation" in education has flourished in the first quarter of the 21st century. The root meaning of "decolonisation" is given in the (Cambridge) dictionary as "the process in which a country that was previously a colony (controlled by another country) becomes politically independent; the process of getting rid of colonies".[30] By extension, the dictionary reports a use in "social science" denoting "the process of changing something such as a curriculum (a list of books, ideas etc to be studied) in a way that considers the cultural beliefs behind it, for example the belief that European writers, artists, or ideas are better and more important than ones from countries that were colonized (controlled) by Europe, and that gives more importance to non-European writers, artists, etc.". We are particularly interested in this extended use of the term as applied to education (and its constituent assessments), both in former colonial powers, such as the UK, France and Spain, and in former colonies, such as the USA, where some ex-European immigrant cultures have become dominant.

The first two examples in this case study are drawn from the higher education sector in the UK. However, the underlying thinking applies more widely. For example, Peters (2015) argues that the widespread protests in the USA following the shooting of Michael Brown in August 2014 demonstrate that "Obama's 'post-racial America' is a kind of mythology. Part of the problem is what scholars call 'internal colonization . . . [which] means that the dominant ideology has become internalized and thus part of the psychological make-up of the oppressed" (p. 642).

In 1869, Matthew Arnold famously defined "culture" as involving "getting to know . . . the best that has been thought and said in the world" (Arnold, 1869/2015, p. viii) and an inherited line of thought is that much of "the best" stems from western European traditions. By implication, colonising powers were thought to be bringing "the best" to indigenous populations in their colonies through education. In an interview with the *New York Times*, Noam Chomsky drew attention to the view of Theodore Roosevelt in 1909[31] that "[t]he expansion of the peoples of white, or European, blood during the past four centuries . . . has been fraught with lasting benefit to most of the peoples already dwelling in the lands over which the expansion took place" (New York Times, 2015).

The first of our cases from the UK concerns a campaign started in 2014 by students at University College London (UCL) and later adopted by some other student groups, entitled "Why is my curriculum white?" In a video[32] promoting the campaign, students express concern about an apparent lack of awareness "that the curriculum is composed of 'white ideas' by 'white authors' and is the result of colonialisation that has normalised whiteness and made blackness invisible". The "UCL collective" further argues[33] that "whiteness" is an "ideology" rather than a "biological" classification: "When we talk about whiteness, we are not talking about white people, but about an ideology that empowers people racialised as white". Their arguments cover the content of the curricula in subject departments, which, they argue, should neither be dominated by white sources nor assume that those sources are "right". They also question the visible celebration of historical figures at the university who supported slavery or pioneered racially divisive thinking such as eugenics.

The second case is a consultation in 2022 by the (UK) Quality Assurance Agency (QAA) for Higher Education, which, among other things, provides guidance to universities through "subject benchmarks".[34] The QAA embarked on a project to review and revise those benchmarks, and one of the revised benchmarks covered Mathematics, Statistics and Operational Research (MSOR) (QAA, 2022). The text of the revised draft guidance included:

> [T]he curriculum should present a multicultural and decolonised view of MSOR, informed by the student voice. Where possible, it should present the work of a diverse group of MSOR practitioners. Students should be made aware of problematic issues in the development of the MSOR content they are being taught, for example some pioneers of statistics supported eugenics, or some mathematicians had connections to the slave trade, racism or Nazism.
>
> *(pp. 6–7)*

Publication of this proposal provoked a backlash from some academics. Dr John Armstrong wrote an article entitled "The sinister attempt to de-colonise mathematics" (Armstrong, 2022) and he and eleven other signatories wrote an open letter to the QAA (Armstrong et al., 2022). They argued that the history of mathematics was not "particularly European" in the first place, and, more fundamentally, they foresaw a risk of "ideological capture by activist academics" who were pursuing a "postmodernist critique of the European paradigm of rational knowledge". In a letter to the *Times Higher Education* (November 2022), they accepted that students might be told about mathematicians who were, say, pro-Nazi, or anti-Nazi, but they regarded such information as an "aside" that might "enliven" a course rather than a core element of the curriculum:

> We struggle to imagine what it would mean to decolonise, for example, a course on the geometry of surfaces. For the most part, the concept of

decolonisation is irrelevant to university mathematics and our students know this.

(Williams, 2022)[35]

Our final case concerns developments in the UK and the USA to train teachers, lecturers and students to be aware of issues including "white privilege and colonialisation". The concept of "white privilege", which has fed into these initiatives, has been traced back to articles by Peggy McIntosh in the 1980s (see McIntosh, 1989, and criticism of the concept in Tobin, 2021) and several courses have made use of tests to recognise examples of white privilege. In Scotland, guidance, bearing the logos of government-funded organisations, has been issued to teachers, and the "Anti-Racist Educator" (a platform for anti-racist education with a Scottish perspective) has published resources with definitions of key terms, including:

In anti-racist work, "white people" refers to a socially-constructed identity based on skin colour. Rather than an identity, "whiteness" is a racial discourse that privileges white people and that asserts white people as the norm.

(Leonardo, 2022, p. 31)[36]

Anti-racism courses, which some universities have made compulsory, have provoked criticism. In England, an article in the *Daily Telegraph* took issue with a course at the University of Kent where students were quizzed on symptoms of "white privilege" and, according to the article, told that "systemic racism . . . is built into the very building blocks of British society" (Somerville, 2021).

In the USA, there was controversy about a programme at the University of Delaware, designed by the university's Office of Residence Life and compulsory for all students. According to Kissel (2009),[37] the students were told, among other things, that the term "racist" "applies to all white people (i.e. people of European descent) living in the United States". Kissel also claimed that students could be referred for follow-up if they questioned the position taken by the course or gave the "wrong" answer to quiz questions.

What is the relevance of these cases to assessment? At the outset, we have to say that assessment is not at the forefront of many of these controversies. In its own words, the "Why is my curriculum white?" campaign is mainly about the curriculum and pedagogy, although it ranges wider into the culture of educational institutions. Curricular changes can feed into changes to the content of curriculum-based assessments, including university examinations, but arguably there is no direct link between a change in, for example, set texts for a literature test and the method of assessing understanding of the (changed) text. We have some sympathy with the mathematician who puzzled what it might mean to decolonise a course on the geometry of surfaces. However, further thought does suggest that there are lessons for assessment from the cases described in this section.

First, as the QAA acknowledges in their draft guidance (Guiding Principles 2, 4, 9, p. 8),[38] the recognised good practice in assessment of universal design (USA) (AERA et al., 2014, Standard 3:1; 3:2; 3:3; 3:4) and fair assessment by design (UK) (Qualifications Wales & CCEA, 2019)[39] support the conclusion that examples and settings used in assessment tasks or test questions should be recognisable by students from all backgrounds, and not provide (construct-irrelevant) barriers to learning for some, because of their race. Although questions on surface geometry may be set without specifying a real-world context, the same cannot be said of all mathematically related assessments.

There is a particular danger for organisations setting tests taken internationally: that the syllabus for the tests or examinations, the assessment tasks and the marking criteria may reinforce the dominance of the culture and intellectual heritage of the host organisation. Even if that is shared explicitly with the candidates and their teachers, it may be open to the legitimate challenge of reinforcing (colonial) power bases.

The second possible challenge is more controversial. It is that "rational knowledge" is argued to be particularly European, and it is thought to be racist to prefer it over "other ways of knowing" (this view is criticised by Armstrong in his Spectator article about the QAA benchmarks for mathematics). If this view were applied to educational assessment, it might be necessary to reconsider assessment criteria and mark schemes to allow for other approaches. However, in our view, there is a danger of racism in assumptions about linking races with different approaches to logic and knowledge in different subjects. It may be more appropriate to see the "rational knowledge" challenge as raising questions rather than answering them. Do our assessment criteria and mark schemes reflect assumptions that stem from a European (or Western) tradition and fail to take account of thinking in other traditions? If so, what is the justification for the approach we are taking?

The third challenge is the use of assessments, including for selection of institutions or tracking/streaming within them. If the effect of these uses is to reinforce power structures that disempower some groups in society, then that should prompt a re-evaluation of the link between the assessment and its use. It is always appropriate to ask "Who will benefit?" when designing an assessment.

Last, the examples of some of the controversial "anti-racism" courses raise questions about formative quizzes and tests used as part of these courses. If the objective is to increase the student's understanding of one point of view, then if that is made clear, it is surely legitimate to test that understanding. For example, we quoted a definition proffered by the Anti-Racism Collective in the "Anti-Racism Educator":

> *In anti-racist work*, "white people" refers to a socially-constructed identity based on skin colour.
>
> *(emphasis added)*

A quiz question along the lines of "How is the phrase 'white people' understood in anti-racist work?" seems appropriate and fair. However, if there is an unstated assumption that only one definition is "right" – or if any other approach to the subject matter of the course is followed up by criticism – then in our view, the purpose of the assessment is skewed.

. . . .

This chapter has identified some trends in thinking about society that have come to the forefront in the first two decades of the 21st century. We have surveyed theoretical and popular challenges from critical theories – and Critical Race Theory in particular – and we have taken "deep dives" into case studies about race-conscious college admissions policies in the USA and decolonising the university curriculum in the UK. Many of the issues discussed have been controversial, and some have proved hugely divisive.

We have begun to ask about the implications for educational assessment, but at this stage we have identified more questions than answers. One feature linking almost all of the trends discussed here has been an emphasis on the importance of the contexts in which assessments are set, taken and used, and a challenge to views of assessments as objective measurements isolated from their contexts. We shall say more about this challenge in Chapter 7. Meantime, in the next chapter, we shall look in more detail at 21st-century changes to thinking about education and assessment.

Notes

1 In the English language, the use of "identify" as a reflexive verb (as in "I identify as . . .") has become common in many fields of discourse, including education.
2 www.insidehighered.com/news/2023/02/20/professors-job-endangered-teaching-about-race
3 A detailed account of the work of the Frankfurt School can be found at https://plato.stanford.edu/entries/critical-theory/
4 For those interested in exploring pragmatism further, there is a very informative summary by Nicholas Rescher in the *Oxford Companion to Philosophy*, Oxford (2005), pp. 749–750.
5 The hashtag #BlackLivesMatter began to be used on social media in July 2013 after the acquittal of George Zimmerman for the shooting of African American teen Trayvon Martin seventeen months earlier.
6 Cited by Geffrey Bell in *The Twilight of Unionism: Ulster and the Future of Northern Ireland*, Verso, London, 2022, at page 203.

7 www.nytimes.com/interactive/2019/08/14/magazine/1619-america-slavery.html
8 See also Joseph, G. G. (2009). Mathematics and Eurocentrism. In R. K. Kanth (Eds.), *The Challenge of Eurocentrism: Global Perspectives, Policy, and Prospects*. Palgrave Macmillan.
9 Increasingly joined on the podium by fairness (e.g. Worrell, 2016).
10 www.officeforstudents.org.uk/advice-and-guidance/promoting-equal-opportunities/effective-practice/black-asian-and-minority-ethnic-students/.
11 *Brown* v. *Board of Education of Topeka*, 347 U.S. 483, 1954.
12 Viewed at www.presidency.ucsb.edu/documents/executive-order-10925-establishing-the-presidents-committee-equal-employment opportunity?utm_source=Iterable&utm_medium=email&utm_campaign=campaign_5294465_nl_Race-in-l Admissions-01_date_20221101&cid=ra01&source=&sourceId=
13 Viewed at www.archives.gov/federal-register/codification/executive-order/11246.html?utm_source=Iterable&utm_medium=email&utm_campaign=campaign_5294465_nl_Race-in-Admissions 01_date_20221101&cid=ra01&source=&sourceId=
14 In this section, we use "college" to refer to post-school educational institutions, including universities.
15 See, for example, the different gradations of "selective" at www.collegetransitions.com/admissions-counseling/college-selectivity/
16 From the Press Release of "Student for Fair Admissions", 3 May 2022, downloaded at https://studentsforfairadmissions.org/students-for-fair-admissions-files-opening-brief-at-u-s-supreme-court-in-students-for-fair-admissions-v-harvard-and-students-for-fair-admissions-v-university-of-north-carolina/
17 *Marco DeFUNIS et al.* v. *Charles ODEGAARD*, President of the University of Washington. 416 U.S. 312. 94 S. Ct. 1704.
18 *Regents of University of California* v. *Bakke*, 438 U.S. 265, 1978.
19 *Los Angeles Times*, 29 June 1978: "Bakke wins but Justices Uphold Affirmative Action" seen at www.rarenewspapers.com/view/668342?utm_source=Iterable&utm_medium=email&utm_campaign=campaign_5294467_nl_Race-in-Admissions-03_date_20221108&cid=ra03&source=&sourceId=
20 *Gratz* v. *Bollinger*, 539 U.S. 244 (2003); *Grutter* v. *Bollinger*, 539 U.S. 306 (2003).
21 *Fisher* v. *University of Texas*, 570 U.S. 297 (2013).
22 *Fisher* v. *University of Texas*, 579 U.S. 365 (2016).
23 *Students for Fair Admissions* v. *Harvard*, 600 U.S. 181 (2023).
24 Fact sheet: US Departments of Education, 29 June 2023 www.ed.gov/news/press-releases/fact-sheet-president-biden-announces-actions-promote-educational-opportunity-and-diversity-colleges-and-universities?utm_source=Iterable&utm_medium=email&utm_campaign=campaign_7173997_nl_Weekly-Briefing_date_20230701&cid=wb&source=&sourceid=
25 Arguments for and against an approach based on wealth are expressed in: "The Path to Diversity at College Now That the Supreme Court Has Struck Down Affirmative Action" by Peter Dreier, Richard D. Kahlenberg, and Melvin L. Oliver. https://slate.com/news-and-politics/2023/02/supreme-court-affirmative-action-wealth-admissions-factor.html#:~:text=The%20Path%20to,FEB%2008%2C%202023; and "The Problem With Wealth-Based Affirmative Action: It's not an adequate substitute for race-based programs" By Richard Rothstein (2021). Atlantic www.theatlantic.com/ideas/archive/2023/06/affirmative-action-race-socioeconomic-supreme-court/674251/
26 The American Freshman: National Norms Fall 2019, obtained at www.heri.ucla.edu/monographs/TheAmericanFreshman2019.pdf
27 See www.pewresearch.org/short-reads/2022/04/26/u-s-public-continues-to-view-grades-test-scores-as-top-factors-in-college-admissions/

28 See Stephanie Saul. "Yale to Require Standardized Test Scores for Admissions". *New York Times*, 22 February 2024. Accessed at www.nytimes.com/2024/02/22/us/yale-standardized-testing-sat-act.html
29 See also *The Spectator*. 14 May 2022. www.spectator.co.uk/article/the-culture-wars-have-crept-into-oxbridge-admissions/
30 *Cambridge Dictionary*: https://dictionary.cambridge.org/dictionary/english/decolonization
31 Theodore Roosevelt's "Expansion of the White Races" Speech, 18 January 1909 – Washington, D.C. Methodist Episcopal Church celebration of the African Diamond Jubilee. https://spiritualpilgrim.net/07_Special-Documents/Historical-Documents/1909_T-Roosevelt%27s%20%27Expansion%20of%20the%20White%20Races%27%20speech.html
32 https://theoccupiedtimes.org/?p=14056
33 See 8 Reasons the Curriculum is White by the 'Why is my Curriculum White?' collective, UCL. 23 March 2015 https://novaramedia.com/2015/03/23/8-reasons-the-curriculum-is-white/
34 "Subject Benchmark Statements describe the nature of study and the academic standards expected of graduates in specific subject areas. They show what graduates might reasonably be expected to know, do and understand at the end of their studies". www.qaa.ac.uk/the-quality-code/subject-benchmark-statements
35 www.timeshighereducation.com/news/professors-say-decolonisation-agenda-politicising-maths-degrees
36 www.theantiracisteducator.com/whiteness
37 How the Dorms Are Politicized: The Case of the University of Delaware. National Association of Scholars. 14 January 2009. www.nas.org/blogs/article/how_the_dorms_are_politicized_the_case_of_the_university_of_delaware
38 UK Quality Code for Higher Education: Advice and Guidance – Assessment. QAA. (2018). www.qaa.ac.uk/docs/qaa/quality-code/advice-and-guidance-assessment.pdf?sfvrsn=ca29c181_4
39 Qualifications Wales & CCEA (Regulation) (2019) Fair Access by Design: Guidance for awarding organisations on designing high-quality and inclusive qualifications, July. Available at: https://qualifications.wales/media/avuda1dk/fair-access-by-design.pdf.

References

Abulafia, D. (2022, May 14). The culture wars have crept into Oxbridge admissions. *The Spectator*. www.spectator.co.uk/article/the-culture-wars-have-crept-into-oxbridge-admissions/

AERA. (2022). *Amicus Curiae brief to the Supreme Court on case of students for fair admissions. Inc. Petitioner, v. University of North Carolina, et al., Respondents, and Students for Fair Admissions, Inc., Petitioner, v. University of North Carolina, et al., Respondents.* www.aera.net/Portals/38/AERA%20SFFA%20Brief.pdf?utm_source=Informz&utm_medium=email&utm_campaign=test

American Educational Research Association, American Psychological Association, and National Council on Measurement in Education. (2014). *Standards for educational and psychological testing.* American Educational Research Association.

Apple, M. W. (2019). On doing critical policy analysis. *Educational Policy, 33*(1), 276–287. http://doi.org/10.1177/0895904818807307

Armstrong, J. (2022, November 14). The sinister attempt to "de-colonise" mathematics. *The Spectator*. www.spectator.co.uk/article/the-sinister-attempts-to-decolonise-mathematics/

Armstrong, J., Ball, J., Dawid, G., Hitchin, N., Kumon, A., Miheisi, N., Rees, M., Reid, M., Salamon, S., Series, C., Sokal, A., Shepard-Barro, N., Reeves, C., Webb,

J. R. L., Gilmour, S., Jacka, S., Gardiner, T., Widmer, M., Koloydenko, A., Hiberdink, T., & Saha, A. (2022). *Open letter about QAA benchmarks for mathematics, statistics and operational research*. Undated. https://nms.kcl.ac.uk/john. armstrong/qaa/QAABenchmarkLetter.pdf

Arnold, M. (1869/2015). *Culture and anarchy and other selected prose*. Penguin Books.

Atewologun, D. (2018). *Intersectionality theory and practice*. Oxford Research Encyclopedia of Business and Management. https://oxfordre.com/business/view/10.1093/acrefore/9780190224851.001.0001/acrefore-9780190224851-e-48

Bell, D. (1992). *Faces at the bottom of the well: The permanence of racism*. Basic Books (Reprint edition, 6 October 1993).

Bell, G. (2022). *The twilight of unionism: Ulster and the future of Northern Ireland*. Verso.

Blum, E. (2022, May 3). *From the press release of "Student for Fair Admissions"*. https://studentsforfairadmissions.org/students-for-fair-admissions-files-opening-brief-at-u-s-supreme-court-in-students-for-fair-admissions-v-harvard-and-students-for-fair-admissions-v-university-of-north-carolina/

Brennan, R. L. (2006). Perspectives on the evolution and future of educational measurement. In R. L. Brennan (Ed.), *Educational measurement* (4th ed., pp. 3–16). American Council on Education/Praeger.

Crenshaw, K., Gotanda, N., Peller, G., & Thomas, K. (Eds.). (1995). *Critical race theory: The key writings that formed the movement*. New Press.

Delgado, R., & Stefancic, J. (2006). *Critical race theory: An introduction*. NYU Press.

Desmond, M. (2019, August 14). In order to understand the brutality of American capitalism, you have to start on the plantation. *The New York Times*.

Dewey, J. (1918/2015). *Democracy and education: An introduction to the philosophy of education*. CreateSpace Independent Publishing Platform.

DiAngelo, R. (2019). *White fragility: Why it's so hard for white people to talk about racism*. Penguin Books.

Dreier, P., Kahlenberg, R. D., & Oliver, M. L. (2023). *The path to diversity at college now that the Supreme Court has struck down affirmative action*. https://slate.com/news-and-politics/2023/02/supreme-court-affirmative-action-wealth-admissions-factor.html#:~:text=The%20Path%20to,FEB%2008%2C%202023

Duncan, O. D. (1968). Social stratification and mobility: Problems in the measurement of trend. In E. B. Sheldon & W. E. Moore (Eds.), *Indicators of social change: Concepts and measurements* (pp. 675–720). Russell Sage Foundation. www.jstor.org/stable/10.7758/9781610446914.15

Economist. (2021, July 30). How has the meaning of the word "woke" evolved? *Economist*. www.economist.com/the-economist-explains/2021/07/30/how-has-the-meaning-of-the-word-woke-evolved

Economist. (2022, July 14). "Critical race theory" is being weaponised. What's the fuss about? *Economist*. www.economist.com/interactive/united-states/2022/07/14/critical-race-theory-is-being-weaponised-whats-the-fuss-about

Elias, J., & Perez, N. (2022, September 2). What would the end of race-conscious admissions mean for minority enrollment? *The Chronicle of Higher Education*. https://www.chronicle.com/article/race-conscious-admission-bans

Ford, R. T. (2022, September 2). How affirmative action was derailed by diversity. *The Chronicle of Higher Education*. www.chronicle.com/article/derailed-by-diversity?utm_source=Iterable&utm_medium=email&utm_campaign=campaign_5411224_nl_Chronicle-Review_date_20221031&cid=cr&source=&sourceid=

Furedi, F. (2021). *100 years of identity crisis: Culture wars over socialisation*. De Gruyter.

Gillborn, D. (2005, July). Education policy as an act of white supremacy: Whiteness, critical race theory and education reform. *Journal of Education Policy, 20*(4), 485–505. http://doi.org/10.1080/02680930500132346

Gillborn, D. (2006). Critical race theory and education: Racism and antiracism in educational theory and praxis. *Discourse: Studies in the Cultural Politics of Education, 27*(1), 11–32. http://doi.org/10.1080/01596300500510229

Hannah-Jones, N. (2019, August 14). Our founding ideals of liberty and equality were false. *New York Times Magazine*, pp. 14–26. www.nytimes.com/interactive/2019/08/14/magazine/black-history-american-democracy.html

Hoover, E. (2023, June 29). *The Supreme Court's decision reveals a gulf between two views of race and merit.* www.chronicle.com/article/the-supreme-courts-decision-reveals-a-gulf-between-two-views-of-race-and-merit?utm_source=Iterable&utm_medium=email&utm_campaign=campaign_7160785_nl_Academe-Today_date_20230630&cid=at&source=&sourceid=

Joseph, G. G. (2009). Mathematics and eurocentrism. In R. K. Kanth (Eds.), *The challenge of eurocentrism: Global perspectives, policy, and prospects.* Palgrave.

Kissel, A. (2009, January 14). How the dorms are politicized: The case of the University of Delaware. *National Association of Scholars.* https://www.nas.org/blogs/article/how_the_dorms_are_politicized_the_case_of_the_university_of_delaware

Ladson-Billings, G. (1998). Just what is critical race theory and what is it doing in a nice field like education? *International Journal of Qualitative Studies in Education, 11*(1), 7–24. http://doi.org/10.1080/095183998236863

Ladson-Billings, G. (2006, October). From the achievement gap to the education debt: Understanding achievement in U.S. schools. *Educational Researcher, 35*(7), 3–12. http://doi.org/10.3102/0013189X035007003

Ladson-Billings, G., & Tate, W. F. I. V. (1995, Fall). Towards a critical race theory of education. *Teachers College Record: The Voice of Scholarship in Education, 97*(1), 47–68. http://doi.org/10.1177/016146819509700104

Leonardo, Z. (2022). The Souls of White Folk: Critical pedagogy, whiteness studies, and globalization discourse. *Race Ethnicity and Education, 5*(1), 29–50. http://doi.org/10.1080/13613320120117180.

Liu, O. L. (2022). Holistic admissions in higher education: Challenges and promises. *Educational Testing Service, Journal of Postsecondary Student Success, 1*(4). https://journals.flvc.org/jpss/article/view/131099/134899

Mac Aogáin, E., Millar, D., & Kellaghan, T. (2010). The bonus for Irish in the leaving certificate examination. *The Irish Journal of Education, 38,* 25–42.

Marmol, E. (2016, Winter). The undemocratic effects and underlying racism of standardized testing in the United States. *Critical Intersection in Education, 4,* 1–9. https://jps.library.utoronto.ca/index.php/cie/article/view/26430/20714

McIntosh, P. (1989). *White Privilege: Unpacking the invisible knapsack.* https://nationalseedproject.org/images/documents/Knapsack_plus_Notes-Peggy_McIntosh.pdf

Mowat, J. G. (2018). Closing the attainment gap – a realistic proposition or an elusive pipe-dream? *Journal of Education Policy, 33*(2), 299–321. http://doi.org/10.1080/02680939.2017.1352033

Newman, D. A., Tang, C., Song, Q. C., & Wee, S. (2022). Dropping the GRE, keeping the GRE, or using GRE-optional admissions? Considering tradeoffs and fairness. *International Journal of Testing, 22*(1), 43–71. http://doi.org/10.1080/15305058.2021.2019750

New York Times. (2015, March 18). Noam Chomsky on the roots of American Racism, by George Yancy and Noam Chomsky. https://archive.nytimes.com/opinionator.blogs.nytimes.com/2015/03/18/noam-chomsky-on-the-roots-of-american-racism/#more-156259

Nisbet, I., & Shaw, S. D. (2020). *Is assessment fair?* SAGE Publications Ltd.

Pearson, P. D. (2004). The reading wars: The politics of reading research and policy – 1988 through 2003. *Educational Policy*, *18*(1), 216–252.

Peters, M. A. (2015). Editorial: Why is my curriculum white? *Educational Philosophy and Theory*, *47*(7), 641–646. http://doi.org/10.1080/00131857.2015.1037227

Pierce, C. S. (1878). How to make our ideas clear. *Popular Science Monthly*, *12*, 286–302. Paragraphs 388–410 (frequently reprinted and cited).

Qualifications Wales & CCEA. (2019, July). *Fair access by design: Guidance for awarding organisations on designing high-quality and inclusive qualifications*. https://qualifications.wales/media/avuda1dk/fair-access-by-design.pdf

Quality Assurance Agency for Higher Education (QAA). (2022, September). *Subject benchmark statement: Mathematics, statistics and operational research* (5th ed.). Version for Consultation.

Rescher, N. (2005). American philosophy. In T. Honderich (Ed.), *Oxford companion to philosophy* (pp. 749–750). Oxford University Press. www.qaa.ac.uk/docs/qaa/quality-code/sbs-mathematics-statistics-and-operational-research-consultation-22.pdf?sfvrsn=f3b9a581_4

Rothstein, R. (2021). The problem with wealth-based affirmative action: It's not an adequate substitute for race-based programs. *Atlantic*. https://www.theatlantic.com/ideas/archive/2023/06/affirmative-action-race-socioeconomic-supreme-court/674251/

Saul, S. (2024, February 22). Yale to require standardized test scores for admissions. *New York Times*. www.nytimes.com/2024/02/22/us/yale-standardized-testing-sat-act.html

Somerville, E. (2021, September 27). Wearing second hand clothes "an example of white privilege", students told. *Daily Telegraph*. www.telegraph.co.uk/news/2021/09/27/wearing-second-hand-clothes-example-white-privilege/

Tate, W. F. (1994, February). Race, retrenchment, and the reform of school mathematics. *The Phi Delta Kappan*, *75*(6), 477–480, 482–484. Published by: Phi Delta Kappa International Stable.

Tobin, S. (2021, September 28). Students at University of Kent must take "white privilege" course. *The Times*. www.thetimes.co.uk/article/students-at-university-of-kent-must-take-white-privilege-course-clc9zm6nl

Trump, D. (2018, September 25). *Remarks by President Trump to the 73rd session of the United Nations General Assembly*. https://trumpwhitehouse.archives.gov/briefings-statements/remarks-president-trump-73rd-session-united-nations-general-assembly-new-york-ny

UCAS. (2023, January). *Future of undergraduate admissions*. www.ucas.com/file/692816/download?token=LueoDrzn

Williams, T. (2022, November 7). *Professors say decolonisation agenda "politicising" maths degrees: New subject guidance mandates "narrowly skewed perspective on the history of mathematics", leading academics claim*. www.timeshighereducation.com/news/professors-say-decolonisation-agenda-politicising-maths-degrees

Worrell, F. (2016). Commentary on perspectives in fair assessment. In N. J. Dorans & L. L. Cook (Eds.), *Fairness in educational assessment and measurement*. Routledge.

5
CHANGES TO THINKING ABOUT EDUCATION AND ASSESSMENT

In Chapters 2 and 3, we described developments in education and wider society in the first part of the 21st century. In Chapter 4, we focused on changes to thinking about society, and in this chapter we turn to changes to thinking about education and assessment and where such thinking stands a quarter of a century on. As we observed in the previous chapter, clearly, developments and thinking are linked. For example, the rapid development of technology to obtain and analyse large amounts of information has prompted thinking about new types of assessment, which these have made possible. It has also challenged some of the assumptions inherited from the days of pens and paper. And sometimes the link has been in the other direction: for example, thinking about the purpose of education or theories about how we learn can lead to changes in paradigms and requirements of assessment.

Almost all of the ideas described in this chapter have their roots in earlier thinking and writing. But they have clustered together in distinctive ways in recent decades, and that is what we are aiming to capture here. This long chapter has been divided into two parts, starting with thinking about education, followed by more specific thoughts about assessment. However, as this book is primarily about assessment, we shall look out for implications for assessment in both parts.

(i) Thinking about education

Purposes

In discussions of the purposes of education – or of schooling (see Chapter 1 for how we distinguish the two concepts) – it is useful to distinguish between descriptive accounts of the role played by education in society and normative

DOI: 10.4324/9781003346166-5

accounts of what education should be for. Both may lead to proposals for change. For example, comparative descriptive accounts of education in different countries may serve as models for others. The normative accounts are closely linked to discussions of the justification of education, a topic to which we shall return in Chapter 6.

Normative thinking about the purposes of education – and of schooling – is by no means new (think Plato, Aristotle, St Thomas Aquinas, Immanuel Kant, John Dewey . . .). In the latter part of the 20th century, the purposes suggested for education broadly fell into three groups: personal development, preparation for democracy and contribution to the economy. The first two purposes were championed in the UK from the 1970s in the work of Hirst and Peters (e.g. Hirst & Peters, 1970), and we have discussed in Chapter 3 how increased emphasis on well-being in the 21st century has drawn attention back to the "personal development" strand. Hirst and Peters saw education as an essential public service in a liberal democracy committed to social justice and freedom, preparing young people to contribute fully to a democratic society.

The third group of purposes – contribution to the economy – itself divides into arguments based on public good (fuelling national – or international – economic growth) and those based on private good (equipping young people to get a job). Private good is closely linked to well-being as getting a good job is widely seen as a source of personal fulfilment and an enabler to raising and supporting a family. As we have seen in Chapter 2, economic purposes were prominent in many international reports about education at the end of the 20th century and continuing into the 21st century. These focused on the purposes of education to serve the needs of national and international economies and to prepare young people for the world of work (recent examples include OECD, 2018 [education] and OECD, 2020 [schooling]).

According to Madgavkar et al. (2022), of the McKinsey Global Institute, the most important resource in any economy is its *human capital* – a concept defined earlier by the OECD as "the knowledge, skills, competencies, and attributes embodied in individuals that facilitate the creation of personal, social, and economic well-being" (OECD, 2001, p. 18). Human capital has been described as based on knowledge, topped by the ability to use the knowledge to generate economic value (Dae-Bong, 2009). The same line of thought leads to products of education being seen as intangible assets driving growth. Lists of these assets include research, patents, copyrights, knowledge processing, data, proprietary software and design skills (Hazan & Smit, 2021).

The term "knowledge economy" has been carried over from the 20th century. It is thought to have been coined by Fritz Machlup, an Austrian American economist, and the term was popularised by Peter Drucker in "The Effective Executive" (2006) to describe a shift from traditional economies (founded on agriculture and, later, manufacturing) to ones where the production and use of knowledge are foremost. A purpose of education is seen as servicing such an economy by creating workers with knowledge and supporting research and the creation of new knowledge.

There is mounting recognition that knowledge-based capital is an all-pervasive feature of the current global marketplace (Wyckoff, 2013). What is meant by "knowledge" in this context is not altogether clear. For example, would Drucker have described the Victorian engineers who designed and built bridges and railways as "knowledge-based"? But the value attributed to "knowledge" in the 21st century has been significant, and we shall explore that further later in this chapter.

What is the relevance to assessment of the continuing debate about the purposes of education? We suggest that it prompts at least two sets of questions for assessment. The first set follows from assessment being seen as an essential support to teaching and learning: What do young people need to learn to be fulfilled (first purpose), to participate in democracy (second purpose) or to contribute to the economy (third purpose)? How can assessment best support that learning? The second set relates to how to measure whether education has fulfilled its purposes for individuals or collections of people. Answering the second set of questions is particularly difficult, as concepts such as personal fulfilment are notoriously difficult to measure. And how should we measure participation in a democracy? By turnout on polling day? Economic growth may be more measurable and international assessments of samples of students at prescribed ages, such as PISA (OECD), can provide data to inform comparisons between countries and enable educational outcomes to be matched against comparative economic performance and conclusions to be drawn about good school systems (see, e.g. McKinsey, 2007). However, the causal link between education and fulfilment of any or all of the three sets of purposes is difficult to test. Correlation is not causation.

We suggest that, at the very least, discussion about the purposes of education prompts important questions about the constructs of assessments and tests. Why is this content being tested? If there is no reply linked to any of the possible purposes of education, why is that content being assessed?

Theories of learning

Although there has never been unanimity about how we learn, as we take stock a quarter of the way into the 21st century, we can trace a broad shift in the previous century from behaviourism to constructivism (in various forms), followed more recently by a reaction against some of the thinking behind constructivism and the associated approaches to teaching. In this section, we shall describe these shifts and consider their implications for assessment.

Definitions of learning are manifold (Jorg et al., 2007), sometimes contentious (Schunk, 2020) and nearly always context-related (Lave & Wenger,

1991). Learning is a process (Ambrose et al., 2010); is a social activity (Dewey, 1938); is a cultural activity (Elwood, 2006); is an invisible neurological process (Lefrançois, 2019); inevitably results in a permanent change in behaviour, knowledge and cognitive skills (e.g. Brown et al., 2014; Krause et al., 2010). What seems to be clear is that learning is something learners themselves *do* whereas assessment is often something *done* to learners.

The advent of cognitive psychology in the late 1950s challenged the prevailing and dominant behaviouristic paradigm of learning. This challenge encouraged thinkers and practitioners in all aspects of education – including assessment – to consider what was going on inside the learner, as well as how the learner was behaving. Thinking in educational assessment was gradually influenced by the literature on cognitive and educational psychology – the two dominant science disciplines informing education practice, interventions and policy (Odendahl, 2011; Pashler et al., 2007).

Although assessment interest in cognitive psychology has burgeoned in recent years, it is not new. Back in the 1980s, Snow and Lohman (1989) had recognised that the cognitive psychology of problem-solving was fundamental to educational measurement. A key principle of test validity applies to test score inferences based on any means of observing consistent test-taker behaviours and the mental processes they employ in responding to and solving test questions. Thus, Snow and Lohman's ideas led to innovations in cognitive diagnostic assessment in the latter half of the 20th and early 21st centuries (Leighton & Gierl, 2007).

With the arrival of constructivist theoreticians such as Jean Piaget and Lev Vygotsky in the early and mid-20th century, constructivism, a learning theory that emphasised the active role of learners in building their own understanding, began to assume primacy in psychology. It took three distinct directions: cognitive constructivism (based on the scholarship of Jean Piaget); social constructivism (grounded in the work of Lev Vygotsky); and radical constructivism (developed by Ernst von Glasersfeld, 1974).[1]

The focus of all these forms of constructivism on the agency of the individual learner has had implications for assessment. New forms of assessment have been sought in which learners have an active role, become aware of their learning processes and needs, and develop a sense of responsibility for their learning (European Commission Education & Culture, 2018; Camacho & Legare, 2016).

Another development from the constructivist vision of learner development is to prompt learners to critically appraise their own knowledge and abilities (Tchibozo, 2011). That in turn raises questions about how (and whether) the skills required for such self-evaluation should be assessed.

Pedagogic practice is – or should be – based on an understanding of how students learn. Given that educational assessments are intended to delineate aspects of learning that should formally be awarded credit as well as having a substantial impact on teaching and learning, it is surprising that the intersection between theories of learning and assessment has received scant attention (Madaus et al., 2009; Pellegrino, 2012). Baird et al. (2017) suggest a relationship between learning and assessment theories, in which assessment design reflects and affects the outcomes of learning. Their approach anticipates that assessment theory and learning theory may have reciprocal effects on one another (p. 318).

In their state of the field review of assessment and learning, Baird et al. (2014) categorise 21st-century learning theories as behaviourist, cognitive constructivist or sociocultural. We shall consider how each of these has developed and the implications for teaching, learning and assessment. Let us turn first to behaviourist theories of learning.

Behaviourism originated in the late 19th century in the early stages of developmental psychology as a reaction against introspective psychology, deemed to be subjective, unquantifiable and heavily reliant on first-person accounts. Championed by the work of Edward Thorndike (1874–1949), Ivan Pavlov (1849–1936) and Burrhus Skinner (1904–1990), the behaviourist approach to learning became a dominant perspective throughout the first half of the 20th century. It focused on the idea that all behaviours (human and animal) are learned through conditional interaction with the environment. Thus, it is primarily concerned with observable behaviour and is founded on "operant (instrumental) conditioning" in which positive responses that are reinforced are strengthened and are probably likely to occur again (Skinner, 1938). From the behaviourist perspective, learners are mostly passive participants in their learning – behaviour is directed by stimuli.

Behaviourist pedagogy explores the observable actions of learners in the classroom, and in many countries 20th-century classrooms aimed to respect Skinner's theory of behaviourism (1972). Traditional teaching and instructional strategies sought to nurture learning through repetition, memorisation and behaviour intervention (both positive and negative). As we have seen, many developments in 21st-century curriculum and pedagogy have reflected a desire to move away from rote learning, acquisition of factual knowledge and memorisation towards real-world application, communication and problem-solving, which require higher-order thinking skills. Arguably, behaviourist methods are somewhat limited in engaging learners in complex, cognitively demanding, thinking such as synthesis, hypothesising, analysis and application.

Behaviourist teaching approaches continue to be effective in learning areas where there is a "correct" response or easily memorised subject material. Advocates of behaviourism evaluate the extent of learning using methods that measure observable behaviour such as test performance. Behaviourism continues to be reflected in some forms of educational assessment, for example, multiple-choice testing (where focus is on performance only), "true-false" tests and short-answer tests (Roblyer et al., 1997; Black, 1999; James et al., 2006).[2] It is difficult to assess higher-order skills or greater depth of processing using drill-and-practice type assessments.[3] However, it needs to be noted that in practice the distinction between assessments of rote-learning and of higher-order thinking may be challenged by instances where learners are drilled to memorise model paragraphs for extended answers purporting to demonstrate higher-order thinking skills.

Dissatisfaction with the shortcomings inherent in behaviourism, in particular its strict focus on observable behaviour, prompted educational psychologists such as Jean Piaget (1896–1980), William Perry (1913–1998) and others to explore other ways to capture the unobservable changes that take place when learning occurs. An approach to learning theory was sought that paid more attention to what went on "inside the learner's head". Such endeavours gave rise in the 1960s to cognitive views of learning (e.g. Neisser, 1967; Sternberg et al., 1981).

In general, cognitivist approaches share the view that knowledge includes symbolic mental representations as well as mechanisms that operate on those representations. Cognitive learning builds on prior knowledge, and new knowledge is perceived as something that is actively constructed by learners based on their existing cognitive structures.

Piaget is celebrated for charting the changes in cognitive development that occur as a child moves from infancy to adulthood. For Piaget, learning takes place when knowledge is constructed by learners because of their experiences in the world. Cognitive development, he argues, is a result of the interaction between innate capabilities (nature) and environmental influences (nurture), and learning can be understood in relation to the learner's stage of cognitive development.

An integral partner to Piaget's view of cognitive development is constructivism – the view that each learner constructs his or her own knowledge (Gandhi & Mukherji, 2021; Piaget & Inhelder, 1969). Constructivists rejected the behaviourists' thesis that learners lack agency in their learning, merely reacting to environmental stimuli such as positive and negative reinforcement. This led to a move from the metaphor of "knowledge-acquisition" to that of "knowledge-construction" – a move that had enormous implications for classroom pedagogy and management (Rogers & Freiberg, 1994).

In essence, the teacher became a cognitive guide of the learner's learning, as opposed to being a knowledge transmitter. Learning was seen as facilitated through the classroom provision of experiences that "induce cognitive conflict and hence encourage learners to develop new knowledge schemes that are better adapted to experience. Practical activities supported by group discussions form[ed] the core of such pedagogical practices" (Driver et al., 1994, p. 6).

What does this mean for assessment? Some of the constructivist criticisms of the limitations of behaviourism can be perceived in the context of assessment. For example, what processing activities in the brain are involved when a student retrieves information or memorised experiences to respond to assessment tasks? Many assessment thinkers and leading practitioners in the early 21st century appeared to be working on a premise of cognitive constructivist theory (see Pellegrino et al., 2001; Baird et al., 2014).

Socio-constructivism was a reaction to the information-processing constructivist approach to cognition and learning, which asserted that cognition and learning processes take place in the mind in isolation, with knowledge regarded as context-independent.[4] Socio-constructivists understood cognition and learning through the lens of interaction between the individual and a particular context or situation. Like cognitive constructivist theories of learning, social constructivism highlights the construction of meaning. However, social constructivism also accentuates the utilisation of cultural tools such as language, mathematics and approaches to problem-solving as a central influence on the construction of meaning. While a learner's cognitive capacities are important, it is the cultural tools at the learners' disposal that fashion learning through authentic, real-life activities to create a common or shared understanding of some phenomenon (Nagel, 2012; Snowman et al., 2009).

Vygotsky's understanding differed from that of Bruner in that Vygotsky considered learning as an activity socially mediated through the symbols and language of a culture, whereas Bruner espoused a discovery approach to learning using problem-solving (Krause et al., 2010). Rogoff (1990) reinforced the idea that language develops in unique cultural contexts. "Situated learning theory", characteristic of the work developed by Lave and Wenger (1991), asserts that all learning is situated and it is within "communities of practice" that learning occurs most efficiently. Situated learning, also referred to as "cognitive apprenticeship" learning, emphasises knowledge that can be applied in real-world settings and attempts to explain the way learning happens in the context of learners working together with a specialist in an environment (see Cakmakci et al., 2020; Rogoff, 1990).

Baird et al. (2014) point to the challenges of applying sociocultural theory to assessment. Sociocultural theory, they contend, "does not sit well with the current state of the field of assessment practice, in large part because standardised, same-for-all assessments have been equated with fairness in the minds of many" (p. 5). However, an understanding of the relationship between assessment and sociocultural theories of learning has gained traction in recent decades (e.g. Baird et al., 2017; Elwood & Klenowski, 2002; Torrance & Pryor, 1998). In particular, formative assessment has become understood to include diverse social interaction practices such as negotiation, mastery learning, the defining and sharing of learning intentions and assessment criteria, and collaborations within and across classroom participants.[5] Thus, the learner is "more actively a subject as well as an object of formative assessment" (Brookhart, 2004, p. 2). This thinking fed into the "Assessment for Learning" initiatives, which we considered in Chapter 2. Writing at the turn of the 21st century, Shepard (2000) suggested that "[i]n order for assessment to play a more useful role in helping students learn it should be moved into the middle of the teaching and learning process instead of being postponed as only the end-point of instruction" (p. 10).

Standing back, we can trace a broad fit between the perceived changing needs of the 21st-century "knowledge" economy and the perceived need for teaching and learning to focus on developing and using cognitive and meta-cognitive skills. However, it has never been easy to reflect a constructivist focus on the learning journey of each individual in plans for shared curricula and assessments, and for public programmes of education there is always a need for some points of reference to guide and evaluate the journey that each individual is taking. Intellectually, there has always been the challenge of the paradox set out by Plato in the *Meno*: how can learning be inquiry if the learner does not know what he is inquiring about? (*Meno*; 80E).[6] But there did seem to be a consensus, at least in the West, at the turn of the century that learning was actively led by the individual learner. However, that consensus was to be challenged in the years that followed.

The knowledge revival

The early 21st century saw a renewed prominence of "knowledge" in policy and theoretical thinking about education. A book by Michael Young in 2007 was entitled *Bringing Knowledge Back In*, with the subtitle *From Social Constructivism to Social Realism in the Sociology of Education*. He and his followers championed "powerful knowledge", which was seen as having the power to be an instrument of social justice.

We shall shortly return to "powerful knowledge", but first, we need to note that, like most of the ideas discussed in this chapter, the 21st-century emphasis on knowledge is not new. We shall see in Chapter 6 that there has been a strain of thought over several centuries seeing the pursuit of knowledge as good in itself, sometimes linked to a Kantian account of what is distinctive in human beings. An extreme version of this saw the value of knowledge as quite separate from any use to which it was put. Cardinal Newman (1852) argued that "cultivation of mind is surely worth seeking for its own sake" and "there is a Knowledge, which is desirable, though nothing come of it" (Part 6, p. 101). This was echoed in the famous (perhaps self-deprecatory) toast at the Mathematical Society of England in Science in the 1880s: "To pure mathematics: may it never be of any use to any man".

In his writings stemming from the 1960s, Paul Hirst developed an account of "forms of knowledge", which, he argued, should be the core of what is offered by a curriculum appropriate for a liberal education (Hirst, 1965). He initially proposed eight forms of logically defined knowledge, each with its own distinctive methods of inquiry: mathematics, physical sciences, human sciences, history, religion, the arts, moral knowledge and philosophy. (Hirst, 1973). He later modified the list and eventually abandoned the approach (Hirst, 1993, p. 184). At the time and beyond, the theoretical basis of Hirst's analysis was criticised, notably by questioning the epistemological basis for the distinctions between the kinds of knowledge involved in the "forms" (see, e.g. White (2018), who draws some parallels with similar criticisms of Michael Young's work). However, Hirst's approach was highly influential in thinking about the school curriculum in England and beyond, not least because the "forms" of knowledge seemed to link conveniently to school subjects. Smith (2023), for example, refers to a Working Paper produced by the Department of Education and Science in England in 1977.[7] The authors of the Working Paper suggested that the curriculum should consider "introducing pupils during the period of compulsory schooling to certain essential areas of experience" (p. 67). While not identical to Hirst's "forms of knowledge", the similarity is striking.

There are aspects of Hirst's thinking that were echoed some decades later in the theories of "powerful knowledge". First, the value that Hirst placed on knowledge did seem to have an ethical basis. It was not just a matter of making conceptual distinctions between different kinds of intellectual activity. This was linked with his work with R.S. Peters, who argued that the concept of "education" had normative implications, including that it involved the transmission of what was worthwhile (Peters, 1966, pp. 25, 31, 45).

Second, a distinction was made between education and "training" (with a clear preference for the former). This seems to have been linked to a distinction between knowledge and skills. In the words of Peters (1966). "There is very little to know about riding bicycles, swimming, or golf. It is largely a matter of 'knowing how' rather than of 'knowing that', of knack rather than of understanding" (p. 159). Later in this chapter, we shall explore – and criticise – the dichotomy between knowledge and skills. But at this stage we would remark that the quote from Peters seems rather quaintly old-fashioned to a 21st-century reader, used to university sports degrees and training qualifications. A quick web search for marketing material for one university found: "You will develop teaching, coaching, academic and scientific skills, and apply your knowledge and understanding to sport, education, health and other contexts in state-of-the-art facilities".[8] But Hirst and Peters would probably want to unpack the description and suggest that the "knowing that" part was the core educational component, and the rest was application to a "field" of sports coaching. Third, the link between "forms" of knowledge and school "subjects" fuelled a debate between disciplinary and interdisciplinary learning, and between generic and specialised knowledge and skills.

Hirst and Peters and their colleagues in England were working in the backcloth of so-called progressive education movements in the earlier 20th century, which promoted child-centred education as a tool for social reconstruction. "Progressive" thinking about education was itself a reaction to the traditional subject-fare of schooling in the 18th and 19th centuries. We do not have space here to do justice to this rich tradition, but names such as Pestalozzi (1746–1827), Froebel (1782–1852) and John Dewey (1859–1952) must be mentioned. In Europe, this was for a time expressed by the post-First World War "New Education Movement" (Horowitz, 1971). These movements saw themselves as child-centred. To an extent that perspective could have been claimed by all good teachers from the earliest times. But the cutting edge was that the progressivists saw education as a development experience for the child, not as a transmission of content from the teacher to the learner. This had implications for epistemology – Dewey, for example, saw education as growth – but also for pedagogy: "Give the pupils something to do, not something to learn; and the doing is of such a nature as to demand thinking; learning naturally results" (Dewey, 1916, p. 191).

Hirst and Peters were not alone in questioning some aspects of this account. The Hungarian-British polymath Michael Polanyi (1891–1976) argued that all learning, whether practical or theoretical, had to have a "fiduciary framework" – a starting point, based on adopting beliefs or following examples (see, e.g. Polanyi, 1958).[9] Polanyi and Peters saw education less as development and more as enculturalisation:

> [Children] start off in the position of the barbarian outside the gates, The problem is to get them inside the citadel of civilisation so that they will understand and love what they see when they get there.
> *(Peters, 1973, p. 104)*

These 20th-century discussions were reinforced with some passion by the knowledge revivalists in the early years of the 21st century. According to E.D. Hirsch (2016), "The idea that education is a natural growth has had a relatively recent birth. One hopes it will grow old and die. It is factually and morally wrong. It intensifies inequalities" (Hirsch, 2016, p. 196). Interestingly, Hirsch's opposition to developmental accounts of education was based not only on intellectual arguments but also on their social consequences. The "progressive" approaches were seen as preventing disadvantaged young people from succeeding in adult life.

This brings us to the development by Michael Young and his colleagues of the principle of "powerful knowledge" (Young, 2009). This school of thought is essentially contextually grounded. Unlike Hirst, who resisted attempts to translate his ideas into prescriptions for the school curriculum, the "powerful knowledge" movement explicitly raises questions about how the school curriculum can be used as a tool for social justice.[10] The "power" in "powerful knowledge" is thus seen as social as well as intellectual, empowering all learners, irrespective of socio-economic background, to be provided with the opportunities to succeed in life. On the intellectual side, Young (2008) said that knowledge is powerful "if it predicts, if it explains, if it enables you to envisage alternatives" (p. 74).

Young saw "powerful knowledge" as having three distinct characteristics. First, it was contrasted with the "common-sense" knowledge acquired through everyday experience. Second, powerful knowledge was described as systematic, which enabled it to be used to extend thinking and apply concepts to new situations (Young et al., 2014, p. 7). And third, it was described as specialised, with distinctions made between different categories of knowledge, each with its own distinctive architecture for developing and extending thinking. This has clear echoes of Hirst's "forms of knowledge" – and John White has argued that it is subject to the same criticisms (White, 2018).

The knowledge revival has fed directly into 21st-century discussions about curriculum policy and practice (see, e.g. Deng, 2018; Mizzi, 2022). Of importance for the assessment focus of this book is the revivalists' support for a subject-based curriculum, as distinct from one based throughout on generalised learning – for example, of "21st century skills" such as creativity or collaboration. E.D. Hirsch pleaded for the wider public to understand that "thinking skills – like critical and creative thinking and problem solving – are" not productive educational aims. Thinking skills are rarely independent of specific expertise.... The goal of imparting all-purpose skills is a delusion" (p. 186). One of the authors attended a lecture by E.D. Hirsch in which he was very dismissive of the value of a period in a school timetable labelled "lap-top hour". We shall return later to the distinction between disciplinary and interdisciplinary learning.

There has been an interesting divergence of approach between the UK countries in their approach to the curriculum. In Scotland and Wales, both reflecting seminal work by Professor Graham Donaldson, there has been a move to group subjects into broader topic areas, linked to stated purposes for the curriculum as a whole. The new "Curriculum for Wales", for example, is structured around six "Areas of Learning Experience": Expressive Arts; Health and Well-being; Humanities; Languages, Literacy and Communication; Mathematics and Numeracy; and Science and Technology.[11] By contrast, in England, there has been explicit (and implicit) support for a more traditionally structured knowledge-based, "content-based", curriculum. Supporters of this approach have cited the higher performance by English students than by their counterparts in Scotland and Wales in PISA in 2022. In the combative words of William Hague, a former (Conservative) Secretary of State for Wales:

> [The new Welsh National Curriculum] ... is officially described as a shift away from being "content-based" to a "broad framework". It has no

prescription of exactly what must be taught, with schools designing their own curriculum around six "areas of learning and experience". In a deep hole of educational decline, "progressive" thinkers are still digging.[12]

It is not only in the UK that the knowledge revival has been controversial and divided opinion. There have been controversies before about what and how children should learn, but it does seem that the latest rounds of these arguments have been incorporated into 21st-century "culture wars" with particular ferocity. Attempting to stand back and take stock, as is the purpose of this book, it seems unarguable that some of the assumptions made at the turn of the century about teaching and learning cannot be taken as "given" as we approach the second quarter of the new century. We have also noted that much of the recent knowledge debate has been dominated by discussion of the education of older children and the high school/secondary school curriculum, while the "progressivists" referred more frequently to early years and the development of infants. It is difficult to see the play-based educational activities of young children as "subject-based",[13] although primary education has seen its own set of 21st-century battles.[14]

The debate between the progressivists and the knowledge-revivalists has obvious implications for curriculum and pedagogy. But what does it mean for assessment? There may be implications for the constructs that curriculum-based assessments should measure. For example, in 1988, E.D. Hirsch published his famous list of 5,000 essential names, phrases, dates and concepts under the heading *Cultural Literacy: What Every American Needs to Know* (Hirsch, 1988). Factual knowledge of dates and the like could presumably be tested, in the classroom and in more formal tests, using questions like "Who gave the Gettysburg Address and what was its date?" With regard to assessment tasks, these would need to reflect the balance sought in the relevant teaching and learning between working from a learned authoritative starting point and creation and discovery by individual learners. Hirsch made his view on this quite clear:

> Tests have always been necessary in education. A better solution is to make tests fewer and better. There's just one way to do that – to base them on well defined, knowledge-based curriculums. There is no other way of making tests fair and productive.
>
> *(Hirsch, 2016, p. 15)*

Hirsch was not saying that all tests should just be about factual knowledge, but he founded his views about testing on his argument that the curriculum being tested must be based on knowledge.

We would add two observations at this point about the implications for assessment of a "knowledge-based curriculum". First, experience tells us that the requirements of national or state high-stakes tests frequently become the driver for what students learn and what their teachers teach. It is a commonplace observation, often made with regret, that "what is assessed is what is taught". It follows that theories of teaching and learning, whether progressivist or knowledge-based, need to include a view on what kind of assessment is appropriate and what kinds of knowledge and skills are required to meet its demands. Without that, proposals for curriculum or pedagogy may never get off the ground. Second, as we have observed in this chapter, there may be a contrast between the intentions of assessment designers regarding the knowledge and skills they will be testing and the realities of how students prepare for the assessment – or are drilled for it by their teachers.

Competence, competencies and competency frameworks

There is a striking difference in emphasis and tone between the thinking about education described in the previous section and this one – about "competence".[15] In 2013, the OECD published "The Future of Education and Skills – Education 2030", which sought to delineate likely challenges in the decade up to 2023. These challenges included economic interdependence, climate change, machine automation, global migration, population growth and confronting inequality and social injustice. UNESCO (2016) spoke of an emerging duality between the local (the traditional foundation of school curricula) and the global, which was transforming the underpinning values of educational institutions. They proposed that to resolve this tension, a sense of curriculum coherence at different levels of education needed to be achieved by focusing on "competencies", that is, "the potential to act thoughtfully on the basis of knowledge" (p. 9). This was working towards an approach that drew from thinking about both knowledge and skills and attempted to draw together the attributes that led to success in the knowledge economy and life in the modern world.

Traditionally, the idea of "competence" has been considered more germane to vocational education and training, given its direct association with the requirements of the workforce (Halász & Michel, 2011). Over time, however, the concept of competence has been propagated across the educational landscape, including not only vocational education and training but also general education from primary school to university.

Developing "workplace competence" has become one of the key ambitions of 21st-century education, gathering momentum in recent years not simply because of its perceived value from an economic perspective but also from learning perspectives, as a means of making learning more effective. Definitions of competencies aim to be applicable in a wide range of contexts. This is an attractive prospect for curriculum and course developers because competencies are not restricted to any national education system or tradition, are not specific to any subject discipline, and are not tied to any education or learning phase. For example, Brassler and Dettmers (2017) suggest that the development of interdisciplinary competencies in Higher Education, that is, "the ability to understand and act in any given interdisciplinary learning or work situation" (p. 1), is closely tied to notions of 21st-century skills and is an important staging post in developing future innovation. They link this educational outcome with particular pedagogies, including problem- and project-based learning (see also McPhail & Rata, 2015).

Competence is conceptually related to the notions of proficiency and mastery used in fields such as mathematics and language (Council of Europe, 2001; Rycroft-Smith & Boylan, 2019). In Chapter 2, we have referred to lists of competencies seen as necessary for the knowledge economy when added to basic core or foundation skills. The skills listed have included problem-solving, decision-making, communication skills, the ability to work in teams and computer skills (see, e.g. Joynes et al., 2019). Knowledge economy workers, it is argued, should be able not only to elicit information but also to evaluate, analyse, create, and apply those skills to address new problems and find new solutions, collaborate effectively and communicate persuasively (see Halpern, 1998, 2001, 2003, 2010). These ideas are closely linked with the lists of so-called 21st-century skills, which we discussed in Chapter 2.

Against this backdrop, there has been an increasing focus on defining what it means to be "competent" in a knowledge-based society. The concept of competence is contested (Ashworth & Saxton, 1990; Rychen & Salganik, 2001), with multiple definitions available that have developed from a variety of epistemological and historical perspectives (see Child & Shaw, 2020; Batt et al., 2019, for a fuller treatment of definitional origins). Wiek et al. (2011) proposed a synthesis definition of competence as "a functionally linked complex of knowledge, skills, and attitudes that enable successful task performance and problem solving" (p. 203). This is interesting, as it includes "attitudes" (as well as knowledge and skills) in the bundle denoted by "competence", although it is not clear what attitudes are intended to be included. The definition also relates competence to the successful performance of tasks in defined functions, presumably in a work context. In contrast, the European Commission & Council of the European Union (2006), see "competence" as binding together knowledge, skills and attitudes "which an individual needs for personal fulfilment and social inclusion" (p. 13).

Mulder et al. (2007) classify notions of competence into three main categories: behavioural, generic and cognitive. Behavioural approaches focus on determining aspects of performance that differentiate successful workers from their less successful counterparts. Generic definitions look to articulate common factors by which variation contributes to overall performance. Finally, cognitive approaches focus on the mental capacities required to perform job-related tasks well.

"Competency frameworks" (or "competence frameworks") have been created in an array of educational, vocational and workplace settings. They seek to provide a structure that conveys overall competence as well as individual competencies (Chartered Institute of Professional Development, 2024). Typically, they describe a range of competencies and the relationships between them, as well as reflecting values held by their developers (Batt et al., 2019). Voogt and Roblin (2012) assert that these frameworks contribute to an understanding of what should be expected from students at different age levels in terms of knowledge, skills and attitudes. Thus, if known and recognised by all involved – and that is a significant "if" – competency frameworks have the potential to direct and influence models of curriculum, learning and assessment at all stages of education.

Interest in workplace competence has extended to influence discussions about learning, curricula, and assessment in general education. According to Siarova et al., "knowledge alone is not sufficient" (2017, p. 7) and "a broader range of skills and abilities is needed to navigate a moving landscape characterised by the increasing importance of information and communications technologies, the decline of functional skills-based professions, and increasing competition" (2017, p. 7). The preoccupation with generic competencies is evident in the raft of OECD initiatives and publications over the last two decades (Biesta & Priestley, 2013). And theoretically, attempts have been made to explore the link between intellectual knowledge and the ability to perform practical tasks. The OECD Learning Compass 2030, for example, recognises four types of knowledge: disciplinary, interdisciplinary, epistemic and procedural.[16]

What are the implications for assessment of the emphasis on competence? As we have seen, the origin of much of the thinking about competency was the demands of the workplace. It might be thought to follow that the final assessment of a person's competency should be in the workplace – does the person display the competency or not? However, if the competency is being developed (and assessed) before the learner enters employment, then evidence may have to be sought from placements or simulations of work situations. These can be problematic – for example, the availability of relevant work placements varies from locality to locality – and they can raise issues of validity. For example, the OECD developed tests of collaborative skills in which the student interacted on a computer with a programmed virtual collaborator (OECD, 2015).[17] But that cannot necessarily test the softer qualities required in collaboration with real people, including willingness to listen and tolerance.

Another problem is that some of the suggested components of generic competence – for example, transversal skills – are notoriously difficult to measure (Stecher & Hamilton, 2014). And if "attitudes" are included, the difficulty becomes more pronounced – how does the assessor know if the student really has the desired attitude, as distinct from being able to write about it or act it out?

The emphasis on the package of abilities shown by each individual student does seem to call for assessment tools that enable the richest possible information to be gathered about each test-taker. As we shall see later, that need has informed thinking about the potential to use technology to capture and use this kind of individualised information.

Finally, the emphasis on bundles of competence raises questions about how the content of assessments should be ordered and titled. For example, should there be separate tests of geography and biology (perhaps with questions about climate change in both) or should there be a generic project or test about climate change? Or should subjects be brought together (and assessed) under generic labels such as "understanding society"? Some choices have to be made when designing national tests and examinations, but we hope that there can be more flexibility in the future to accommodate a variety of approaches in order to enable students to provide better evidence of what they know and can do (though the practicalities of organising this in schools present a real challenge).

Misleading dichotomies

Before leaving the contrasting thought-worlds of knowledge, skills and competencies, we would suggest that there is a pressing need to question and jettison some dichotomies that have polarised debate. The first is between knowledge and skills. Use of this distinction can harm perceptions of both: "knowing that", "knowing how" and "knowing why" are all involved in much intellectual thinking as well as in practical skills (Reiss & Oates, 2014). Mathematicians will say that they teach their students "how to do mathematics" and universities catering for elite athletes will link their coaching with explanation. The now-high-status occupation of surgery, informed by detailed factual knowledge and understanding of interrelationships between different organs and blood vessels, also requires the development of manual dexterity and practical skill. Historically, surgeons were accorded a very low status, comparable to the status of barbers, in comparison with doctors who were seen to use their minds more. The truth is that the competencies required for both involve practical knowledge, understanding, manual skills and human qualities. The historical prejudice against surgeons was a kind of anti-skills snobbery, which is theoretically unfounded and socially harmful.

The second misleading distinction is between disciplinary and interdisciplinary knowledge – or between generic and subject-specific knowledge. There is no question that many of the pressing problems of our time – climate change, well-being, the impact of AI – are "interdisciplinary", in the sense that they bring together and use concepts derived from different disciplines.

However, it does seem that to do that requires disciplinary knowledge to be brought together. We have seen how E.D. Hirsch denounced generic educational objectives such as "critical thinking". No doubt Hirsch thought that it was very important for students to become critical thinkers – but his point was that there was a need to have a (disciplinary) base for critical thinking, and he claimed that trying to teach it without such a base was problematic.

To an extent we agree with Hirsch on that point. However, we would make two observations: first, that there does not seem to be a case for the relationship between disciplinary and interdisciplinary education always to be chronological, with disciplinary education coming first. We have commented on the apparently interdisciplinary nature of the play of young children. In practice, we suggest that learners of all ages can be encouraged to combine some disciplinary learning while still being encouraged to bring together what they have learned from different disciplines. The relationship may be seen as episodic rather than chronological.

Second, the definitions of "disciplines" are not static and can be redefined over time – partly as the result of interdisciplinary thinking. We have seen how Hirst's and Young's "forms" or "categories" of knowledge were vulnerable to questions about whether they were distinct and meaningful, to the extent that Hirst eventually abandoned them. This line of questioning seems to be particularly apposite for younger disciplines, such as the social sciences. Is social geography part of the same discipline as physical geography? In the real world, subject distinctions may well reflect the practical constraints of dividing up the school timetable into recognisable and manageable chunks[18] rather than epistemology.

Information – "big data"

In Chapter 2, we described the explosion of information now available for education (including assessment) to use and for its outcomes to be measured and analysed. Two main points were clear (1) there is a great amount of it, and (2) it is readily and affordably available. Here we consider the implications for thinking about education and assessment.

The 21st century has seen a succession of "Vs" used in popular discussion to chart the progression of big data, starting with the 3 Vs – volume, velocity and variety – and later adding two more: value and veracity. The advent and availability of big data has been described as a "revolution that will transform how we live, work, and think" (Mayer-Schönberger & Cukier, 2013, p. 1). The term denotes large volumes of data – both structured and unstructured – that are too unwieldy or complex to be dealt with by traditional data-processing application software. Academically, the definitions offered include "storage of large quantities of data in accessible form that can be used to analyse, predict and to make decisions" (see Murchan & Siddiq, 2021, p. 5).[19]

Interest in how big data can be employed in education has given rise to new subdisciplines: Educational Data Mining (EDM) (see Angeli et al., 2017) and Learning Analytics (see Pena-Ayala, 2018; Zhang et al., 2018). They each have their own conferences and even their own journals: the *Journal of Educational Data Mining* and the *Journal of Learning Analytics*.

EDM has been described (for the lay user) as "the process of finding anomalies, patterns and correlations within large data sets to predict outcomes".[20] It clearly has commercial uses,[21] and in education settings it involves developing approaches for investigating increasingly large-scale and often "noisy" data sets and utilising those approaches to advance understanding of learners, and the contexts within which their learning occurs. As a process, EDM can use a range of techniques, including statistical analyses and machine learning (Bienkowski et al., 2012; Gobert et al., 2013; Angeli et al., 2017). EDM can obtain, analyse and interpret data garnered from learners' use of interactive learning environments, such as log files, keystrokes, clickstream data and discussion threads in natural language (Baker & Siemens, 2014), digitised-supported collaborative learning, or administrative data from schools and higher education (Cope & Kalantzis, 2016).

The field of Learning Analytics is concerned with the measurement, collection, analysis and reporting of "structured" data generated by learners as they work within a digital environment with the underlying purpose of enhancing and optimising learning and the settings in which teaching, learning and assessment take place (e.g. Avella et al. (2016); Pena-Ayala (2018); Wintrup (2017); Zhang et al. (2018) and The Society for Learning Analytics Research – SoLAR (online)). Learning analysts collect and examine data from different educational sources in order to understand the performance of learners better and with a view to improving it (Baker & Inventado, 2014). The Horizon Report: 2019 Higher Education Edition, produced by EDUCAUSE learning initiatives (Alexander et al., 2019) identifies learning analytics as one of the digital strategies and technologies predicted to penetrate mainstream education in the near future. For example, it could be used to help teachers assess the efficacy of their learning and teaching practices or by researchers to understand the outcomes of teaching interventions, even analysing at the level of individual learners. And organisations could use learning analytics to inform their policymaking and strategies. However, such uses would require understanding of data and judgement in their use – yet another training need for hard-pressed teachers.

Before considering what this expanding field means for assessment, it is important to note crucial ethical concerns. Discussion of the five Vs of big data has led to a sixth V being suggested – vulnerability.[22] In educational contexts, this points up the risk that extensive data about individual learners – including young children – could be lost, stolen or used for commercial or criminal purposes. The easy manipulation and potential abuse of digital photographic images of children – or recordings of their performances – is more widely recognised in the 2020s than it was at the turn of the century. There is a clear duty of care that applies to all educational (and other) users of big data.

Beyond the risk of abuse, there are issues of privacy raised by the collection, processing and analysis of sensitive and private data (Jones, 2019). One of the authors attended a conference at which a researcher presented the results of a project that involved filming, recording and analysing every movement of a class of young children for a week. The educational value to the teacher was considerable, but a conference attendee sitting next to the author commented "I will not send my daughter to that school". Do all learners have a right to have aspects of their private lives protected from data mining? Do all teachers need ethics training?

There are also ethical questions about transparency (What should learners be told about the information regarding them that will be obtained and how it will be used?). And what consent should be required for data to be obtained and used? If children are involved, the role of the parent or carer/guardian becomes relevant and important. If consent is given, does it relate to all or some of the data? Often, assumptions are made that consent can be taken as "implied" – for example, by students enrolling at a university. But in our view, that assumption should often be questioned. The views of data subject of all ages and in all contexts (including the workplace) cannot be taken for granted. There are also issues of security in the storing of data obtained – including important questions about computerised storage in the cloud or through other systems. Regarding the retention of the data, how long should it be retained? Should it be destroyed, and if so, after how long? Who is the owner and the data processor and controller of data collected for educational purposes? What are their responsibilities? And finally, who is responsible for the interpretation of the data (including misinterpretation or inaccurate data analysis)?[23]

What are the implications of these developments for thinking about education? There are three areas of potential impact: theory, practice and research. The possibilities offered by the use of big data encourage efforts to reconceptualise current teaching, learning and assessment practices (Shute et al., 2013). The concept of a "lesson" may need to be reconsidered, as will be the desirable balance for learners between retaining personal knowledge and being able to obtain and critically assess information. In practice, if the use of big data is made practicable and understandable for busy teachers, there is considerable potential to enhance the personalised learning of each student. And the potential for research and analysis of education data is vast. However, the ethical concerns here are very important.

In our view, there is scope for the education research world to learn from thinking in related fields about research ethics in the world of big data. For example, in the UK, a committee established to advise the National Statistician on data ethics has developed a set of principles to be addressed in research proposals involving big data. They are:

1. The use of data has clear benefits for users and serves the public good.
2. The data subject's identity (whether person or organisation) is protected, information is kept confidential and secure and the issue of consent is considered appropriately.
3. The risks and limits of new technologies are considered, and there is sufficient human oversight so that methods employed are consistent with recognised standards of integrity and quality.
4. Data used and methods employed are consistent with legal requirements, including the common law duty of confidence.
5. The views of the public are considered in light of the data used and the perceived benefits of the research.
6. The access, use and sharing of data are transparent and communicated clearly and accessibly to the public.[24]

These seem to be a good starting point for considering the use of big data for educational research at this time.[25]

What are the implications for assessment? There are clearly both opportunities and challenges in several respects: the evidence available for assessment; the methods of obtaining that evidence; how to make valid assessment conclusions from evidence of many different kinds (the "variety" V of big data); and how to interpret and use the outcomes. We shall suggest in chapter 6 that, taken together, this poses a high-level moral question for assessment in the 21st century – from the vast amount of data available, what should be used for assessment and how?

Clearly, there has been a great increase in the scale, types and immediacy of information available (Herold, 2016; Raikes, 2019). Combining and using such a variety of information can present theoretical and practical challenges, both at the level of the classroom teacher and for external assessment bodies. How does one bring together in a single assessment evidence from a film, records of everyday interactions and answers to examination questions? This kind of question has been dealt with in the past in assessments involving practical work or performances requiring different skills, but big data presents it in an extreme form.

Within computer-mediated educational environments, Cope and Kalantzis (2016) have categorised three major sources of evidence of learning according to their technology and data type. While these kinds of data were not new at the time of writing, what is novel is the sheer quantity of data that can now be generated, the likelihood that they can be produced continuously, their multiplicity, and the prospect of examining data sets aggregated and combined across diverse sources. For example (p. 3):

Machine assessments data: Computer Adaptive Testing (e.g. Select response assessments genre) and Natural language processing (e.g. Automated essay scoring genre).
Structured, embedded data: Argument-defined processes and Machine learning processes (e.g. Semantic tagging and annotation genres).
Unstructured, incidental data: Incidental "data exhaust" (e.g. Keystroke patterns, clickstream and navigation paths genres)

The challenge for assessment theorists is how to combine such a variety of kinds of data in a judgement that produces a defensible outcome and interpretation. In Chapter 7, we consider how the theoretical model of the "assessment argument" may have to be reconsidered in the future for those and other reasons.

Gibson and Webb (2015) and Timmis et al. (2016) have written on the risks associated with big data in a technology-enhanced assessment.[26] In addition, the impact of big data has underscored the necessity to develop assessment literacy in teachers, learners and others in the world of educational assessment (Gibson & Webb, 2015). And arguably, there are implications for the understanding of teachers' professionalism by teachers themselves and by those with whom they interact (Wyatt-Smith et al., 2021).

Artificial intelligence in education

The impact of Artifical Intelligence (AI) at this point in the 21st century has been described by Sundar Pichai, Google's Chief Executive Officer, as "more profound than fire or electricity or anything we have done in the past"[27] while Bill Gates argues that "this new wave of AI is as fundamental as the creation of the microprocessor, the personal computer, the Internet, and the mobile phone".[28] AI is already beginning to revolutionise and challenge teaching, learning and assessment.

UNICEF has offered a definition of AI:

AI refers to machine-based systems that can, given a set of human-defined objectives, make predictions, recommendations, or decisions that influence real or virtual environments. AI systems interact with us and act on our environment, either directly or indirectly. Often, they appear to operate autonomously, and can adapt their behaviour by learning about the context.
(2021, p. 16)

The distinctive feature of AI, which marks it out in this educational stocktake, is its generative capacity to create new material. This is different in kind from the super-analytic facilities associated with big data.

The lists of potential benefits of AI for education include the capacity to: personalise learning to promote students' autonomy and agency (e.g. Herder et al., 2017; McMurtrie, 2018); improve student outcomes; automate assessment systems (including marking) to aid teachers; automate formative assessment (Foster, 2019). The lists go on: AI can connect students and teachers through social media outlets (Krutka et al., 2019); tailor learning content based on student-specific learning patterns or knowledge levels (Hwang et al., 2020); apply facial recognition systems to generate insights about learners' behaviours; support students with learning disabilities (Barua et al., 2022); diagnose learning disabilities (Anuradha et al., 2010); and prepare students for success in the digital age.

Recognition of the opportunities offered by AI is widespread and growing. UNESCO, for example, is committed to supporting its member states and associate members to harness the huge potential of AI technologies for achieving the Education 2030 Agenda while maintaining integrity, inclusion and equity in the application of AI to educational contexts. However, the enthusiasm has tended to be matched by some notes of caution, particularly about the need for humans to retain a role in AI and the risks that it can be abused or cause harm. At the International Conference on Artificial Intelligence and Education, held in Beijing in 2019 and co-organised by UNESCO and the government of the People's Republic of China, representatives from Member States and the United Nations agreed:

> that the development of AI should be human-controlled and centred on people; that the deployment of AI should be in the service of people to enhance human capacities; that AI should be designed in an ethical, non-discriminatory, equitable, transparent and auditable manner; and that the impact of AI on people and society should be monitored and evaluated throughout the value chains.
>
> *(UNESCO Education 2030, 2019, p. 4)*

Arguably, AI is forcing us to reconsider what it means to be human, as it is taking over some of the tasks hitherto seen as essentially human. For accounts of education that are linked to the development of what is distinctive in a person, that is a significant challenge.

We have considered the ethical challenges to the use of big data and the perceived risks. Many of them, including issues around privacy and consent, are cited with increased force about AI, and the possibility of AI being misused or causing harm is frequently raised. In March 2023, in an open letter,

Tesla and SpaceX founder Elon Musk, with more than 1,000 other technology leaders, argued for a pause on giant AI experiments, stating "AI systems with human-competitive intelligence can pose profound risks to society and humanity" (22 March 2023).[29] The ethical questions raised in the open letter included:

- *Should* we let machines flood our information channels with propaganda and untruth?
- *Should* we automate away all the jobs, including the fulfilling ones?
- *Should* we develop nonhuman minds that might eventually outnumber, outsmart and replace us?
- *Should* we risk loss of control of our civilization?

(emphases in original).

Holmes et al. (2022) consider the use of AI in education through the lens of the Council of Europe's three core values: human rights, democracy and the rule of law, highlighting some of the key issues (Holmes & Tuomi, 2022, p. 558):

- *Right to human dignity*: "Teaching, assessment, and accreditation of learning (and related educational decisions) should not be delegated to an AI system."
- *Right to autonomy*: Children should not be subject to decisions made solely by AI systems
- *Right to be heard.* Children (or their parents/guardians) should be afforded the right to decline any engagement with AI classroom tools without it resulting in adverse effects on their education
- *Right not to suffer from discrimination.* All children should be able to benefit from the use of technology, not just those from privileged socio-economic groups
- *Right to data privacy and data protection*: "Children should be ensured a free and unmonitored space of development and upon moving into adulthood should be provided with a "clean slate" of any public or private storage of data related to them" (Council of Europe, 2019, p. 2).
- *Right to withhold or withdraw consent.* Children[30] should have genuinely consented to their data being collected in AI systems, and parental consent should only be given with sufficient understanding.

One of the risks associated with AI is that material used for education, and generated in an educational context, could contain bias. AI systems learn from the data they are trained on, and if the data contains biases, those biases can be learned and perpetuated by the AI system replicating them. In other words, AI algorithms are not objective, value-neutral tools but reflect the values and principles of their constructors and society's historical and systemic biases. This is especially troubling in the context of education, as bias in AI algorithms could bolster existing stereotypes (Stahl & Wright, 2018).

What does this mean for assessment? One of the earliest risks recognised in generative AI was to the integrity of students' work submitted for assessment, for example, if an essay or presentation was generated by AI rather than by the student. Concerns about cheating and plagiarism in assessment are not new, and to some extent, existing guidance on signs of plagiarism (e.g. inconsistent use of language), together with the use of anti-plagiarism software can still be sensible precautions. However, there may be more profound implications for the kinds of thinking skills that will be required to use generative AI intelligently and ethically and to assess such use. There has been particular debate about this in Higher Education, including an article by Georgina Chami (2023) which concluded:

> As AI becomes ubiquitous, universities must equip students with the necessary skills and understanding to use these tools responsibly. Universities that embrace AI thoughtfully to ensure that human interaction, critical thinking and the value of in-depth education are preserved will likely thrive in this new educational landscape.[31]

As we enter the second quarter of the 21st century, many would agree with Bill Gates that AI is the biggest development hitting us and that the potential effect on our thinking about education and assessment is huge. Lists of benefits and risks have been offered, and we have quoted from some of them here. However, the balance of risk and benefit is still unclear, while the development of widely accessible and affordable AI tools is fast-moving. If a sequel to this book is written at the half-century mark, AI is the area where the authors will probably report the greatest amount of change.

(ii) Thinking about assessment

In our accounts of developments in thinking about education, we have asked from time to time about the implications for educational assessment, the subject of this book. We now turn to consider some developments in thinking about assessment itself. At the turn of the 21st century, in an anniversary issue celebrating the first ten years of the journal *Assessment in Education: Principles, Policy and Practice*, Broadfoot and Black (2004) highlighted some of the more prominent debates that had characterised international assessment research in the pages of the journal up to that point. They summarised the leading issues as: Purposes, International Trends, Quality Concerns and Assessment for Learning, and concluded that throughout its history, educational assessment had played a powerful role in facilitating social progress.

Twenty years on, would the list be the same? And in 2009, Broadfoot observed that, despite all the discussions of change in the modern world and in education, examinations and assessment practices across international jurisdictions "remain strikingly similar to those that prevailed a century or more ago" (Broadfoot, 2009, p. vii). Would we say the same today?

In 2021, in an introduction to a special issue of "Educational Research", Twist (2021) described promising indications of development in approaches to assessment at the student, teacher and system level. The eight papers comprising the special issue demonstrated how assessment had responded to, and was ultimately fashioned by, the requirements of the contexts in which assessments were being applied. However, Twist noted that there remained a prevailing tension in the assessment world between the desire for change and the extent to which change was implemented.

Assessing higher-order thinking skills

We have seen how discussions of the demands of the "knowledge economy" and the various lists of "21st century skills" emphasised the importance of critical thought. The emphasis on higher-order thinking skills, including thinking-about-thinking ("metacognition") was not new in the 21st century. Bloom's taxonomy of educational objectives was first produced in 1956 (revised half a century later), and distinctions between different levels of thinking have been used for many years to inform assessment design and the classification of assessments and qualifications (see, e.g. Webb, 1997, 2007). However, understanding the basis for assessing higher-order thinking skills has never been easy and remains challenging as the century has progressed.

Take, for example, the conceptualisation and assessment of student reflection. As with assessments in traditional academic subjects, tasks can be designed to elicit behaviours that require students to use reflective internal thought processes. However, it is important to define clearly the indicators of such processes. There is an argument that reflection should not be assessed in an educational setting at all, although it should be established and nurtured in the classroom. For example, Ixer (2016) claims that by attempting to assess reflection we are distorting the construct. Students may also become confused about what they are actually being assessed on (Wilson, 2013). And it is difficult to establish whether reflections (irrespective of how they are captured) resemble students' authentic experiences (Ryan & Ryan, 2013).

Nevertheless, there are several good reasons why assessing reflection remains desirable in the 21st century. First, students often focus on assessment in their learning, and their learning becomes motivated by assessment (Watkins et al., 2005). The assessment of reflection may, therefore, increase the value of reflection in the eyes of students. Second, a function of assessment can be to make student learning visible. A third important function of assessment is diagnosis. In this regard, assessment can be part of the process used to determine students' strengths and weaknesses. It should therefore be expected to identify students who struggle with reflection or who are particularly good at it.

Similar questions could be asked about the assessment of other skills highly valued in 21st-century thought about education – critical skills, creativity, communication skills, collaboration, and so on. And we have commented earlier about the difficulty of assessing attitudes. Conceptualising these skills and attributes and identifying what would count as evidence for them is an essential need. We may agree with Ixer (2016) that some of these are better left unassessed, but for the reasons we have given it is problematic to omit from assessment some of the most important components of education.

Innovation in assessment: use of technology

As we observed at the beginning of this chapter, the availability of different media and tools for assessment can offer opportunities for changing our thinking about what assessment can do. Of course, a mere change of tool does not necessarily stimulate innovation, any more than a change in the kind of pen used for traditional written examinations. In 2002, Bennett argued that the advance of technology would force fundamental changes in the format and content of assessment and that there would be a "need to go beyond the initial achievement of computerising traditional multiple-choice tests to create assessments that facilitate learning and instruction in ways that paper measures cannot" (p. 1).

The most frequently cited justification for innovative approaches to assessment is the potential to measure skills that are not easily assessed through multiple-choice items and other traditional assessment approaches. Stecher and Hamilton (2006) suggest that a test might be innovative if it:

- incorporates prompts that are more complex than are typical in a printed test, such as hands-on materials, videos or multiple types of materials;
- offers different kinds of response options – such as written responses, collections of materials (portfolios) or interactions with a computer – and therefore requires more sophisticated scoring procedures; or
- is delivered in an innovative way, usually by computer.

Timmis et al. (2016) identify a number of potential benefits from innovation in assessment in response to a changing world and learning needs. They refer to the potential to capture traditionally difficult-to-measure learning skills and competences, together with "the use of multiple forms of representation to enable learners to represent their learning in ways of their choice" and "developing ways of capturing" (p. 9). But each of those potential benefits needs to be debated on its merits. Innovation is not necessarily good – for example, there may be arguments against giving learners too wide a choice about how to represent their learning. However, the opportunity for innovation has been presented.

In the early 2000s, the Joint Information Systems Committee, which supports post-16 and higher education and research in the UK, described the term "e-assessment" as

> "broadly-based . . . covering a range of activities in which digital technologies are used in assessment. Such activities include the designing and delivery of assessments, marking – by computers, or humans assisted by scanners and online tools – and all processes of reporting, storing and transferring of data associated with public and internal assessments".
>
> *(JISC, 2007, p. 6)*

Back in 2004, Ken Boston, the then head of the Qualifications and Curriculum Authority in England, said that "On-screen assessment will shortly touch the life of every learner in this country". Despite his ambitious expectations for England, there has been slow progress there (and in many other countries) regarding the implementation of on-screen and online high-stakes educational assessment, though this has not been the case for routine adoption of such methods in professional and vocational qualifications.

Practical developments throughout the first quarter of this century have included the advance of computer-based assessment following the transition from paper-and-pencil assessments in many – though by no means all – countries and the greater use of computer adaptive testing. In adaptive testing, candidates are set different test questions or tasks depending on their previous performance before or during the test. Computer Adaptive Testing (CAT) is a computerised assessment that has gained traction in licensure and certification testing and over the last few decades has found greater application in educational settings.[32] For example, adaptive tests are administered to young learners in literacy and numeracy in Scotland (the Scottish National Standardised Assessments), and in Wales, individualised assessments in reading and numeracy are currently statutory for learners in maintained schools from Years 2 to 9. Examples of CATs beyond the UK include the Graduate Record Examination (GRE), the Graduate Management Admission Test (GMAT) and the Test of English as a Foreign Language (TOEFL).[33]

CAT uses AI algorithms to control the level of difficulty of the questions, thereby personalising the test for every test-taker. The algorithms select the items for test takers (through a detailed item bank) in response to their success or otherwise in answering initial or subsequent test questions (see Weiss, 1983). Arguably, this provides more pedagogically useful feedback to teachers and students to inform their practices. Each student gets a more tailored opportunity to show what he or she can do, but the information obtained about each candidate is not identical.

Wyatt-Smith et al. (2019) trace the progression of assessment from simple adaptive learning to AI-based assessment in authentic learning environments and provide a helpful outline of the evolution of digitally mediated ways to assess student progress authentically in context. They describe a raft of new AI-related technologies, collectively known as Immersive Assessments, designed to augment the experiential and cognitive potential of digital learning assessment. Technologies include Augmented Reality (AR), Virtual Reality (VR), Mixed Reality (MR) and Extended Reality (XR), all of which are "being used to provide authentic, conceptually and perceptually enriched experiences in which assessment could occur" (p. 5). However, Wyatt-Smith *et al.* wrote in 2019 that the uses of these technologies remain "mostly aspirational" (p. 3).

These and other technology-enabled innovations have continued through the first quarter of the century and should be expected to continue. However, they have prompted questions and concerns, which themselves have changed over time. An early concern has been how comparable the outcomes are between traditional paper tests and their screen counterparts (see, e.g. Mead & Drasgow, 1993; Schaeffer et al., 1998; Schaeffer et al., 1995). A growing number of studies have focused on the score equivalence of computer-based tests (CBT) and paper-based tests (PBT), exploring the impact of factors such as computer familiarity and attitudes, test modality, mode order, question types and gender differences.[34]

International guidelines on computer-based tests and internet-delivered testing promote good practice in test adaptations (Van de Vijver & Hambleton, 1996) and good practice in test use (ITC, 2001).[35] By way of illustration, the "International Test Commission Guidelines on Computer-Based and Internet Delivered Testing" (ITC, 2005) suggest that test developers "provide clear documented evidence of the equivalence between the CBT/Internet test and non-computer versions (if the CBT/Internet version is a parallel form)" (p. 24). The guidelines make it clear that when an assessment is administered in two modes and two sets of statistically similar outcome scores are obtained, the scores must be able to be considered equivalent, valid and reliable.

However, these questions of comparability only remain important if the construct being assessed is the same (or similar). And after a while, when it has become custom and practice to use a more modern medium (e.g. a word processor), detailed comparisons over time with outcomes using the old mode (pen and paper) arguably matter less. We agree with Bennett (2002) that concern for comparability at a time of change can constrain innovation by preventing the computer-based version from fully utilising the technology to widen measurement beyond what traditional methods permit.

Reflecting this quandary, two broad approaches to transitioning to computer-based assessment have emerged in recent years (e.g. Threlfall et al., 2007; Ripley, 2009; Hughes, 2021):

- a *migratory* strategy includes computer-based tests that have been migrated directly from paper, as well as new computer tests that still faithfully reproduce many of the features of the traditional paper versions (the "paper behind glass" approach). There is no innovative impact on the assessment model or on curriculum, teaching and learning.
- a *transformational* strategy – employing technology to create a new, innovative and authentic assessment that is "designed to influence (or minimally to reflect) innovation in curriculum design and learning" (Ripley, 2009, p. 94). With transformative assessments, the question items and tasks are different.

Bennett (2002) described the then current generation of computer-assisted assessments as "migrational" and argued that the migration of tests in general neglected to encompass the striking improvements that the innovations could allow. Bennet contended that the first-generation e-assessments failed to make use of the opportunities offered by the technology to change tests for the better.

Despite clear motivations for migrating to greater use of technology (lessening costs; enhanced marking reliability; hastening marking and reporting; improving diagnostic analysis), Hughes (2022) delineates three risks of migrating paper tests to screens. The first is a threat to validity through inaccurate replication of measurement standards, different modes of interaction and unintended demands placed on test candidates when using onscreen tools. The other risks are a potential mismatch between learning and assessment and limitations to achieving comparability. Ofqual (2020), the regulator of assessments in England, identified three further issues – differences in information technology provision across schools, practical implementation challenges and issues of fairness to all students during or after implementation (pp. 3–4).

We welcome Ofqual's reporting of differences across schools in information technology provision. This is echoed by differences in online access for young people at home and unequal ease and familiarity with the medium. Issues of digital inequality and poverty became particularly evident during the pandemic. In a literature review on digital inequality relevant to assessment, Coleman (2021) distinguished several aspects of the difference in access: physical access (devices and internet), material access (device type, internet speed), conditional access (shared devices, data poverty) and motivational access (attitudes towards using technology). She also identified skill differences: the idea that "digital natives" in the 2020s do not require to learn internet skills is as questionable as an assertion that they do not need to learn to read and write. To that we can add geographical and income-related differences in internet connectivity in many countries.

All these are transitional issues, though important ones. However, it is important not to lose sight of the most telling arguments in favour of using technology for assessment – contextual fit, and validity for use. Young people taking tests or examinations at school in the 2020s will not be expected to write extended papers with a pen in a work context or, increasingly, at college or university. They will be expected to have editing skills and the ability to communicate effectively online. The skills required to sit a PBT are increasingly irrelevant in any other life context. So why should they be required and learned for the purposes of educational assessment?

Alignment with curricular thinking

We have considered some strands of 21st-century thinking about the goals of education. Whether these goals are expressed in terms of knowledge or competency (or both), there does seem to be agreement that curriculum, pedagogy and assessment should be aligned (Kim et al., 2019). Assessment is fundamental to learning and teaching. While what is assessed circumscribes what is taught and how it is learnt, the actual processes of assessment necessarily fashion institutional practice and affect a learner's perspective on the value of engaging in learning. Curriculum, assessment and instruction are seen as closely involved in the process of effective learning (Pellegrino et al., 2001), and assessment cannot be decoupled from the other elements (Phelan et al., 2011).

Alignment occurs when curriculum, pedagogy and assessment are mutually supportive; that is, they identify and support the learning of agreed knowledge, skills and competencies. The curriculum enshrines the learning objectives that influence the suggested teaching and learning activities, promoting active engagement and thinking on the part of the learners. The impact of the curriculum-pedagogy-assessment triad is well-attested (Pellegrino, 2006; Pellegrino et al., 2001; Achtenhagen, 2012): a direct relationship exists between how the curriculum is taught, a learner's exposure to the curriculum and their performance on summative (and formative) assessments (Schmidt et al., 2002).

Impact on assessment thinking in cognitive and educational psychology

Thinking in educational assessment is being increasingly influenced by the literature on cognitive and educational psychology (Pashler et al., 2007). Developmental cognitive neuroscience is also thriving, and knowledge from human brain mapping is having an impact on assessment,[36] helped by the emergence of innovative imaging technologies (Goswami, 2006). Non-invasive neuroscience techniques, including magnetic resonance imaging, functional magnetic resonance imaging, electroencephalography and event-related potentials, provide data on neural processing within tasks. Neuroscience has the potential to lead to innovative teaching and test-development practices (Dhawan, 2014, p. 46).

The application of cognitive psychology to thinking about assessment has continued from the late 20th century into the 21st century, a key source being ideas advanced by Snow and Lohman in their chapter "Implications of Cognitive Psychology for Educational Measurement" in Educational Measurement (1989). Snow and Lohman recognised that not only was the cognitive psychology of problem-solving fundamental to educational measurement but, more comprehensively, educational assessment "cut across the matrix of cognitive psychology" (p. 265). (A key principle of test validity applies to test score inferences based on any means of observing consistent test-taker behaviours and the mental processes they employ in responding to and solving test questions.)

Formative assessment

As we have seen in Chapter 2, talk of "assessment for learning" (AfL) as opposed to "assessment of learning" began to dominate the educational assessment arena towards the end of the 20th century, with many touting the former as one of the most promising approaches for initiating improvement in student learning. However, as well as conceptual confusions and definitional ambiguities, practical barriers to the integration and implementation of AfL classroom practices continue to remain evident in many countries, and a quarter of a century later the eagerly awaited benefits of AfL are not yet fulfilled (Swaffield, 2009; Coe, 2013; Baird et al., 2014). Bennett's (2011) critical review of six interrelated issues[37] in formative assessment led him to conclude that "'formative assessment' does not yet represent a well-defined set of artefacts or practices" (p. 5).

The aim of the UK-based Assessment Reform Group[38] at the turn of the century was to ensure that assessment policy and practice at all levels took account of emerging research evidence. That need continues, intensified by the experience of the pandemic, which forced assessment providers to make short-term changes to sources of evidence for assessment and the way assessment was carried out. Can or should these changes form the foundation for more sustained and systemic change as the century progresses?

Inclusive assessment

Changes to assessment have also been driven by considerations about the role of assessment in society and its effects on students, including its impact on socio-economically disadvantaged students, those who are overlooked and underprivileged, other marginalised students and those with disabilities and learning difficulties. Interest in inclusive practice in learning, teaching and assessment is gaining momentum in the assessment world and inclusivity is perceived to be a critical factor in assessment design.

There are two arguments in favour of inclusive assessment. One is based on fairness, justice and equality – that it is fair for all learners, including disadvantaged ones, to be able to show what they can do. Hanesworth (2019) equates inclusive assessment with social justice and refers to a social justice approach (an "inclusive+" approach), in which social justice is envisioned as an inherent feature and underlying learning outcome of assessment.

The second argument is that inclusive assessment is part of an inclusive approach to curriculum, teaching and assessment that benefits all learners, not just disadvantaged ones. Hockings (2010) defines inclusive teaching, learning and assessment as:

> the ways in which pedagogy, curricula and assessment are designed and delivered to engage students in learning that is meaningful, relevant and accessible to all. It embraces a view of the individual and individual difference as the course of diversity that can enrich the lives and learning of others.
>
> *(p. 1)*

Montenegro and Jankowski (2017) argue that inclusive, diversified assessment strategies seek to meet the objectives of improved learning for all students, in ways that authentically capture what they know and can do.

The first argument for inclusivity is based on fairness. A test that is fair (in the sense being used here) will reflect the same constructs for all test-takers, and scores will have the same meaning for all individuals in the intended population (AERA et al., 2014, p. 219). Until recently, the prevailing belief has been to measure students in the same manner if an assessment is to be fair. But identical assessment tasks may not always provide the same information about the knowledge and skills of all test-takers (Mislevy, 2018). Mislevy proposes "conditional fairness" as a reasoned foundation for adapting to the interests and previous knowledge of the test-taker. He argues that the performance of a task must be understood by taking into account the person, background, tasks, settings and situations. There is, therefore, a need to locate the "assessment argument" (the tasks, evidence and inferences drawn from the assessment outcomes) in context. We shall return to this important point in Chapter 7.

We have argued (Nisbet & Shaw, 2022) that, from the perspective of fairness, there are contexts in which Mislevy's argument can be extended further. Is equivalence always required for fairness? Assessment arrangements that have had to be adapted because of Covid-19 have led to outcomes which may not be equivalent for students in different settings and with different experiences of loss of learning and personal hardship. Nevertheless, the adapted assessment arrangements may be fair in the sense that they have given as many students as possible an opportunity to show what they can do. And, beyond the special circumstances of Covid-19, there are arguably many purposes for assessment where equivalence of consideration for all test-takers is not the highest priority. For example, in countries where the norm is for students to proceed from high school to the local university or college, it may be more important to obtain relevant information about the learning of each student than to apply equivalent criteria to each and every one of them (though there are practical challenges about collecting this kind of individualised information at scale).

Accessibility takes the principle of fairness one step further and requires that careful thought be given to what construct(s) the test is intended to measure, as these need to be accessible to all test-takers. That leaves the question of whether/how to test constructs that are not available to all but may be essential for the requirements of a particular profession. However, the effect of the fairness argument for inclusivity is that, at the very least, claims that any non-inclusive assessment is required should be rigorously scrutinised.

Recent work undertaken by colleagues from Advance HE[39] and the University of Worcester (UK) has attempted to develop a typology for praxis to practicalise theory developed by Jan McAthur (2016), especially in relation to her work on the role of assessment in achieving social justice (Hanesworth, 2019). This work is underpinned by research contributing to an inclusive education agenda in which Waitoller and Thorius (2016) seek to bring together Culturally Sustaining Pedagogy, which aims to enhance inclusivity and nurture learners' understanding of, and engagement with, culture and society, and Universal Design for Learning,[40] a scientific framework for guiding educational practice. Hanesworth (2019) argues a social justice approach to assessment builds on inclusivity, thereby addressing aspects of assessment inequality and supporting the design of assessment practices and processes that are strengthened by the foundational tenet of concern for individual, economic and cultural difference.

Socioculturally responsive assessments

In the United States, the debate about the role and efficacy of using standardised tests for assessment has intensified in recent years (Polster et al., 2021). Long claims that "educators have long known that standardized tests are an inaccurate and unfair measure of student progress" (Long, 2023). As we have seen in Chapter 4, one outcome of the controversy is that many US universities and colleges have been moving away from the use of standardised testing in admissions, although we reported possible very recent signs of a reversion to standardised tests because of concerns about the alternatives.

Standardised tests are "designed to be objective measures . . . intended to provide an accurate, unfiltered measure of what a student knows" (Churchill, 2015). Yet assertions of objectivity, according to Yosso (2005), can serve as "a camouflage for the self-interest, power, and privilege of dominant groups in U.S. society" (p. 7). Bennett (2023) argues that opposition to standardised tests has been driven by the perception that traditional standardised tests perpetuate social injustice (p. 34). Bennett counsels that testing as an enterprise must reconsider its practices and respond more appropriately to today's demands for equity. He offers an initial rationale and theory of socioculturally responsive assessment and suggests provisional principles that might serve to guide the design of such assessments, thereby making the overarching concept more tangible.

According to Bennett (2023), socioculturally responsive assessment "is assessment that people can see and affirm themselves in and from which they can learn" (p. 96). He lists five distinguishing features. Socioculturally responsive assessment, he suggests:

> (1) includes problems that connect to the cultural identity, background, and lived experiences of all individuals, especially from traditionally underserved groups; (2) allows forms of expression and representation in problem presentation and solution that help individuals show what they know and can do; (3) promotes deeper learning by design; (4) adapts to personal characteristics including cultural identity; and (5) characterizes performance as an interaction among extrinsic and intrinsic factors.
>
> *(p. 96)*

In the 21st century, assessment designers aiming for cultural responsiveness have been exhorted to consider the ways in which the assessment makes reference to culture; how the assessment allows students to draw from their cultural influences; and how the assessment supports students in bridging their social/cultural identities with their academic identities.[41]

Putting this approach into practice has raised some issues linked to the "culture wars" discussed in Chapter 4. Ladson-Billings (2014) comments, with disapproval, that "the idea that adding some books about people of colour, having a classroom Kwanzaa[42] celebration, or posting 'diverse' images makes one 'culturally relevant' seem to be what the pedagogy has been reduced to" (p. 82). However, there is much support for the view that students learn more when they are valued, engaged and empowered – three tenets of cultural relevance (Lyons et al., 2021). To develop culturally competent students, they need to possess an understanding of their own culture (beginning at the basics, but always growing towards mastery); a willingness to learn about the cultural practices and world views of others; a positive attitude towards cultural differences; and a readiness to accept and respect those differences (McFarlan, 2022). In order to develop academically successful students, it is necessary to re-imagine the format of assessments so that it allows students to demonstrate their understanding in a way that is relevant to them.

A large body of research relating to culturally responsive assessment is focused on student-centred, culturally sustaining classroom practice that engages students, values their cultural identities and empowers students as agents of change (Nortvedt et al., 2020). However, attention is shifting towards inequities in large-scale, high-stakes assessment design. It is much more of a challenge to make large-scale testing more culturally responsive. This will be a priority in assessment development in the second quarter of the 21st century.

Conclusion

In this chapter we have identified and discussed strands of thinking about education and educational assessment that are particularly influential or important as we move into the middle period of the 21st century. In the first part, about changes to thinking about education, we have described trends in thinking about the purposes of education and different theories of learning, with a 20th century move from behaviourism to different forms of constructivism, followed by challenges to any constructivist consensus and a revival of support for "knowledge". A different tradition has been the increased use of ideas about "competence" as an aim of education and a subject for assessment. We have discussed "big data" and the thunderbolt of AI. All have implications for how we shall think about assessment (and education) in the future.

In the second part, we turned to thinking about assessment itself. We charted the impact of technology on how we conceptualise assessment, and we outlined some of the thinking behind approaches to assessment that reflect an increased recognition of the importance and relevance of the social context in which assessments take place. We agreed with Bennett (2013) that the experience of the early 21st century may invite a rethinking of the relationships between – and comparative priority of – fundamental assessment principles, including validity, reliability, fairness and impact. In Chapter 7, we shall take this further. But before doing that, we need to stand back and ask some moral questions about assessment at this time. That will be the focus of the next chapter.

Notes

1 Radical constructivism asserted that the learner is the sole constructor of knowledge and meaning, and their reality is incomplete, subjective and continuously developing – a theory of knowing that provides a pragmatic approach to questions about reality, truth and human understanding (Walshe, 2020, p. 359).
2 Teachers still employ Skinner's theories by setting clear learning objectives, optimising the stimulus-response association and using appropriate reinforcement of behaviours (see Rogti 2021).
3 At the dawn of the 21st century, esteemed assessment scholars like Lorrie Shepard were criticising the legacy of behaviourism and its impact on assessment: "the continued intellectual kinship between one-skill-at-a-time test items and instructional processes aimed at mastery of constituent elements" (2000, p. 5).
4 The pioneering works of Lev Vygotsky (1896–1934), Jerome Bruner (1915–2016), Barbara Rogoff (1950–present), Jean Lave (1939–present) and Etienne Wenger (1952–present) are associated with sociocultural orientations of learning.
5 However, Torrance and Pryor (1998) also recognise formative assessment classroom practices that align with behaviourist thinking.
6 "For [a man] cannot inquire about what he knows, because he knows it, and in that case is in no need of inquiry; nor again can he inquire about what he does not know, since he does not know about what he is to inquire" (trans Lamb, Loeb edition, Heinemann, London, 1968).
7 *Curriculum 11–16: Working Papers* by H.M. Inspectorate, 1977 (p. 67).
8 University of Loughborough, accessed at www.lboro.ac.uk/study/undergraduate/courses/sport-coaching-and-physical-education/
9 For a (largely approving) critical discussion of Polanyi's views and their implications for education, see Kitchen (2014, chapter 5).
10 Young and Muller (2013) clarify the notion of "powerful knowledge" as a sociological concept and as a curriculum principle.
11 https://hwb.gov.wales/curriculum-for-wales.
12 William Hague, "Welsh education failure is a lesson for Labour" in *The Times*, 4 March 2024.
13 We are indebted for this point to Dr Keir Bloomer.
14 See, for example, James S. Kim, "Research and the Reading Wars" (2008).
15 We accept that the knowledge-revivalists might claim that they were arguing for knowledge as a basis for competence, not as an alternative. However, the stylistic differences between the two sets of literature remain striking.
16 www.oecd.org/education/2030-project/teaching-and-learning/learning/learning-compass-2030/
17 www.oecd.org/pisa/innovation/collaborative-problem-solving/
18 We are grateful to Dr Mick Walker for this observation.
19 See, for example, Zitter (2022).
20 www.sas.com/en_gb/insights/analytics/data-mining.html
21 The website quoted above continues, "Using a broad range of techniques, you can use this information to increase revenues, cut costs, improve customer relationships, reduce risks and more".
22 Forbes note at www.forbes.com/sites/bernardmarr/2016/12/20/big-data-the-6th-v-everyone-should-know-about/
23 Slade and Prinsloo (2013), using a socio-critical perspective on the use of learning analytics, highlight the role of power, the impact of surveillance, the need for transparency and links with different understandings of student identity. Exemplified by a number of case studies covering schools, universities and the workplace, ethical concerns about Learning Analytics and how data collection methods

may differ significantly and ethically from traditional methods are scrutinised by Griffths et al. (2016).
24 Ethical Principles – UK Statistics Authority. See also the UK GDPR guidance and resources website – https://ico.org.uk/for-organisations/uk-gdpr-guidance-and-resources/
25 See also the Nuffield Council on Bioethics – The collection, linking and use of data in biomedical research and healthcare: ethical issues. Published February 2015. The report considers the ethical questions raised by advances in information technology and data science in the context of healthcare and biomedical research.
26 Gibbs and Webb (2015) identify four measurement challenges: "1. Dealing with change over time via time-based data. 2. How a digital performance space's relationships interact with learner actions, communications and products. 3. How layers of interpretation are formed from translations of atomistic data into meaningful larger units suitable for making inferences about what someone knows and can do. 4. How to represent the dynamics of interactions between and among learners who are being assessed by their interactions with each other as well as with digital resources and agents in digital performance space" (p. 1).
27 https://fortune.com/2023/04/17/sundar-pichai-a-i-more-profound-than-fire-electricity/
28 www.gatesnotes.com/The-Age-of-AI-Has-Begun
29 https://futureoflife.org/open-letter/pause-giant-ai-experiments/
30 Providing that they have sufficient intelligence, competence and understanding of the pertinent issues, otherwise, someone with parental responsibility can consent for them. This concept is referred to in the UK as "Gillick competence". See, for example, www.ncbi.nlm.nih.gov/pmc/articles/PMC4962726
31 Georgina Chami, "Artificial intelligence and academic integrity: striking a balance A look at how universities can encourage the ethical and transparent use of artificial intelligence tools to support learning while guarding against misconduct". *Times Higher Education Supplement*, 23 October 2023, accessed at www.timeshighereducation.com/campus/artificial-intelligence-and-academic-integrity-striking-balance.
32 The Centre for Evaluation and Monitoring (CEM, Cambridge) introduced its adaptive test for primary schools in 2003 and its computer-adaptive baseline test, MidYIS (ages 11–14) for secondary schools two years later, in 2005. Currently, around 350,000 students take a CEM adaptive test each year.
33 Bimpeh and West (2022) offer examples of personalised CATs: American Society of Clinical Pathologists-Board of Registry Certification Examinations (ASCP), USA; A Flexible Testing System in Mathematics Education for Adults (MATH-CAT), Netherlands; Computerized Assessment System for English Communication (CASEC), Japan; Business Language Testing Service (BULATS) computer test, offered by Cambridge English; North American Pharmacist Licensure Examination (NAPLEX), USA (pp. 2–3).
34 As well as on the cognitive processes of constructing an essay on paper versus on-screen. See, for example, Barkaoui (2016), Shiell et al. (2011).
35 See, for example, the Association of Test Publishers (ATP). Guidelines for Computer Based Testing; British Psychological Society Psychological Testing Centre (2002) Guidelines for the Development and Use of Computer-Based Assessments.
36 Neuroimaging allows mapping of brain processes to cognitive performance.
37 (1) The definition of formative assessment; (2) claims commonly made for its effectiveness; (3) limited attention given to domain considerations in its conceptualisation; (4) under-representation of measurement principles in that conceptualisation; (5) teacher-support demands formative assessment entails; (6) impact of the larger educational system.
38 Assessment Reform Group www.nuffieldfoundation.org/project/the-assessment-reform-group.

39 *Advance HE* – a British charity and professional membership scheme promoting excellence in higher education.
40 Universal design is an "approach to assessment development that attempts to maximise the accessibility of a test for all its intended examinees" (AERA et al., 2014, p. 189). See Lazarus et al. (2022) for a brief overview of what a universally designed assessment is, followed by a set of steps for US states to consider when designing and developing, or revising, their summative assessments.
41 Culturally Responsive Assessment: Goals, Challenges, and Implications. Institute of Education Sciences. REL Pacific. https://ies.ed.gov/ncee/rel/infographics/pdf/REL_PA_Culturally_Responsive_Assessment.pdf.
42 Kwanzaa – a secular festival observed by many African Americans from 26 December to 1 January as a celebration of their cultural heritage and traditional values.

References

Achtenhagen, F. (2012). The curriculum-instruction-assessment-triad. *Empirical Research in Vocational Education and Training*, 4, 5–25.
Alexander, B., Ashford-Rowe, K., Barajas-Murphy, N., Dobbin, G., Knott, J., McCormack, M., Pomerantz, J., Seilhamer, R., & Weber, N. (Hrsg.) (2019). *EDUCAUSE Horizon report: 2019 Higher education edition*. EDUCAUSE.
Ambrose, S. A., Bridges, M. W., DiPietro, M., Lovett, M. C., & Norman, M. K. (2010). *How learning works*. John Wiley & Sons.
American Educational Research Association, American Psychological Association, and National Council on Measurement in Education. (2014). *Standards for educational and psychological testing*. American Educational Research Association.
Angeli, C., Howard, S. K., Ma, J., Yang, J., & Kirschner, P. A. (2017). Data mining in educational technology classroom research: Can it make a contribution? *Computers & Education*, 113, 226–242. https://doi.org/10.1016/j.compedu.2017.05.021
Anuradha, J., Dhiman, T., Ramachandran, V., Arulalan, K. V., & Tripathy, B. K. (2010). Diagnosis of ADHD using SVM algorithm. In *Proceedings of the third annual ACM Bangalore conference* (pp. 1–4). Association for Computing Machinery. https://doi.org/10.1145/1754288.1754317
Ashworth, P. D., & Saxton, J. (1990). On "competence". *Journal of Further and Higher Education*, 14(2), 3–25. https://doi.org/10.1080/0309877900140201
Association of Test Publishers (ATP). (2002). *Guidelines for computer-based testing*: ATP. https://www.testpublishers.org/assets/documents/CBTGuidelines.pdf
August, D. E., & Hakuta, K. E. (1997). *Improving schooling for language-minority children: A research agenda*. National Academies Press.
Avella, J. T., Kebritchi, M., Nunn, S. G., & Kanai, T. (2016). Learning analytics methods, benefits, and challenges in higher education. A systematic literature review. *Online Learning*, 20(2), 17p. https://fles.eric.ed.gov/fullt ext/EJ1105911.pdf
Baird, J. A., Andrich, D., Hopfenbeck, T. N., & Stobart, G. (2017). Assessment and learning: Fields apart? *Assessment in Education: Principles, Policy & Practice*, 24(3), 317–350. http://doi.org/10.1080/0969594X.2017.1319337
Baird, J. A., Hopfenbeck, T. N., Newton, P., Stobart, G., & Steen-Utheim, A. T. (2014). *State of the field review: Assessment and learning*. Norwegian Knowledge Centre for Education (case number 13/4697). Oxford University Centre for Educational Assessment Report OUCEA/14/2.
Baker, R. S, & Inventado, P. S. (2014). Educational data mining and learning analytics. In J. Larusson & B. White (Eds.), *Learning analytics*. Springer.
Baker, R. S., & Siemens, G. (2014). Educational data mining and learning analytics. In K. Sawyer (Ed.), *Cambridge handbook of the learning sciences* (2nd ed., pp. 253–274). Cambridge University Press.

Barkaoui, K. (2016). What and when second-language learners revise when responding to timed writing tasks on the computer: The roles of task type, second language proficiency, and keyboarding skills. *Modern Language Journal*, 100(1), 320–340. http://doi.org/10.1111/modl.12316

Barua, P. D., Vicnesh, J., Gururajan, R., Oh, S. L., Palmer, E., Azizan, M. M., Kadri, N. A., & Acharya, U. R. (2022). Artificial intelligence enabled personalised assistive tools to enhance Education of children with neurodevelopmental disorders – A review. *International Journal of Environmental Research and Public Health*, 19(3), 1192.

Batt, A. M., Tavares, W., & Williams, B. (2019). The development of competency frameworks in healthcare professions: A scoping review. *Advances in Health Sciences Education*. http://doi.org/10.1007/s10459-019-09946-w

Bennett, R. E. (2002). Inexorable and inevitable: The continuing story of technology and assessment. *Journal of Technology, Learning, and Assessment*, 1(1). https://ejournals.bc.edu/index.php/jtla/article/view/1667/1513

Bennett, R. E. (2011). Formative assessment: A critical review. *Assessment in Education: Principles, Policy & Practice*, 18(1), 5–25. http://doi.org/10.1080/0969594X.2010.513678

Bennett, R. E. (2013). *Preparing for the future: What educational assessment must do*. Published by the Gordon Commission on the Future of Assessment in Education. http://www.gordoncommission.org/publications_reports/assessment_paradigms.html

Bennett, R. E. (2023). Toward a theory of socioculturally responsive assessment. *Educational Assessment*, 28(2), 83–104. https://doi.org/10.1080/10627197.2023.2202312

Bienkowski, M., Feng, M., & Means, B. (2012). *Enhancing teaching and learning through educational data mining and learning analytics. An issue Brief*. U.S. Department of Education, Office of Educational Technology. https://tech.ed.gov/wp-content/uploads/2014/03/edm-la-brief.pdf

Biesta, G., & Priestley, M. (2013). Capacities and the curriculum. In M. Priestley & G. Biesta (Eds.), *Reinventing the curriculum: New trends in curriculum policy and practice* (pp. 35–49). Bloomsbury.

Bimpeh, Y., & West, D. (2022). Adaptive testing: An introduction. *AQA Assessment Research and Innovation*. https://filestore.aqa.org.uk/content/research/AQA-ADAPTIVE-TESTING-AN-INTRODUCTION.PDF

Black, P. (1999). Assessment, learning theories and testing systems. In P. Murphy (Ed.), *Learners, learning and assessment* (pp. 118–134). Paul Chapman.

Boston, K. (2004). *Speech to e-assessment conference*. QCA. www.qcda.gov.uk/libraryAssets/media/6998_kb_speech_20040420_e assessment.rtf

Brassler, M., & Dettmers, J. (2017). How to enhance interdisciplinary competence – interdisciplinary problem-based learning versus interdisciplinary project-based learning. *Interdisciplinary Journal of Problem-Based Learning*, 11(2). http://doi.org/10.7771/1541-5015.1686

Broadfoot, P. (2009). Signs of change: Assessment past, present and future. In C. Wyatt-Smith & J. Cummings (Eds.), *Educational assessment in the 21st century. Connecting theory and practice* (pp. v–xi). Springer.

Broadfoot, P., & Black, P. (2004). Redefining assessment? The first ten years of assessment in education. *Assessment in Education: Principles, Policy & Practice*, 11(1), 7–26. http://doi.org/10.1080/0969594042000208976

Brookhart, S. M. (2004). Classroom assessment: Tensions and intersections in theory and practice. *Teachers College Record*, 106(3), 429–458.

Brown, P. C., Roediger, H. L., & McDaniel, M. A. (2014). *Make it stick: The science of successful learning*. Harvard University Press. www.hup.harvard.edu/catalog.php?isbn=9780674729018

Cakmakci, G., Aydeniz, M., Brown, A., & Makokha, J. M. (2020). Situated cognition and cognitive apprenticeship learning. In B. Akpan & T. J. Kennedy (Eds.), *Science education in theory and practice*. Springer Texts in Education. Springer. https://doi.org/10.1007/978-3-030-43620-9_20

Camacho, D. J., & Legare, J. M. (2016). Shifting gears in the classroom – movement toward personalised learning and competency-base education. *The Journal of Competency-Based Education*, 1, 151–156.

Chami, G. (2023, October 23). Artificial intelligence and academic integrity: Striking a balance A look at how universities can encourage the ethical and transparent use of artificial intelligence tools to support learning while guarding against misconduct. *Times Higher Education Supplement*. www.timeshighereducation.com/campus/artificial-intelligence-and-academic-integrity-striking-balance

Chartered Institute of Professional Development. (2024, January 4). *Competence and competency frameworks*. www.cipd.org/uk/knowledge/factsheets/competency-factsheet/#what

Child, S. F., & Shaw, S. D. (2020). A purpose-led approach towards the development of competency frameworks. *Journal of Further and Higher Education*, 44(8), 1143–1156. http://doi.org/10.1080/0309877X.2019.1669773

Churchill, A. (2015). Bless the tests: Three reasons for standardised testing. *Thomas Fordham Institute*. Retrieved March 18, 2023, from https://fordhaminstitute.org/national/commentary/bless-tests-three-reasons-standardized-testing

Coe, R. (2013, June 18). Improving education: A triumph of hope over experience. *Inaugural Lecture of Professor Robert Coe*, Durham University. http://eachandeverydog.net/wp-content/uploads/2015/05/ImprovingEducation2013.pdf

Coleman, V. (2021). *Digital divide in UK education during COVID-19 pandemic: Literature review*. Cambridge Assessment Research Report, accessed at Digital divide in UK Education During COVID-19 Pandemic: Literature Review. cambridgeassessment.org.uk

Cope, B., & Kalantzis, M. (2016). Big data comes to school: Implications for learning, assessment and research. *AERA Open*, 2(2), 1–19. http://doi.org/10.1177/2332858416641907

Council of Europe. (2001). *Common European framework of reference for languages: Learning, teaching, assessment*. Cambridge University Press.

Council of Europe. (2019, September 11). *Consultative committee of the convention for the protection of individuals with regard to automatic processing of personal data (convention 108)*. Report on Data in Education. Children's Data Protection in Education Systems: Challenges and Possible Remedies. Recommendations Summary Directorate General of Human Rights and Rule of Law. T-PD(2019)06BIS. https://rm.coe.int/children-s-data-protection-in-education-systems-challenges-and-possibl/1680973671

Dae-Bong. K. (2009, October 27–30). Human capital and its measurement. *The 3rd OECD World Forum on "Statistics, knowledge and policy": Charting progress, building visions, improving life*, pp. 1–15. https://www.trueval-uemetrics.org/DBpdfs/HumanCapital/Prof-Dr-Kwon-Human-Capital-Measurement.pdf

Deng, Z. (2018). Bringing knowledge back in: Perspectives from liberal education. *Cambridge Journal of Education*, 48(3), 335–351. http://doi.org/10.1080/0305764X.2017.1330874

Dewey, J. (1916). *Democracy and education*. Macmillan.

Dewey, J. (1938). *Experience and education*. Collier Books.

Dhawan, V. (2014). Education and neuroscience. *Research Matters: Cambridge Assessment Publication*, 17, 46–55. www.cambridgeassessment.org.uk/Images/466322-education-and-neuroscience.pdf

Driver, R., Asoko, H., Leach, J., Mortimer, E., & Scott, P. (1994). Constructing scientific knowledge in the classroom. *Educational Researcher, 23*(7), 5–12. http://doi.org/10.3102/0013189X023007005

Drucker, P. F. (2006). *The effective executive.* HarperCollins.

Elwood, J. (2006). Gender issues in testing and assessment. In C. Skelton, B. Francis, & L. Smulyan (Eds.), *The SAGE handbook on gender and education* (pp. 262–278). SAGE Publications Ltd.

Elwood, J., & Klenowski, V. (2002). Creating communities of shared practice: The challenges of assessment use in learning and teaching. *Assessment and Evaluation in Higher Education, 27*(3), 243–256.

European Commission & Council of the European Union. (2006, December 30). Recommendation of the European Parliament and of the Council of 18 December 2006 on key competences for lifelong learning. *Official Journal of the European Union, 394*, 10–18.

European Commission Education & Culture. (2018). Commission staff working document. *Proposal for a council recommendation on key competencies for lifelong learning.* https://eur-lex.europa.eu/legal-content/EN/TXT/PDF/?uri=CELEX:52018SC0014&from=EN

Foster, S. (2019). What barriers do students perceive to engagement with automated immediate formative feedback. *Journal of Interactive Media in Education, 2019*(1), 1–5. https://eric.ed.gov/?id=EJ1228614

Gandhi, M. H., & Mukherji, P. (2021). Learning theories. *StatPearls.* Retrieved November 5, 2021, from www.ncbi.nlm.nih.gov/books/NBK562189/

Gibson, D. C., & Webb, M. (2015, December). Data science in educational assessment. *Education and Information Technologies, 20*(4). http://doi.org/10.1007/s10639-015-9411-7

Gobert, J. D., San Pedro, M., Raziuddin, J., & Baker, R. S. (2013). From log files to assessment metrics: Measuring students' science inquiry skills using educational data mining. *The Journal of the Learning Sciences, 22*, 521–563.

Goswami, U. (2006). Neuroscience and education: From research to practice? *National Review of Neuroscience, 7*(5), 406–411.

Griffiths, D., Drachsler, H., Kickmeier-Rust, M., Steiner, C., Hoel, T., & Greller, W. (2016, January 6). Is privacy a show-stopper for learning analytics? A review of current issues and their solutions. *Learning Analytics Review.* ISSN: 2057–7494. LACE Project.

Halász, G., & Michel, A. (2011). Key competences in Europe: Interpretation, policy formulation and implementatio. *European Journal of Education, 46*(3), 289–306.

Halpern, D. F. (1998). Teaching critical thinking for transfer across domains: Dispositions, skills, structure training, and metacognitive monitoring. *American Psychologist, 53*(4), 449–455.

Halpern, D. F. (2001). Assessing the effectiveness of critical thinking instruction. *Journal of General Education, 50*(4), 270–286.

Halpern, D. F. (2003). *Thought and knowledge: An introduction to critical thinking.* Erlbaum.

Halpern, D. F. (2010). *Halpern critical thinking assessment manual.* Schuhfried GmbH.

Hanesworth, P. (2019). Inclusive assessment: Where next? *Advance HE.* www.advance-he.ac.uk/news-and-views/inclusive-assessment-where-next

Hazan, E., & Smit, S. (2021, July 13). How defining intangible investments can help grow the knowledge economy. *World Economic Forum.* www.mckinsey.com/mgi/overview/in-the-news/how-defining-intangible-investments-can-help-grow-the-knowledge-economy

Herder, E., Sosnovsky, S., & Dimitrova, V. (2017). Adaptive intelligent learning environments. In D. Erik, S. Mike & S. Rosamund (Eds.), *Technology enhanced learning* (pp. 109–114). Springer International Publishing.

Herold, B. (2016, February 5). Technology in education: An overview. *Education Week*. www.edweek.org/technology/technology-in-education-an-overview/2016/02

Hirsch, E. D. (1988). *Cultural literacy: What every American needs to know*. Vintage Books.

Hirsch, E. D. (2016). *Why knowledge matters: Rescuing our children from failed educational theories*. Harvard Educational Press.

Hirst, P. H. (1965). Liberal education and the nature of knowledge. In R. D. Archambault (Ed.), *Philosophical analysis and education* (pp. 113–138). Routledge and Kegan Paul.

Hirst, P. H. (1973). Liberal education and the nature of knowledge. In P. H. Hirst (Ed.), *Knowledge and the curriculum: A collection of philosophical papers* (pp. 30–53). Routledge and Kegan Paul.

Hirst, P. H. (1993). Education, knowledge and practices. In R. Barrow & P. White (Eds.), *Beyond liberal education: Essays in honour of Paul H. Hirst* (pp. 184–199). Routledge.

Hirst, P. H., & Peters, R. S. (1970). *The logic of education*. Routledge & Kegan Paul.

Hockings, C. (2010). *Inclusive learning and teaching: A synthesis of the research*. Higher Education Academy. www.heacademy.ac.uk/resources/detail/resources/detail/evidencenet/Inclusive_learning_a nd_teaching_in_higher_education

Holmes, W., Persson, J., Chounta, I.-A., Wasson, B., & Dimitrova, V. (2022). *Artificial intelligence and Education. A critical view through the lens of human rights, democracy, and the rule of law*. Council of Europe.

Holmes, W., & Tuomi, I. (2022). State of the art and practice in AI in education. *European Journal of Education, 57*, 542–570. https://doi.org/10.1111/ejed.12533

Horowitz, H. L. (1971, Spring). Review: The progressive education movement after World War I. *History of Education Quarterly, 11*(1), 79–84. Cambridge: Cambridge University Press.

Hughes, S. (2021, November 18). *What do we mean by "digital" and how does that impact assessment?* www.cambridge.org/news-and-insights/insights/what-do-we-mean-by-digital-assessment

Hughes, S. (2022, January 6). Why don't we just put our high stakes exams on screen? *Cambridge Assessment*. www.cambridge.org/news-and-insights/insights/Why-don%E2%80%99t-we-just-put-our-high-stakes-exams-on-screen

Hwang, G. J., Xie, H., Wah, B. W., & Gašević, D. (2020). Vision, challenges, roles and research issues of artificial intelligence in education. *Computers and Education: Artificial Intelligence, 1*, 100001.

International Test Commission. (2001). International guidelines for test use. *International Journal of Testing, 1*, 93–114.

International Test Commission. (2005). *International guidelines on computer-based and internet delivered testing*. www.intestcom.org

Ixer, G. (2016). The concept of reflection: Is it skill based or values? *Social Work Education, 35*(7), 1470–1227. http://doi.org/10.1080/02615479.2016.1193136

James, M., Black, P., Carmichael, P., Conner, C., Dudley, P., Fox, A., Frost, A., Honour, L., Macbeth, J., McCormack, R., Marshall B., Pedder, D., Procter, R., Swaffield, S., & Wiliam, D. (2006). *Learning how to learn: Tools for schools*. Routledge.

Joint Information Systems Committee (JISC). (2007). *Effective practice with e-assessment: An overview of technologies, policies and practice in further and higher education (online)*. www.jisc.ac.uk/media/documents/themes/elearning/effpraceassess.pdf

Jones, K. M. L. (2019). Learning analytics and higher education: A proposed model for establishing informed consent mechanisms to promote student privacy and autonomy. *International Journal of Educational Technology in Higher Education, 16*(24), 1–22. https://doi.org/10.1186/s41239-019-0155-0

Jorg, T., Davis, B., & Nickmans, G. (2007). Position paper: Towards a new, complexity science of learning and education. *Educational Research Review*, 2(2), 145–156. http://doi.org/10.1016/j.edurev.2007.09.002

Joynes, C., Rossignoli, S., & Fenyiwa Amonoo-Kuofi, E. (2019). 21st century skills: Evidence of issues in definition, demand and delivery for development contexts. *K4D Helpdesk Report*. Institute of Development Studies. https://assets.publishing.service.gov.uk/media/5d71187ce5274a097c07b985/21st_century.pdf

Kim, H., Care, E., & Vista, A. (2019, January 30). Education systems need alignment for teaching and learning 21st century skills. *Brookings Focus on Assessment*. www.brookings.edu/articles/education-system-alignment-for-21st-century-skills/

Kim, J. S. (2008, January). Research and the reading wars. *The Phi Delta Kappan*, 89(5), 372–375.

Kitchen, W. H. (2014). *Authority and the teacher*. Bloomsbury Academic.

Krause, K.-L., Bochner, S., Duchesne, S., & McMaugh, A. (2010). *Educational psychology for learning and teaching* (3rd ed.). Cengage Learning Australia.

Krutka, D., Manca, S., Galvin, S., Greenhow, C., Koehler, M., & Askari, E. (2019). Teaching "against" social media: Confronting problems of profit in the curriculum. *Teachers College Record*, 121(14), 1–42.

Ladson-Billings, G. (2014). Culturally relevant pedagogy 2.0: A.k.a. the remix. *Harvard Educational Review*, 84(1), 74–84. https://doi.org/10.17763/haer.84.1.p2rj131485484751

Lave, J., & Wenger, E. (1991). *Learning in doing: Social, cognitive, and computational perspectives. Legitimate peripheral participation*. Cambridge University Press. https://doi.org/10.1017/CBO9780511815355

Lazarus, S. S., Johnstone, C. J., Liu, K. K., Thurlow, M. L., Hinkle, A. R., & Burden, K. (2022). An updated state guide to universally designed assessments. *NCEO Report 431*. National Center on Educational Outcomes.

Lefrançois, G. R. (2019). *Theories of human learning: Mrs Gribbin's cat (Seventh/Guy R. Lefrançois.)*. Cambridge University Press. www.cambridge.org/gb/academic/subjects/psychology/educational-psychology/theories-human-learning-mrs-gribbins-cat-7th-edition

Leighton, J. P., & Gierl, M. J. (2007). Why cognitive diagnostic assessment? In J. P. Leighton & M. J. Gierl (Eds.), *Cognitive diagnostic assessment for education: Theory and applications* (pp. 3–18). Cambridge University Press. https://doi.org/10.1017/CBO9780511611186.001

Long, C. (2023, March 30). Standardized testing is still failing students. *NEA Today*. www.nea.org/nea-today/all-news-articles/standardized-testing-still-failing-students

Lyons, S., Johnson, M., & Hinds, B. F. (2021, July). A call to action: Confronting inequity in assessment. *Lyons Assessment Consulting*. www.lyonsassessmentconsulting.com/assets/files/Lyons-JohnsonHinds_CalltoAction.pdf

Madaus, G., Russell, M., & Higgins, J. (2009). *The paradoxes of high stakes testing: how they affect students, their teachers, principals, schools and society*. Sage Publications, Inc.

Madgavkar, A., Schaninger, B., Smit, S., Woetzel, J., Samandari, H., Carlin, D., Seong, J., & Chockalingham, K. (2022, June 2). Human capital at work: The value of experience. *McKinsey Global Institute*. www.mckinsey.com/capabilities/people-and-organizational-performance/our-insights/human-capital-at-work-the-value-of-experience#/

Mayer-Schönberger, V., & Cukier, K. (2013). *Big data: A revolution that will transform how we live, work, and think*. Houghton Mifflin Harcourt.

McArthur, J. (2016). Assessment for social justice: The role of assessment in achieving social justice. *Assessment & Evaluation in Higher Education*, 41(7), 967–981. https://doi.org/10.1080/02602938.2015.1053429

McFarlan, C. (2022, January 19). Cultural relevance versus construct relevance: How do we create culturally responsive assessments? *2022 NCME equity in assessment webinar*. National Council on Measurement in Education. Renaissance. https://higherlogicdownload.s3.amazonaws.com/NCME/4b7590fc-3903-444d-b89d-c45b7fa3da3f/UploadedImages/Equity_in_Assessment_Resources/NCME_2022_Equity_in_Assessment_Webinar_1_-_Slides.pdf

McKinsey & Company. (2007). *How the world's best performing school systems come out on top*. www.mckinsey.com/industries/education/our-insights/how-the-worlds-best-performing-school-systems-come-out-on-top

McMurtrie, B. (2018). How artificial intelligence is changing teaching. *The Chronicle of Higher Education*. www.chronicle.com/article/How-Artificial-Intelligence-Is/244231

McPhail, G., & Rata, E. (2015). Comparing curriculum types: "Progressive knowledge" and "21st century learning". *New Zealand Journal of Educational Studies*. https://doi.org/10.1007/s40841-015-0025 9

Mead, A. D., & Drasgow, F. (1993). Equivalence of computerized and paper-and-pencil cognitive ability tests: A meta-analysis. *Psychological Bulletin, 114*(3), 449–458. https://doi.org/10.1037/0033-2909.114.3.449

Mislevy, R. J. (2018). *Sociocognitive foundations of educational measurement*. Routledge.

Mizzi, E. (2022). Conceptualising powerful knowledge in economics. *Journal of Curriculum Studies, 55*(4), 409–423. http://doi.org/10.1080/00220272.2023.2225194

Montenegro, E., & Jankowski, N. (2017). *Equity and assessment: Moving towards culturally responsive assessment (Occasional Paper No. 29)*. University of Illinois and Indiana University, National Institute for Learning Outcomes Assessment (NILOA). www.learningoutcomesassessment.org/wp-content/uploads/2019/02/OccasionalPaper29.pdf

Mulder, M., Weigel, T., & Collins, K. (2007). The concept of competence in the development of vocational education and training in selected EU member states: A critical analysis. *Journal of Vocational Education and Training, 59*(1), 67–88. http://doi.org/10.1080/13636820601145630

Murchan, D., & Siddiq, F. (2021). A call to action: A systematic review of ethical and regulatory issues in using process data in educational assessment. *Large-scale Assessments in Education, 9*(25), 1–27. https://doi.org/10.1186/s40536-021-00115-3

Nagel, M. (2012). Student learning. In R. Churchill, P. Ferguson, S. Godinho, N. Johnson & A. Keddie (Eds.), *Teaching making a difference* (Vol. 2, pp. 74–88). Wiley Publishing.

Neisser, U. (1967). *Cognitive psychology*. Appleton-Century-Crofts.

Newman, J. H. (1852). *The idea of a university* (C. F. Harrold, Ed.). Longmans, Green, and Co.

Nisbet, I., & Shaw, S. D. (2022). Fair high-stakes assessment in the long shadow of Covid-19. *Assessment in Education: Principles, Policy & Practice*. http://doi.org/10.1080/0969594X.2022.2067834

Nortvedt, G. A., Wiese, E., & Brown, M. (2020). Aiding culturally responsive assessment in schools in a globalising world. *Educational Assessment, Evaluation and Accountability, 32*(1), 5–27. https://doi.org/10.1007/s11092-020-09316-w

Odendahl, N. V. (2011). *Testwise: Understanding educational assessment* (Vol. 1). Rowman & Littlefield Education.

OECD. (2001). *The well-being of nations: The role of human and social capital*. Author.

OECD. (2013). *The future of education and skills. Education 2030*. OECD Publishing. www.oecd.org/education/2030/E2030%20Position%20Paper%20(05.04.2018).pdf

OECD. (2015). *PISA 2015 collaborative problem solving.* https://www.oecd.org/en/topics/sub-issues/student-problem-solving-skills/pisa-2015-collaborative-problem-solving.html

OECD. (2018). *The future of education and skills: Education 2030.* www.oecd.org/education/2030-project

OECD. (2020). *Back to the future of education: Four OECD scenarios for schooling, educational research and innovation.* OECD Publishing. https://doi.org/10.1787/178ef527-en

Ofqual. (2020). Online and on-screen assessment in high stakes, sessional qualifications. A review of the barriers to greater adoption and how these might be overcome. *Ofqual/20/6723/1.* https://www.gov.uk/government/publications/online-and-on-screen-assessment-in-high-stakes-sessional-qualifications

Pashler, H., Bain, P., Bottge, B., Graesser, A., Koedinger, K., McDaniel, M., & Metcalfe, J. (2007). *Organizing instruction and study to improve student learning (NCER 2007–2004).* National Center for Education Research, Institute of Education Sciences, U.S. Department of Education. http://ncer.ed.gov

Pellegrino, J. W. (2006). *Rethinking and redesigning curriculum, instruction, and assessment: What contemporary research and theory suggests.* Paper commissioned by the National Center on Education and the Economy for the New Commission on the Skills of the American Workforce. National Center on Education and the Economy.

Pellegrino, J. W. (2012). Chapter 10. Teaching, learning and assessing 21st century skills. *OECD iLibrary.* www.oecd-ilibrary.org/sites/9789264270695-12-en/index.html?itemId=/content/component/9789264270695-12-en#:~:text=The%20cognitive%20domain%20involves%20reasoning,responding%20to%20messages%20from%20others

Pellegrino, J. W., & Hilton, M. L. (Eds.). (2012). *Committee on defining deeper learning and 21st century skills.* Center for Education, Division on Behavioral and Social Sciences and Education, National Research Council.

Peña-Ayala, A. (2018). Learning analytics: A glance of evolution, status, and trends according to a proposed taxonomy. *Wiley Interdisciplinary Reviews: Data Mining and Knowledge Discovery, 8*(3), e1243. https://doi.org/10.1002/widm.1243

Peters, R. S. (1966). *Ethics and education.* Allen and Unwin.

Peters, R. S. (1973). *Authority, responsibility and education.* Allen & Unwin.

Phelan, J., Choi, K., Vendlinski, T., Baker, E., & Herman, J. (2011). Differential improvement in student understanding of mathematical principles following formative assessment intervention. *The Journal of Educational Research, 104*(5), 330–339.

Piaget, J., & Inhelder, B. (1969). *The psychology of the child.* Basic Books.

Polanyi, M. (1958). *Personal knowledge: Towards a post-critical philosophy.* University of Chicago Press.

Polster, P. P., Detrich, R., & States, J. (2021). *Standardized testing: The controversy surrounding it.* The Wing Institute. www.winginstitute.org/student-standardized-tests

Raikes, N. (2019). Data, data everywhere? Opportunities and challenges in a data-rich world. *Research Matters: A Cambridge Assessment Publication, 27,* 16–19.

Reiss, M., & Oates, T. (2014). Powerful knowledge and national curriculum. *Cambridge Assessment.* www.cambridgeassessment.org.uk/news/video/view/the-importance-of-powerful-knowledge-in-the-national-curriculum-michael-reiss-and-tim-oates/

Ripley, M. (2009). Transformational computer-based testing. In F. Scheuermann & Julius Björnsson (Eds.), *The transition to computer-based assessment new approaches to skills assessment and implications for large-scale testing.* JRC *scientific and technical reports. EUR 23679 EN – 2009* (pp. 92–98). European Commission Joint Research Centre Institute for the Protection and Security of the Citizen.

Roblyer, M. D., Edwards, J., & Havriluk, M. J. (1997). *Integrating educational technology into teaching*. Prentice Hall.

Rogers, C., & Freiberg, J. (1994). *Freedom to learn* (3rd ed.). Merrill Publishing.

Rogoff, B. (1990). *Apprenticeship in thinking: Cognitive development and social context*. Oxford University Press.

Rogti, M. (2021). Behaviorism as external stimuli: Improving student extrinsic motivation through behavioral responses in Algerian college education. *Global Journal of Human-Social Science, 21*(1), 28–41.

Ryan, M., & Ryan, M. (2013). Theorising a model for teaching and assessing reflective learning in higher education. *Higher Education Research & Development, 32*(2), 244–257. http://doi.org/10.1080/07294360.2012.661704

Rychen, D. S., & Salganik, L. H. (2001). *Defining and selecting key competencies*. Hogrefe & Huber Publishers.

Rycroft-Smith, L., & Boylan, M. (2019). *Summary of evidence for elements of teaching related to mastery in mathematics* (Espresso 16). Cambridge Mathematics. www.cambridgemaths.org/Images/espresso_16_mastery_in_mathematics.pdf

Schaeffer, G. A., Bridgeman, B., Golub-Smith, M. L., Lewis, C., Potenza, M. T., & Steffen, M. (1998). Comparability of paper-and-pencil and computer adaptive test scores on the GRE© general test. *GRE Professional Report No. 95–08P*. ETS Research Report 98–38. http://www.iacat.org/content/comparability-paper-and-pencil-and-computer-adaptive-test-scores-gre-general-test

Schaeffer, G. A., Steffen, M., Golub-Smith, M. L., Mills, C. N., & Durso, R. (1995). *The introduction and comparability of the computer-adaptive GRE General Test* (Research Rep. No. 95–20). Educational Testing Service.

Schmidt, W., Houang, R. T., & Cogan, L. (2002). A coherent curriculum: The case of mathematics. *American Educator, 26*, 1–17. www.aft.org/sites/default/files/media/2014/curriculum.pdf

Schunk, D. H. (2020). *Learning theories: An educational perspective* (8th ed.). Pearson Education. www.pearson.com/us/higher-education/program/Schunk-Learning-Theories-An-Educational-Perspective-8th-Edition/PGM1996609.html

Shepard, L. A. (2000). The role of assessment in a learning culture. *Educational Researcher, 29*(7), 4–14.

Shiell, H., Johnson, M., Hopkin, R., Nádas, R., & Bell, J. (2011, January). Extended essay marking on screen: Does marking mode influence marking outcomes and processes? *Research Matters: A Cambridge Assessment Publication*, Issue 11. www.cambridgeassessment.org.uk/Images/471465-extended-essay-marking-on-screen-does-marking-mode-influence-marking-outcomes-and-processes-.pdf

Shute, V. J., Ventura, M., & Kim, Y. J. (2013). Assessment and learning of qualitative physics in Newton's playground. *The Journal of Educational Research, 106*(6), 423–430. https://doi.org/10.1080/00220671.2013.832970

Siarova, H., Sternadel, D., & Mašidlauskaitė, R. (2017). Assessment practices for 21st century learning: Review of evidence. *NESET II Report*. Publications Office of the European Union. http://doi.org/10.2766/71491

Skinner, B. (1972). Utopia through the control of human behavior. In J. M. Rich (Ed.), *Readings in the philosophy of education*. Wadsworth.

Skinner, F. (1938). *The behavior of organisms: An experimental analysis*. Appleton Century-Crofts.

Slade, S., & Prinsloo, P. (2013). Learning analytics: Ethical issues and dilemmas. *American Behavioral Scientist, 57*(10), 1509–1528.

Smith, R. (2023). Forms of knowledge and forms of philosophy. *Journal of Philosophy of Education*, 57, 65–76. https://doi.org/10.1093/jopedu/qhad007

Snow, R. E., & Lohman, D. F. (1989). Implications of cognitive psychology for educational measurement. In R. L. Linn (Ed.), *Educational measurement* (pp. 263–331). Macmillan Publishing Co, Inc; American Council on Education.

Snowman, J., McCown, R., & Biehler, R. (2009). *Psychology applied to teaching* (12th ed.). Houghton Mifflin.

SoLAR [Society for Learning Analytics Research] (online). *What is learning analytics?* www.solar esearch.org/about/what-is-learning-analytics/

Stahl, B. C., & Wright, D. (2018). Ethics and privacy in AI and big data: Implementing responsible research and innovation. *IEEE Security and Privacy*, 16(3), 26–33. http://doi.org/10.1109/MSP.2018.2701164

Stecher, B. M., & Hamilton, L. S. (2006, April). Using test-score data in the classroom. *WR-375-EDU*. RAND Education. www.rand.org/content/dam/rand/pubs/working_papers/2006/RAND_WR375.pdf

Stecher, B. M., & Hamilton, L. S. (2014). *Measuring hard-to-measure student competencies: A research and development plan*. Rand.

Sternberg, R. J., Conway, B. E., Ketron, J. L., & Bernstein, M. (1981). People's conceptions of intelligence. *Journal of Personality and Social Psychology*, 41(1), 37–55. https://doi.org/10.1037/0022-3514.41.1.37

Swaffield, S. (2009). *The misrepresentation of assessment for learning – and the woeful waste of a wonderful opportunity*. www.aaia.org.uk/content/uploads/2010/07/The-Misrepresentation-of-Assessment-for-Learning.pdf

Tchibozo, G. (2011). Emergence and outlook of competence-based education in European education systems: An overview. *Education, Knowledge and Economy*, 4(3), 193–205.

Threlfall, J., Pool, P., Homer, M., & Swinnerton, B. (2007). Implicit aspects of peer and paper and pencil mathematics assessment that come to light through the use of the computer. *Educational Studies in Mathematics*, 66(3), 335–348. www.jstor.org/stable/27822709

Timmis, S., Broadfoot, P., Sutherland, R., & Oldfield, A. (2016). Rethinking assessment in a digital age: Opportunities, challenges and risks. *British Educational Research Journal*, 42(3), 454–476.

Torrance, H., & Pryor, J. (1998). *Investigating formative assessment*. Open University.

Twist, L. (2021). Changing times, changing assessments: International perspectives. *Educational Research*, 63(1), 1–8. http://doi.org/10.1080/00131881.2021.1876590

UNESCO. (2016). *A conceptual framework for competencies assessment*. https://unesdoc.unesco.org/ark:/48223/pf0000245195

UNESCO Education 2030. (2019). *Beijing Consensus on artificial intelligence and education*. Outcome Document of the International Conference on Artificial Intelligence and Education 'Planning education in the AI era: Lead the leap', 16–18 May 2019, Beijing, People's Republic of China.

UNICEF. (2021). *Policy guidance on AI for children*. Author. www.unicef.org/globalinsight/media/2356/file/UNICE F-Global-Insight-policy-guidance-AI-children-2.0-2021.pdf.pdf

Van de Vijver, F., & Hambleton, R. (1996). Translating tests: Some practical guidelines. *European Psychologist*, 1, 89–99.

von Glasersfeld, E. V. (1974). Piaget and the radical constructivist epistemology. *Epistemology and Education*, 1–24. www.aippc.it/wp-content/uploads/2019/04/2014.02.094.107.pdf

Voogt, J., & Roblin, N. P. (2012). A comparative analysis of international frameworks for 21st century competencies: Implications for national curriculum policies. *Journal of Curriculum Studies*, 44(3), 299–321. http://doi.org/10.1080/00220272.2012.668938

Waitoller, F. R., & Thorius, K. A. K. (2016). Cross-pollinating culturally sustaining pedagogy and universal design for learning: Toward an inclusive pedagogy that accounts for dis/ability. *Harvard Educational Review*, 86(3), 366–389. https://doi.org/10.17763/1943-5045-86.3.366

Walshe, G. (2020). Radical constructivism – von Glasersfeld. In B. Akpan & T. J. Kennedy (Eds.), *Science Education in Theory and Practice*. Springer Texts in Education. Springer. https://doi.org/10.1007/978-3-030-43620-9_24

Watkins, D., Dahlin, B., & Ekholm, M. (2005). Awareness of the backwash effect of assessment: A phenomenographic study of the views of Hong Kong and Swedish lecturers. *Instructional Sciences*, 33(4), 283–309. http://doi.org/10.1007/s11251-005-3002-8

Webb, N. L. (1997). *Research Monograph Number 6: "Criteria for alignment of expectations and assessments on mathematics and science education*. CCSSO.

Webb, N. L. (2007). Issues related to judging the alignment of curriculum standards and assessments. *Applied Measurement in Education*, 20(1), 7–25.

Weiss, D. J. (1983). *New Horizons in testing*. Academic Press.

White, J. (2018). The weakness of "powerful knowledge". *London Review of Education*, 16(2), 325–335. https://doi.org/10.18546/LRE.16.2.11

Wiek, A., Withycombe, L., & Redman, C. L. (2011). Key competencies in sustainability: A reference framework for academic program development. *Sustainable Science*, 6, 203–218.

Wilson, G. (2013). Evidencing reflective practice in social work education: Theoretical uncertainties and practical challenges. *British Journal of Social Work*, 43(1), 154–172.

Wintrup, J. (2017). Higher education's panopticon? Learning analytics, ethics and student engagement. *Higher Education Policy*, 30, 87–103.

Wyatt-Smith, C., Lingard, B., & Heck, E. (2019, October). Digital learning assessments and big data: Implications for teacher professionalism.25 Education Research and Foresight: Working papers. https://unesdoc.unesco.org/ark:/48223/pf0000370940

Wyatt-Smith, C., Lingard, B., & Heck, E. (Eds.). (2021). *Digital disruption in teaching and testing: Assessments, big data, and the transformation of schooling*. Routledge.

Wyckoff, A. (2013). Knowledge is growth. *OECD Yearbook 2013*. www.oecd.org/innovation/knowledge-is-growth.html

Yosso, T. J. (2005). Whose culture has capital? A critical race theory discussion of community cultural wealth. *Race Ethnicity and Education*, 8(1), 69–91. http://doi.org/10.1080/1361332052000341006

Young, M. (2008). *Bringing knowledge back in: From social constructivism to social realism in the sociology of education*. Routledge.

Young, M. (2009). Education, globalisation and the "voice of knowledge". *Journal of Education and Work*, 22, 193–204. http://doi.org/10.1080/13639080902957848

Young, M., Lambert, D., Roberts, C., & Roberts, M. (2014). *Knowledge and the future school: Curriculum and social justice*. Bloomsbury.

Young, M., & Muller, J. (2013). On the powers of powerful knowledge. *Review of Education*, 1(3), 229–250. http://doi.org/10.1002/rev3.3017

Zhang, J., Zhang, Y., Zou, Q., & Huang, S. (2018). What learning analytics tells us: Group-behavior analysis and individual learning diagnosis based on long-term and large-scale data. *Educational Technology & Society*, 21(2), 245–258.

Zitter, L. (2022, November 23). What are the 5 V's of big data? *TechnologyAdvice*. https://technologyadvice.com/blog/information-technology/the-four-vs-of-big-data/

6
THE MORAL COMPASS

So far, we have considered developments in education and society in the first quarter of the current century (Chapters 2 and 3) and contemporaneous changes in thinking, together with their implications for educational assessment (Chapters 4 and 5). In this chapter we apply a moral compass to educational assessment as we enter the second quarter of the 21st century. Is the morality of educational assessment being considered at all? If so, what is the current thinking? Do we agree with it? What moral challenges have been made to educational assessment? Are there persuasive answers to them? And what moral principles should guide the world of assessment in the years to come?

Some readers may be surprised to find a book of this kind about assessment including a chapter about "morality". Some of that surprise may be a matter of terminology: Why is the chapter not entitled "The ethics of education (or of assessment)"? Historically, in English, the two terms have often been used interchangeably: we translate Aristotle's seminal work as the "Nicomachean Ethics" (2009), reflecting the Greek "ethicos" which relates to character or virtue in individuals, promoted and supported by good social practices and rules. Almost two thousand years later, Kant's seminal work, with its title translated into English as the *Groundwork of the Metaphysic of Morals*, focused on the moral imperative as based on the essence of what is of value in humanity. One school of thought fashionable in 20th-century moral philosophy was "meta-ethics",[1] including reflections on the language and logic of moral statements. And the academic world contains professors of ethics and professors of moral philosophy, doing much the same thing, with their titles largely a matter of custom and practice.

DOI: 10.4324/9781003346166-6

This interchangeability notwithstanding, there is a sense in which morality is seen as bigger than ethics. "Ethics" is sometimes used to refer to that part of morality that applies to a particular context, such as a profession or a form of activity. For example, "business ethics" or "medical ethics" refer to rules or principles governing the behaviour of business people or doctors. In that sense, the reader might expect this book to discuss what might be included in "assessment ethics" – for assessment practitioners – and how thinking on that has changed in recent years (if it has). Indeed, we do propose some such principles later in this chapter. However, if morality is to be applied in a particular context, there needs to be a fundamental understanding of what this "morality" is that is being applied in that context and how the rules governing life in a particular profession or activity relate to rules governing life beyond that context.

There are also some senses in which ethics is seen as bigger than morality. In the 20th century, Bernard Williams, drawing on the approach of Socrates and his followers, saw "ethics" as concerned with the wide question "how do I live?", while morality was about a particular kind of obligation (Williams, 1985). And as our book is about thinking in the 21st century, we also need to consider the influence of the views of (critical) sociologists, social theorists and philosophers writing at the turn of the century and beyond about "postmodernism", morality and ethics.

In his highly influential *Postmodern Ethics* (written in 1993), Zygmunt Bauman wrote of the "ethical crisis of postmodernity" (Bauman, 1993, see also Lukes, 1995; Mason, 2001). The description of this "crisis" sees "morality" as being about universally applicable codes of right and wrong, which should be able to be rolled out from the personal realm into wider society through accepted codes of "ethics". The problem, say Bauman and others, is that the bases for doing so seem to have collapsed in postmodern society. Our actions have such wide-reaching consequences that they defy utilitarian calculations. We have multiple, often conflicting, roles in life. And, most importantly, there are no shared beliefs in codes of right and wrong that give them authority to be applied in society through ethical codes.

Bauman (1993) states the problem at the beginning of his book:

[T]he moral thought and practice of modernity was animated by the belief in the possibility of a *non-ambivalent, non-aporetic ethical code*. Perhaps such a code has not been found yet. But it surely waits round the next corner. Or the corner after next. It is the *disbelief* in such a possibility that is postmodern.

(pp. 9–10) [emphases in original]

Bauman does not use "postmodern" as a chronological term, referring to years after the "modern" age, but is talking about a progression of ideas, where beliefs held in the "modern" age are no longer appropriate. He proceeds to offer a new approach to the moral foundation for ethics, founded on a revaluation of one-to-one human relationships ("The Moral Party of Two"). Other writers have also sought to build bridges between (personal) morality and (societal) ethical codes – for example, Mason, in an educational context, does so through the concept of "integrity" (Mason, 2001).

Jürgen Habermas (1929–present), one of the "Frankfurt School" of 20th-century critical theorists, saw ethics as a field of discourse across contexts. He championed "ethical discourse", involving rational discussion and seeking to bring together different moral views in societal contexts. His main purpose was not to distinguish between ethics and morality – or to reject morality – but to offer a rational structure for ethical discussion in real-life contexts. In the sense that Habermas's ethical discourse involves people in social contexts, it is in a sense bigger than (personal) morality (Habermas, 1990).

In the 20th century, while some were distinguishing between morality and ethics, others – notably W.D. Ross (Ross, 1930) – were distinguishing between the "right" and the "good",[2] with the language of morality linked to the first (which is about interpersonal constraints to conduct and what is right or wrong) and the language of ethics linked to the second (which is about value and what is good or bad). But whatever labels writers have given to these distinctions, they need to wrestle with the question of how the two domains (as depicted by them) are linked. And those who have concentrated on the "ethical" rather than the "moral" still need to ask what fundamental principles should inform ethical discussions in real-life contexts. We would argue that the pressing 21st-century agenda of issues affecting education – and educational assessment – needs moral debate and guidance more than ever. The fact that traditional sources of moral authority are questioned (and such questioning is not unique to the 21st century) makes that quest more difficult but even more important. We are, therefore, unashamed about using the language of morality in this chapter. And if we apply Ross's right/good distinction to educational assessment, which is very much about the norms governing a particular field of interpersonal engagement, then that would place it in the realm of the right rather than the good.

We are therefore seeking to apply the moral compass to education and subsequently to educational assessment. Before proceeding to do so, however, it is important to distinguish two sets of questions:

(a) What moral principles apply to education – and educational assessment in particular?
(b) What should be taught (and assessed) in moral education (seen as a curriculum subject or as a cross-curricular objective)?

This chapter is about (a). Question (b) is also interesting and important, and has been addressed by thinkers from ancient times to now. In the late

20th century, the work of John Wilson and his colleagues was highly influential in the UK and beyond (see, e.g. McLaughlin & Halstead, 2000), as was Paul Hirst's *Moral Education in a Secular Society* (Hirst, 1975). And Michael Hand is prominent among contemporary writers (e.g. Hand, 2017).

Curriculum designs produced in many countries include sections on "moral [and religious] education".[3] Many of the concerns raised by the postmodernists are relevant, particularly for teachers in contexts where, in Mason's words, "the culturally plural classroom does face us with competing moral claims codified in the ethical paradigms of different cultures" (Mason, 2001, p. 59). But we shall put aside question (b) for the present and return to question (a). In the structure of this book, our focus here is on questions such as "What is the moral justification for educational assessment" and "What moral principles should govern educational assessment"?

What we mean by morality

As we are using the term "morality", it falls to us to define what we mean by it. This could be the subject of a separate book (e.g. Wallace & Walker, 1970), but we shall confine ourselves here to setting out the basis on which we shall apply the moral compass to education and educational assessment in this chapter.

Our main premise is that the moral domain is, in a sense, bigger than all others because – by definition – moral principles and judgements transcend context. We realise that this statement may surprise readers used to discussions where the application of values varies with context, but we ask them to bear with us while we outline our position further. It means that teachers or assessment professionals cannot take their moral hat off when they go to work. This is not to deny that they may be subject to professional codes as educators or assessors. But we are following Kant and 20th-century writers, including R.M. Hare, in our understanding that moral considerations are understood as trumping all others – as "overriding" (Hare, 1952, 1963, 1981).

Kant compared the "categorical imperative" to act morally (whatever the circumstances) with "hypothetical imperatives" (in circumstances X, do Y) (Kant, 1785, p. 43).[4] Hare's account of "overridingness" is helpful here:

> Sometimes, when two evaluations . . . conflict (not in the sense that they contradict each other, but in the sense that, the facts being what they are, we cannot act on both) we allow one to *override* the other. I interpret this term as meaning, not only that we in fact act on the one and not the other, but that we think we *ought* to act on one even though it involves disregarding the other.
>
> *(Hare, 1963, pp. 167–168) (emphases in original)*

This is not the place to evaluate in detail other characteristics of moral language and judgements discussed by some analytic moral philosophers in the late 20th century, with conscious echoes of Kant: namely that moral considerations are "universalizable"[5] (a way of thinking which some of the postmodernists might now question) and – particularly according to Hare – "prescriptive". Our premise for the discussion that follows in this chapter is that moral considerations are, by definition, the biggest considerations that we can apply to living our lives. They are also personal in that – unlike some conceptions of the "ethical" domain – they apply to us as individuals, not just to social groupings.

We would add that agreeing that moral judgements are overriding does not require a belief in the objectivity of moral judgements. Even those who, like Bertrand Russell, think that moral sentiments are expressions of emotion, may feel, as Russell did, that moral emotions trump other feelings and want to urge others to share them.[6] A more recent proponent of a similar view is Simon Blackburn (see, e.g. his essays on the "quasi-realism" of moral statements) (Blackburn, 1993).

The adjective "moral" has been applied to many kinds of things – to language (expressing judgements or beliefs), to choices, dilemmas and decisions, to principles and rules, to government action (Downie, 1964) and to virtues and character traits (MacIntyre, 1981). In this chapter we are applying the moral compass to educational assessment, which is a field of activity. Thus, to talk of the "morality of assessment" is like talking about the "morality of warfare": we are concerned here with the moral principles that apply to assessment as a field for actions, within the larger field of education, and to choices and decisions for action within that field.

The moral justification for educational assessment

What is the moral justification for educational assessment? If the question is asked about the justification for doing any assessment at all, it may seem trivial or pointless. Surely questions and answers are part of almost all approaches to education? Indeed, where moral questions have been asked about assessment, they have often been about particular ways of assessing rather than about assessment per se. Thus, the US pressure group "FairTest" enjoins parents to "Just say No to standardised tests".[7] However, their more detailed text after this headline states that "Opting out calls for better assessment models" (arguing that "Opting out demands better ways to assess and promote student learning"). They claim that the way standardised tests are used in some states is harmful to children, but they seem to be advocating "better assessment" rather than none.

However, there is benefit in standing back and considering what – if anything – is the moral justification for any/all educational assessments. The answer may provide criteria for answering questions about how and when to assess. But the premise for considering that question must be the moral justification for education. If education is not justified, then neither is educational assessment. It is now generally accepted that education is a good thing and that the state has a moral duty to provide it or enable it to be provided. This consensus was reflected in Articles 28 and 29 of the UN Convention on the Rights of the Child, adopted in 1989. There have been episodic challenges to education (or to schooling) by the Romantics, Rousseau ("Emile") and Wordsworth ("Shades of the prison-house begin to close Upon the growing Boy"),[8] followed in the 20th century by the de-schoolers (e.g. Illich, 1971) and echoed by Pink Floyd in 1979.[9] However, even the de-schoolers were arguably in favour of (non-institutional) education, and there does seem to be a commitment in almost all countries to the value of education and to providing it to children, normally in schools. The 19th and 20th centuries saw debate about the education of girls and women, and this has been revived in the second decade of the 21st century by measures taken by the Taliban in Afghanistan.[10] But there is no question that the Taliban are seen as outliers in this respect and heavily condemned by almost all other countries. In the UK, expenditure on education (public and private) in 2018 totalled over 6% of the gross domestic product,[11] and levels of spending were similar in the USA.[12] In many countries, including the UK, education is second only to health in its demands on the public purse.[13]

There are linguistic differences in debates about the purposes and justification of education. German discussion differentiates between "Bildung" (education and personal development), "Ausbildung" (vocational training/apprenticeship) and "Erziehung" (upbringing and nurturing) (Keiner, 2002). There are also differences in English between "education" and "training". A web search of sites aimed at the non-specialist public quickly found:

> Education provides students with theoretical knowledge, while training provides practical skills. Training is typically job-specific and practical, while education can be more general and provides a theoretical foundation.[14]

Such distinctions have for some time been criticised for not taking account of the importance of theoretical knowledge in learning practical skills (see, e.g. Dearden, 1984) and for undervaluing the relevance of theoretical understanding and intellectual skills to the world of work. Concepts such as "knowledge", "skills", "understanding" and "competence" are found in both domains, and in Chapter 5, we have criticised the dichotomy of knowledge versus skills. Nevertheless, there remains a broad distinction between the worlds of "education" and "training". Discussion of the formation of young children is normally conceptualised as "education" (or "schooling", if the emphasis is on a child's right to go to school).

There have been three main approaches to providing a moral justification for education (White, 2005). The first is utilitarian: education brings benefits to the individual (living a happy and fulfilled life, getting a good job) and to society (economic growth and social harmony). In 2011, the UK government used these terms to justify its proposals (subsequently implemented) to increase the statutory minimum age for ending participation in education or training in England:

> Participating in education or training has clear benefits: increasing skills and qualifications, and leading to improved earnings and career prospects. Ensuring that all our young people are able to access high quality education and training drives social mobility and economic growth.[15]

The second approach to justifying education, often implied rather than stated, is to state that education is self-justifying – it just is a good thing (World Vision, 2023).[16] This can refer to the process of education or its outcome (knowledge, learning) – or to both – and can be combined with valuing the utilitarian benefits of education.

The third justification, which is close to, but distinct from, the second, justifies education as developing what is distinctive and most worthy in human nature. Around 1780, Kant urged this view on his students in his *Lectures on Pedagogy*, using language that it would be hard to find in modern institutions providing initial teacher training:

> The human being can only become human through education. He is nothing except what education makes of him. . . . Providence has willed that the human being shall bring forth by himself that which is good, and he speaks, as it were, to him: "Go forth into the world," so might the creator address humanity, "I have equipped you with all predispositions toward the good. It is up to you to develop them, and thus your own happiness and unhappiness depend on you yourself".
>
> *(9:443 & 9: 446)*

With the insights of later centuries, it is important to remark that Kant's understanding of what was good in the cultural inheritance of humanity was limited to western European society as experienced by him, and his references in the "Lectures" to uneducated "savages" can, with some justice, now be seen as racist. Distinguished Professor at The Whare Wānanga o Awanuiārangi (New Zealand), Linda Tuhiwai Smith has argued that colonial powers have appropriated values developed by indigenous cultures elsewhere and claimed ownership of them (Tuhiwai Smith, 2022). However, as she has illustrated in her writings, indigenous cultures too have linked education to what is distinctively human. John White has suggested that this post-Kantian line of thought has influenced some late 20th-century writers in England, including Paul Hirst (White, 2005), and it has also influenced the authors of this book. Of course, these three justifications for education are not mutually exclusive. Many would acknowledge the utilitarian benefits of education even if they went beyond those in justifying it, and we would join them in doing so.

Education is also often seen as a human right. For example, the UN Declaration of Human Rights (1948) includes, in Article 26:

> Everyone has a right to education. . . . Education shall be directed to the full development of the human personality and to the strengthening of respect for human rights and fundamental freedoms.

Such a view can be derived from any of the three justifications of education. If something is not morally justified, it cannot be a right. There is also a requirement for an element of private good as well as public good to lead to a human right – why should people have a right to something that does not benefit them in any way? There is a related concept of the rights of children, who are in need of protection and for whom arguably there is the richest return on investment in their education. As we have seen, such thinking prompted the UN to adopt their Declaration of the Rights of the Child in 1989.

A moral justification for education is a necessary but not sufficient condition for justifying educational assessment. If assessment is part of education, and education is not morally justified, then neither are its constituent parts (unless as a means to some other good). A link to the justification of education is necessary. However, it is not sufficient – a justifier of education might not justify its inclusion in assessment. So, we turn now to the justification of assessment.

As we outlined in Chapter 1, we are using the term "assessment" to denote a judgement based on evidence. "Educational assessment" refers to such judgements about constructs that are relevant to the content and/or purposes of education. So, for example, a judgement of the height of children in order to design a school doorway is not an educational assessment (although it is in an educational context), but a judgement of whether they can multiply numbers by two is. Judgements about X and Y can be based on evidence thought to be relevant to X and Y (the validity of the assessment will depend on how well-founded that thought is).

Of course, there are different methods and purposes of assessment. Justifying assessment as a whole does not imply justifying all kinds of assessment. As we have seen, the US organisation "FairTest" takes exception to specific uses of standardised testing methods but seems to approve of other forms of assessment. The same can be said about different purposes for assessment.

Using the familiar distinction between formative purposes (informing further teaching and learning) and summative purposes (judging and reporting on what the student knows or can do) (see, e.g. Black & Wiliam, 1998), the question can be asked of whether either or both kinds of purpose are morally justified and, if so, why. In asking that, we acknowledge that for some day-to-day informal assessment for formative purposes – such as asking a question or asking a student to repeat something in a different language – the justification seems so obvious that it is almost trivial, as long as it is part of education that is justified. However, asking ourselves why that seems so obvious may help inform our wider discussion about the justification of assessment.

Many possible and actual purposes have been identified for assessment. Newton (2007) listed eight such purposes, and the list has grown since. We can group them broadly into three subgroups. The first is the classic formative use of assessment at a fixed point in time – to support the teaching and learning of students by describing what they have learned, identifying strengths and gaps and guiding them and their teachers in what to do next.

The second subgroup of purposes involves checking what individual students know or can do to compare them against benchmarks. The benchmarks can be preset standards or competencies or the comparison may be with the achievements of others. The outcomes of these assessments may be used to provide information to institutions, parents, teachers and students themselves. It can also be seen as a reward for learners to receive a report of what they have learned and what they can do. The uses of the information by others can include processes that may have supporters and detractors, such as selection or "setting" within schools. And even if a purpose – say, selection – is supported, if the assessment does not provide valid evidence to justify the selection decision, that can be a ground for moral criticism.

The third subgroup covers the use of assessment outcomes for evaluation, often for the further purpose of accountability. The evaluation may be of the level(s) of learning or performance attained in a school, region or country. This purpose may not require each learner to be assessed but can be approached through the testing of a sample, often with little or no feedback to the students themselves.

These subgroups of purposes of assessment can be distinguished from the purposes of qualifications following assessment, although the moral questions posed are similar. One purpose of qualifications is certification – to provide learners with something to show what they know and can do. For that to be of much use to the learner, the assessment needs to be valid and reliable and the certificate needs to be understood and respected. All these features have been debated in the context of the US High School Diploma.[17]

A second purpose of qualifications is to support progression to continuing education or into/within work. Qualifications do this by claiming to provide valid and reliable evidence to inform selection by educational establishments or employers. This is clearly linked with the second subgroup of purposes of assessment that we described earlier. However, the currency of the qualification can add assurance for learners, educators or employers that learners have the necessary knowledge and skills to progress. And some qualifications can be a requirement for progression in education (a "hurdle") or for entry into a trade or profession (a "licence to practise").

Wherever an assessment – and its resulting qualification, if there is one – sits in our taxonomy of purposes, there are moral questions to ask. Is the identified purpose morally justified? On what grounds? If so, does the assessment used (who? how? when?) achieve that purpose? If not, what is its justification? Are there moral arguments against the assessment process involved (even if the purpose is morally justified)? For example, there might be issues of injustice or inequality in the comparative opportunities for learners to do well. Or the process itself might be thought to cause harm through imposing stress or anxiety (Putwain & Daly, 2014). If so, are there better ways of achieving the justified purpose? Does the moral balance justify continuing with the assessment, perhaps in a way that minimises morally bad aspects?

We shall use these questions in the remainder of this chapter when we look at moral challenges to assessment and suggest moral principles for the assessment world. But before doing so, we return to the question at the head of this section – what is the moral justification for doing assessment at all? That question is not asked as often as it should be (Winch & Gingell, 1999) but one attempt to answer it was made by Antony Flew in the 1970s, based on the concept of sincerity, in his book *Sociology, Equality and Education*:

> If someone is sincerely trying to learn something or trying to teach someone to learn something, then they must, necessarily, be concerned whether, and how far, they are succeeding.
>
> *(1976, p. 89)*

Thus, according to Flew, sincere teaching or learning requires checks on what has been learned, and assessment is justified as providing such a check.

In response to Flew, John White argued that checking on how teaching and learning are succeeding only requires periodic monitoring, possibly using sampling, rather than testing each individual student (White, 1999, p. 205). We would add that the argument from sincerity does not justify asking how much pupils know compared with each other.[18] Why should a teacher (or student) need to know that if they want to check how the class (or individual learners) are getting on?

There is also the familiar argument that too much testing can distort the learning experience – the content of learning can be skewed to what will be in the test, and test preparation can take up scarce teaching and learning time

(Alderson, 1999; Klein et al., 2000; Linn, 2000). Assessment which distorted learning would not be able to be justified by Flew as an effective check for the sincere teacher or learner, as it would, in effect, create another objective – doing well in the test – and would leave open the question of how the pursuit of that objective was justified.

However, on balance, we do think that there is some common sense in Flew's argument. It does seem sensible to check from time to time how the learning is going, in the same way that walkers might consult a map to check how far they have gone. And we accept that at the level of informal feedback in the course of a normal teaching session, the justification of assessment becomes almost trivial. It's just part of the everyday process of teaching and learning, and its justification is the same as the justification of the education of which it forms a part.

Moral challenges to educational assessment

As we have said earlier in this chapter, many challenges to assessment are really challenges to particular types of assessment (e.g. standardised tests or traditional written examinations) or to particular uses (e.g. for entry into selective schools), rather than to all kinds of assessment or testing. However, there are possible moral challenges to educational assessment, and we shall consider two in this chapter – one at a very high level of generality and one more specialised challenge to a particular aspect of some high-stakes assessments taken by school pupils.

The high-level challenge is about power. Assessment, this argument claims, is a morally objectionable instrument to reinforce the power of the assessor over the assessed. The French 20th-century philosopher and social theorist Michel Foucault wrote *Discipline and Punish: The Birth of the Prison* in 1975. Readers of our book may be surprised to find that Foucault's volume includes a chapter headed "Examinations". He writes about disciplinary power across society as a form of control through the monitoring and surveillance of populations.

A student assessment or examination is an arena where disciplinary power – particularly between the assessor and the assessed – is most evident. Foucault writes about the assessors as the "judges of normality" and argues that they are present everywhere. Disciplinary power (and its success) produces individuals in hierarchy and observation, normalisation and judgement, and their combination in examination. In hierarchical observation, the practice of discipline assumes a mechanism that intimidates by means of observation. Foucault gives illustrations of classroom doors with windows that allow observation to take place at any time. Normalising and judgement refer to the quasi-judicial privileges of authorities in establishing and enforcing the rules. Examination (in which he includes both school and medical examinations) unites the elements of observation and normalisation. In an examination, the individual is observed by the hierarchy, who can reward or punish by awarding ranks – or, in the case of examinations, marks.

A challenge to assessment derived from this account would be that the power relationships manifested in educational assessment situations are an abuse of power and are not morally justified. This may be illustrated by a random web search for newspaper or media illustrations of school pupils sitting traditional examinations. In the UK, such pictures nearly always show a room full of anxious-looking youngsters, in enforced spatial separation from their peers, writing under the supervision of a stern-looking invigilator. It is very evident who the power figure is in the examination hall. The students are trying to please the authority figures who will be marking their test, and their future may depend on whether they succeed in doing so. Such an unequal power relationship, the challenge concludes, is not compatible with the moral purposes of education.

In reply to the power critique, it is helpful to distinguish between power and authority. Defenders of assessment might argue that, while some instances of the exercise of power may be wrong, the kind of authority exercised in setting, supervising and marking assessments is appropriate and morally justifiable. William Kitchen (2014) defends authority in education, both in a disciplinary and a teaching context. He cites with approval Michael Polanyi's argument in the mid-20th century[19] that intelligence must be developed within a "fiduciary framework" of a cultural inheritance, which the student must learn from the master. It follows, the assessment defender might add, that it is appropriate for the student to seek to please the authority figure by showing that he or she has absorbed this cultural inheritance.

Some centuries before, in his *Lectures on Pedagogy*, Kant had spoken of education as involving a first stage of "formation and instruction", where the child imitates his parents and teachers, like a little bird learning to sing by imitating the mother bird, followed by "tutoring", where the pupil "learned to think how to make the world better than before" (Kant, 1776–1784). Similarly, learning established mathematical arguments and principles, as formulated in the textbooks, might be thought of as an essential first step equipping the learner to develop more novel mathematical ideas later. The assessment defender might argue that testing the learner to produce the answers specified by the authority figure of the assessor was justified and appropriate, at least at the earlier stage. And if the assessment defender had read Confucius, he or she might describe the pupil as learning to imitate the "master", who had authority by virtue of knowing more. This concept of authority is sometimes translated as "sapiential authority", based on the authority figure's superior knowledge and experience. In other words, the right to be heard by reason of a person's superior knowledge and experience – the "sage on the stage".

And, of course, it may be to a student's advantage to be able to show in an assessment that he or she has learned the things that a relevant authority has said need to be known, say, for entry into a profession or for recruitment or selection to a desired destination. That requirement may be subject to moral scrutiny, but if it exists, it is surely beneficial to the learner to offer an assessment opportunity to show whether he or she meets it.

None of these defences justifies abuse of power – for example, by making assessment candidates feel humiliated or belittled, or by inflicting excessive stress and causing unhappiness. Also, if we follow Kant in seeing a justification of education as developing the capacity for students to think for themselves and develop fully as free human beings, then an assessment with narrow constructs or one that feels overpowering may not contribute to that overall educational purpose. But if those abuses are avoided, it may be beneficial to learners to be able to show that they have learned what the authorities require.

The second, more specialised, challenge, has been voiced in the context of high-stakes national examinations in England but may find echoes in other national assessment systems. It relates to the approach taken by public authorities to set mark schemes[20] and grade boundaries for each examination. A reader from the United States may refer to these designs as "rubrics". The objection is to mark schemes where the design of the test – and the setting of grade boundaries – is designed to achieve a "bell curve" of outcomes, showing a range of levels of attainment across all candidates. In England, for much of the first quarter of the 21st century and for some years before that, grading of national examinations has been informed both by a statistically led attempt to achieve a spread of marks, and by defined requirements for certain grades in the mix, all in an attempt to maintain standards year-on-year – a uniquely British compromise between criterion-based and norm-based assessment.[21]

The moral challenge to this approach is that, *by design*, there will always be some candidates who get low marks. In the words of Brighouse and Waters (2021), whose book *About Our Schools* is based on interviews with a large number of actors in English education over the past decades:

> In what way is it fair to imply to pupils that their knowledge, skills and understanding will be recognised if the measure is applied not to the extent to which they meet the criteria but to a comparison with the performance of others? Do . . . parents, pupils and teachers . . . realise that pupils are not being challenged to demonstrate their learning against clear benchmarks, but are, in fact, in a race with their peers to be awarded a predetermined number of top grades?
>
> *(Brighouse & Waters, 2021, p. 210)*

In conversation with one of the authors of this book, the moral challenge was put bluntly in these terms: Statistically, most of the low achievers will be from disadvantaged backgrounds, so if their teachers tell them that they can do well if they work hard, they are telling lies. The mark scheme is designed to create failures and is, therefore, immoral – it fails to meet the necessary condition of the justification for education.

What are we to say about this challenge? First, we would remark that it should not be dismissed lightly: it is strongly felt – and voiced – by many teachers, often motivated by their experience in working with disadvantaged youngsters and wider concerns about social and economic injustice. However, in our view, there is a moral justification for providing opportunities in a mark scheme for a wide range of levels of achievement to be displayed and recognised in a grade. That justification is particularly strong for a national assessment that is intended to be taken by a large proportion of the relevant age cohort, as is the case with the GCSE in England. It is not "telling lies" for a teacher to say to individuals that if they work hard they can do well. That is a true statement. However, if in one year there was an unprecedented major improvement in aggregate performance, then, in our view, there would be a moral imperative to redesign the mark scheme to answer the challenge posed by Brighouse and Waters.

And it should be noted that this objection does not normally apply to vocational assessments or skills tests, where the sole objective is to measure the individual against competency standards. In those assessments, it would be highly unusual for the mark scheme to aim for a bell curve. If all the candidates were to demonstrate validly and reliably that they could meet the required standard, then the teacher and the assessor would be satisfied.

In this section we have explored only two of the many possible moral challenges to educational assessment, one at a high level and one aimed at a particular aspect of one assessment system. There are many more, including challenges to the uses made of assessment outcomes (e.g. in holding schools and teachers to account)[22] and questioning the fairness of assessment design and tasks set. We hope that this chapter will stimulate an analysis of more of these moral challenges. Doing that illuminates – and tests – a view of the moral strengths and vulnerabilities of assessment, and should inform policymaking.

Moral principles governing assessment practice

We have considered the moral justification of educational assessment and two of the many possible moral challenges. Neither has been a killer blow against all assessment, so we shall move on to ask what moral principles should govern assessment practice. In our view, the time is overdue for the assessment profession to follow the example of other professions by addressing this question. We referred at the beginning of this chapter to the use of "ethics" to refer to rules or principles governing a particular profession or context within a broader moral framework. In that sense, the principles we outline here are a starting point for developing "assessment ethics". We shall start by suggesting two such principles, but we hope that readers will explore this area further.

Our first suggested principle is borrowed from medical ethics – "Primum non nocere": "First do no harm". Although attributed to Hippocrates, this principle has more recently been thought to have been coined by 18th-century French medical thinkers,[23] in the context of a world where demonstrations of medical prowess were a form of show business. As adopted into medical thinking since then, the principle requires doctors to consider whether there is a risk of harm in procedures that may have justified medical aims such as diagnosing illness, repairing injury or carrying out research for wider public benefit. Considering this risk is particularly apposite for procedures that involve "invasion" of the human body. Although that principle was first applied to individual procedures carried out by doctors, it has more recently been applied to clinical policies and practices more generally.[24] It has also been cited to criticise overtreatment, defined as "interventions that do not benefit the patient, or where the risk of harm from the intervention is likely to outweigh any benefit the patient will receive".[25]

A memorable application of this principle was in the Nuremberg trials, where experiments involving subjecting prisoners to grievous harm (such as replicating battlefield injuries) were justified in well-written and referenced academic papers as producing evidence for the public good (Gaw, 2006).

What relevance does this principle have for educational assessment? By analogy with medicine, it states that even if the purposes of an assessment are morally justified, that does not justify any means of carrying out the assessment. As we have seen, it can be argued that pressurised preparation for high-stakes assessments and the processes involved in a strictly supervised examination hall (including separation from peers and taking away phones) can produce stress and anxiety for students (see, e.g. Denscombe, 2000). Meta-analyses of research suggest that higher levels of examination anxiety are associated with lower student well-being and an elevated risk of poor mental health. Examination anxiety is associated with lower examination performance, although the causes are difficult to judge. Leaving aside for now the question of whether such stress threatens the validity of educational conclusions from the examination, this situation raises the question of whether it is morally right to cause it.

One answer is that examination stress can be "good stress", helping young people to learn how to handle stress in later life (Hazell, 2019). We have sometimes referred to this view as the "cold shower theory of examinations".

But it is not persuasive. Why should educational assessments that affect people's futures be the best training ground for such skills? And we have not seen research supporting the hypothesis that those who have had to handle examination stress in traditional written examinations as youngsters have proved better able to handle other kinds of stress in adult life than those who were spared such examination stress.

Clearly, most terminal assessments need to involve some constraints on students and may require them to devote time to preparation when they would rather be doing something else. Of course, the students might themselves be glad later that they did some work instead of playing computer games. But for the assessors, the moral calculus requires a balance of risk, just as the doctor's does. As the discomfort of inserting an intravenous line comes before the benefit of the effects of the medication delivered down the line, the doctor has to calculate whether the later benefit justifies the initial discomfort. Similarly, we suggest that the assessment industry needs to ask the question of whether any harms of the assessment process itself are justified in terms of benefit for the students involved.

The concept of "overtreatment" may also be relevant to educational assessment. Many teachers and educational thinkers, when asked, will support the proposition that there is "too much assessment". Their reasons may be educational – that too much test preparation can distort and limit teaching and learning. But they may also have moral concerns. For example, in some UK countries, students aged 16–18 may have three consecutive years facing batteries of high-stakes examinations, each preceded by preparatory "mocks". Is that "overassessment"?

Our second suggested moral principle is "The context of an assessment always matters". This goes back to our understanding of morality, set out at the beginning of this chapter, in which we see morality as, by definition, the big picture. A moral judgement cannot choose to ignore uncomfortable aspects of a situation when coming to a judgement. This means seeing each assessment in context: the circumstances of the time, the background of the teachers and learners, who took the test (and who didn't), the intended use and so on.

Taking account of these factors, as distinct from finding ways to exclude them from consideration, is unfamiliar and difficult for many intellectual disciplines in educational assessment, which tend to be analytic rather than synthetic. Also, many professionals – for example, test developers or researchers who work in organisations providing tests or assessments – see their work as technical and highly specialised. Surely, they could argue, it is not reasonable to expect assessment professionals to try to make the world better each day that they go to work?

In reply, we would say that the assessment profession, collectively and individually, should be considering whether the processes in which they are involved are morally justified, taking all the contextual factors into consideration. If they are not, even if the assessments concerned are technically sound under some criteria, then we all need to consider what we can or should do about it.

Looking forward

This book is concerned with taking stock of educational assessment at the end of the first quarter of the 21st century and looking forward. But many of our references have been backward-looking – to Kant, no less, not to mention Antony Flew and other writers in the late 20th century. We have also visited some perennial philosophical questions, such as the definition of morality. Why have we included a chapter on "the moral compass"?

In our view, the second quarter of the 21st century is a ripe time to revisit some of these important moral questions and apply them to educational assessment. Techniques and technology of assessment have been moving fast, as we have described in earlier chapters, and at the time of writing, the assessment world is beginning to come to grips with the opportunities and challenges of AI. Theoretical thinking has also been on the move, with different applications of Critical Theory making their presence felt in many contexts, including education (see Chapter 4). And, as we have seen in this chapter, there is a postmodern critique of morality itself.

We have set out our understanding of morality and considered the moral justification for assessment. We have identified two of the many possible moral challenges to educational assessment and attempted to address them. We have also sought to stimulate work on moral principles governing assessment by suggesting two: First do no harm; and second, the context of an assessment always matters. Are there moral challenges that are particularly important for the mid-21st century?

As our earlier chapters have illustrated, at this time there is a huge mass of evidence available to show what students – including young children – can do and what they know. Technical means of recording learners' behaviour – science fiction in the 20th century – are now affordable and easy to use. Primary teachers talk of their 7-year-olds contributing to "show and tell" with films made on their phones. So, what evidence from this pile is it morally right to use to make assessment judgements? And what processes are morally justified to obtain that evidence?

These questions need to be explored morally as well as educationally. It would clearly be morally wrong as well as educationally inappropriate to use information that did not support a valid conclusion. The moral arguments against such an approach might be that it involved some kind of deceit in the reported conclusions, or that it was unfair to use this evidence as a basis for a conclusion (such as a "grade") that benefitted some candidates at the expense of others, for construct-irrelevant reasons. But what about the processes involved? Are there moral considerations regarding learners' rights to privacy and "safe" learning spaces? And what about the scope for malpractice and cheating?

In 1998, Messick wrote:

> The primary measurement standards that must be met to legitimize a proposed test use are those of reliability, validity, and fairness, *which are also value-laden concepts*.
>
> *(emphasis added) (Messick, 1998, p. 1, 2000; see also Black & Wiliam, 2009)*

We leave the application of the moral compass with questions: Is validity a moral concept? What is morally wrong with invalidity? Or unreliability? What assessment processes are morally justifiable in the 21st century, with so much information available and so much information causing harm? We opened this chapter with Steven Lukes' question of whether "universal morality" is a "pre-post-modern illusion". We conclude that moral issues are timely and relevant to educational assessment in the mid-21st century.

Notes

1 Meta-ethics is concerned with the meaning of moral judgements, such as calling something right or wrong, rather than with what is actually right or wrong (Ross Harrison in the Oxford Companion to Philosophy, 1995).
2 We are indebted to Ben Colburn for drawing our attention to the relevance of Ross's distinction here.
3 For example, in the Scottish "Curriculum for Excellence" at https://education.gov.scot/curriculum-for-excellence/curriculum-areas/religious-and-moral-education/
4 At p. 80 of Paton's translation in *The Moral Law*.
5 The concept of "universalizability" is set out in Kant's *Groundwork of the Metaphysics of Morals* (1785/1993).
6 Russell, "Reply to Criticisms" *RoE*: 149/*Papers* 11: 51 ("Russell on Ethics", ed Charles Pigden, London, Routledge, 1999).
7 https://fairtest.org/get-involved-opting-out/
8 *Ode on Intimations of Immortality*, from *Recollections of Early Childhood*.
9 "Another Brick in the Wall" (including "Hey, teacher, leave them kids alone").
10 See, for example, UNESCO, 18 January 2023: "Let girls and women in Afghanistan learn" www.unesco.org/en/articles/let-girls-and-women-afghanistan-learn
11 https://commonslibrary.parliament.uk/research-briefings/sn01078/
12 www.globaldata.com/data-insights/macroeconomic/expenditure-on-education-as-a-of-gdp-in-the-united-states/
13 See https://data.oecd.org/eduresource/public-spending-on-education.htm#indicator-chart. For the UK, see https://ifs.org.uk/microsite/education-spending
14 What is the difference between training and education? (edubrite.com) www.edubrite.com/training-and-education
15 House of Commons Education Committee. (2011). Participation by 16–19-year-olds in education and training: Government Response to the Committee's Fourth Report.

Eight Special Report of Session 2010–12. Ordered by the House of Commons to be printed 26 October 2011.
16 Why is education important and how does it affect one's future? World Vision. 29 August 2023. www.worldvision.ca/stories/education/why-is-education-important#
17 See, for example, Grant Wiggins, "A Diploma Worth Having", Educational Leadership, March 2011.
18 There is a more technical argument about rank ordering (or use of comparisons between candidates) as a means to achieving more valid assessment outcomes (see, for example, Bramley & Oates, 2011). However, our point here is that the *aim* of providing a rank order is not justified by Flew's argument from sincerity.
19 For example, in his *Personal Knowledge* (1958).
20 Mark schemes are statements that set out the knowledge or skills that must be demonstrated to gain a particular mark.
21 A controversial application of this approach ("comparable outcomes") is examined in Benton (2016). There is also a short explanatory guide by Pearson at https://qualifications.pearson.com/content/dam/pdf/GCSE/support-documents/Comparable-Outcomes-a-Guide.pdf
22 For a comparison of international practice in this regard, see Meyer and Benevot (2013).
23 See Herranz (2002).
24 In the UK, the General Medical Council and the Medical Schools Council provided guidance applying the principle to undergraduate medical education, at www.gmc-uk.org/-/media/documents/first-do-no-harm-patient-safety-in-undergrad-education-final_pdf-62483215.pdf
25 A classic statement of principles, including this one, is in Beauchamp and Childress (2001).

References

Alderson, C. J. (1999, May). Testing is too important to be left to testers. *Plenary address to the third annual conference on current trends in English language testing*. United Arab Emirates University, Al Ain and Zayed University, Dubai Campus.
Aristotle. (2009). *Nichomachean ethics* (c330 BCE) (D. Ross, Trans.; L. Brown, Ed.). Oxford World's Classics.
Bauman, Z. (1993). *Postmodern ethics*. Blackwell.
Beauchamp, T. L., & Childress, J. F. (2001). *Principles of biomedical ethics*. Oxford University Press.
Benton, T. (2016). Comparable outcomes: Scourge or scapegoat? *Cambridge assessment research report*. Cambridge Assessment. 344467-comparable-outcomes-scourge-or-scapegoat-tom-benton.pdf (cambridgeassessment.org.uk).
Black, P., & Wiliam, D. (1998). Inside the black box: Raising standards through classroom assessment. *Phi Delta Kappan, 80*, 139–148. www.jstor.org/stable/20439383
Black, P., & Wiliam, D. (2009). Developing the theory of formative assessment. *Educational Assessment, Evaluation and Accountability, 21*(1), 5–31.
Blackburn, S. (1993). *Essays in quasi-realism*. Oxford University Press.
Bramley, T., & Oates, T. (2011, January). Rank ordering and paired comparisons – the way Cambridge Assessment is using them in operational and experimental work. *Cambridge Assessment, Research Matters*, (11). https://doi.org/10.17863/CAM.100519
Brighouse, T., & Waters, M. (2021). *About our schools*. Crown House Publishing Limited.
Convention on the Rights of the Child. (1989). Treaty no. 27531. *United Nations Treaty Series, 1577*, pp. 3–178. https://treaties.un.org/doc/Treaties/1990/09/19900902%2003-14%20AM/Ch_IV_11p.pdf

Dearden, R. (1984). Education and training. *Westminster Studies in Education*, 7(1), 57–66. https://doi.org/10.1080/0140672840070104

Denscombe, M. (2000). Social conditions for stress: Young people's experience of doing GCSEs. *British Educational Research Journal*, 26(3), 359–374. http://doi.org/10.1080/713651566

Downie, R. S. (1964). *Government action and morality in the democratic state*. Macmillan.

Flew, A. (1976). *Sociology, equality and education*. Macmillan.

Foucault, M. (1975). *Discipline and punish: The birth of the prison* (A. Sheridan, Trans.). Allen Lane, 1977. Penguin Books, 1979, 1991. Penguin Classics, 2000.

Gaw, A. (2006, April). Beyond consent: The potential for atrocity. *Journal of the Royal Society of Medicine*, 99(4), 175–177.

Habermas, J. (1990). Discourse ethics: Notes on a program of philosophical justification. In *Moral consciousness and communicative action*. MIT Press.

Hand, M. (2017). *A theory of moral education*. Routledge. https://doi.org/10.4324/9781315708508

Hare, R. M. (1952). *The language of morals*. Oxford University Press.

Hare, R. M. (1963). *Freedom and reason*. Oxford University Press.

Hare, R. M. (1981). *Moral thinking: Its levels, method and point*. Clarendon Press.

Harrison, R. (1995). *The Oxford companion to philosophy* (T. Honderich, Ed.). Oxford University Press.

Hazell, W. (2019, January 25). Exclusive: "High stress" in exams is good, says exam board chief. But Cambridge Assessment's Saul Nassé also admits exam stress is a "live concern right around the world". *Times Educational Supplement (TES) Magazine*. www.tes.com/magazine/archive/exclusive-high-stress-exams-good-says-exam-board-chief

Herranz, G. (2002, June 15). Why the Hippocratic ideals are dead. *BMJ*, 324. https://doi.org/10.1136/bmj.324.7351.1463

Hirst, P. H. (1975). *Moral education in a secular society* (2nd ed.). Hodder Arnold H&S.

House of Commons Education Committee. (2011, October 26). Participation by 16–19 year olds in education and training: Government response to the committee's fourth report. *Eight special report of session 2010–12*. Ordered by the House of Commons to be Printed.

Illich, I. (1971). *Deschooling society*. Marion Boyars Publishers Ltd.

Kant, I. (1776–1784). Lectures on Pedagogy, published online by Cambridge University Press (2013). See also Kant (1900). Kant on Education (über Pädagogik). Translated by Annette Churton. With an Introduction by C. A. Poley Rhys Davids. D.C. Heath & Co.

Kant, I. (1785). *Groundwork of the metaphysic of morals* (H. J. Paton, Trans.). The Moral Law, 1948. Hutchinson.

Kant, I. (2007). Lectures on pedagogy (R. B. Louden, Trans.). In G. Zöller & R. B. Louden (Eds.), *Anthropology, history, and education* (pp. 434–485). Cambridge University Press (Päd, AA 09: 443).

Keiner, E. (2002). Education between academic discipline and profession in Germany after World War II. *European Educational Research Journal*, 1(1), 83–98. https://doi.org/10.2304/eerj.2002.1.1.14

Kitchen, W. H. (2014). *Authority and the teacher*. Bloomsbury Academic.

Klein, S. P., Hamilton, L. S., McCaffrey, D. F., & Stetcher, B. M. (2000). *What do test scores in Texas tell us?* The RAND Corporation.

Linn, R. L. (2000). Assessments and accountability. *Educational Researcher*, 29(2), 4–16.

Lukes, S. (1995). Moral diversity and relativism. *Journal of Philosophy of Education*, 29(2), 173–179. https://doi.org/10.1111/j.1467-9752.1995.tb00351.x

MacIntyre, A. (1981). *After virtue*. University of Notre Dame Press.

Mason, M. (2001). The ethics of integrity: Educational values beyond postmodern ethics. *Journal of Philosophy of Education*, 35(1), 47–69. https://doi.org/10.1111/1467-9752.00209

McLaughlin, T. H., & Halstead, J. M. (2000). John Wilson on moral education. *Journal of Moral Education*, 29(3), 247–268. http://doi.org/10.1080/03057240050137328

Messick, S. (1998). Consequences of test interpretation and use: The fusion of validity and values in psychological assessment. *ETS Research Report RR-98-48*. https://www.ets.org/research/policy_research_reports/publications/report/1998/ihem.html

Messick, S. (2000). Consequences of test interpretation and use: The fusion of validity and values in psychological assessment. In R. D. Goffin & E. Helmes (Eds.), *Problems and solutions in human assessment: Honoring Douglas N. Jackson at seventy* (pp. 3–20). Kluwer Academic Publishers.

Meyer, H.-D., & Benavot, A. (2013). PISA and the globalization of education governance: Some puzzles and problems. In H.-D. Meyer & A. Benavot (Eds.), *PISA, power, and policy: Oxford studies in comparative education* (pp. 7–26). Symposium Books.

Newton, P. E. (2007). Clarifying the purposes of educational assessment. *Assessment in Education: Principles, Policy & Practice*, 14(2), 149–170. https://doi.org/10.1080/09695940701478321

Polanyi, M. (1958). *Personal knowledge: Towards a post-critical philosophy*. Routledge & Kegan Paul.

Putwain, D. W., & Daly, A. L. (2014). Test anxiety prevalence and gender differences in a sample of English secondary school students. *Educational Studies*, 40(5), 554–570.

Ross, W. D. (1930). *The right and the good*. Clarendon Press (New edition, 2003).

Russell, B. A. W. (1999). *'Reply to criticisms' RoE: 149/papers 11: 51. "Russell on ethics"* (C. Pigden, Ed.). Routledge.

Tuhiwai Smith, L. (2022). *Decolonizing methodologies: Research and indigenous peoples*. Bloomsbury Academic.

Wallace, G., & Walker, A. D. M. (Eds.). (1970). *The definition of morality* (1st ed.). Routledge. https://doi.org/10.4324/9781003051961.

White, J. (1999). Thinking about Assessment. *Journal of Philosophy of Education*, 33(2), 201–212.

White, J. (2005, July). Reassessing 1960s philosophy of the curriculum. *London Review of Education*, 3(2), 131–144. http://doi.org/10.1080/14748460500163914

Wiggins, G. (2011). A diploma worth having. *Educational Leadership*, 68(6), 28–33. www.ascd.org/publications/educational-leadership/mar11/vol68/num06/A-Diploma-Worth-Having.aspx

Williams, B. (1985). *Ethics and the limits of philosophy*. Routledge (Taylor and Francis) (New edition, 2011).

Winch, W., & Gingell, J. (1999). *Key concepts in the philosophy of education*. Routledge.

World Vision. (2023, August 29). *Why is education important and how does it affect one's future?* www.worldvision.ca/stories/education/why-is-education-important#

7
LESSONS LEARNED AND THE PATH AHEAD

At the beginning of this book, we recalled the millennium celebrations and thinking about them. We referred to Caroline Gipps's *Beyond Testing*, written in 1994, which she described as "an attempt to reconceptualise assessment in education in the 1990s" (p. 1). It is well worth revisiting in full the words that we quoted from her first page:

> There has been over the last decade an explosion of developments in assessment and a number of key actors have been reconceptualising the issues. The aim of this book is to bring together much of this work to discuss and synthesize it in an attempt to further our understandings and practice in educational assessment: to develop the theory of educational assessment.
>
> *(Gipps, 1994, p. 1)*

A quarter of a century on, this book is a fresh attempt to discuss and synthesise developments and thinking about society, education and assessment. In this concluding chapter, we recall the main lessons from the earlier chapters, and we set out our proposed path ahead for educational assessment, both in theory and in practice.

Lessons learned

For Chapters 2–6, we selected examples from developments and thinking about education and assessment in the early 21st century. We could have selected many others, and several of those we have discussed deserve a book of their own. There is a danger of oversimplifying contrasts between the last century and this. Few, if any, of the 21st-century developments that we have described were new (perhaps with the exception of generative AI). In education, there was much debate throughout the previous century about knowledge, learning and assessment. Aspects of assessment, such as intelligence testing, were highly controversial and links with wider societal issues were identified and explored. Fairer use of assessment was one of the themes pursued by anti-discrimination campaigners in the second half of the 20th century. And on the negative side, links between some kinds of testing and eugenics had such horrendous associations in the mid-century that they have remained taboo ever since. Critical theory, which we discuss in Chapter 4, can arguably be traced back to ideas in American pragmatism at the end of the 19th century. Even the Covid-19 pandemic, which came as such a shock to so many of us, had been planned for in most countries (although perhaps not really expected) and was prefigured in the Spanish flu outbreak a century before. And the authorities cited in our previous chapters include Plato and Kant.

However, in our view, the first quarter of the 21st century has seen changes in priorities and in the underlying feelings reflected in public and academic discourse about society and education. In 2023, Gordon Brown and his co-authors wrote:

> There's no scarcity of evidence that old assumptions must go. The world is tilting from one divided between manual and non-manual workers to an era where the real division is between the education-poor and the education-rich.
>
> *(Brown et al., 2023, p. 10)*

Over and above the developments described in this book, events such as the terrorist attack on the USA on 11 September 2001 ("9/11") and the economic downturn of 2008 (the "Great Recession"),[1] together with the increasingly bitter cultural divides in much academic and public discourse, have called a check on some of the millennial assumptions about worldwide linear progress, international cooperation and the purposes of education and schooling.

Twenty-two years after the optimistic speech by Bill Clinton, which we quoted at the beginning of this book, *Collins Dictionary*'s Word of the Year was "permacrisis", defined as "the feeling of living through a period of war, inflation, and political instability".[2] The famous line from Yeats: "Things fall apart; the centre cannot hold" (W. B. Yeats, 1920, first stanza, line 3) has been used (changed to the past tense) as the title of a popular UK podcast about culture wars.[3] Turning to education, if it ever was defensible to assume a consensus in thinking about the purposes of education, learning and testing, it certainly isn't now.

In Chapter 2 ("Developments in education and assessment"), we trace some of the changes in views by policymakers and commentators about the kinds of knowledge and skills that are important for the 21st century, ranging from basic numeracy, literacy and IT user skills to the so-called 21st-century skills such as collaboration, critical thinking and working in teams, and increased interest in the importance of affective traits and emotional intelligence. These raise questions of how – or, indeed, whether – such attributes should be assessed and the role of any such assessments in supporting, and reflecting, best practice in teaching. They also question one of the main assumptions behind most received practice in educational assessment – that it is always (or almost always) individuals who are being assessed.

Chapter 2 also charts the rise of the "Assessment for Learning" ("AfL") movement, which has been more influential, and for longer, in some countries than in others. It does seem to have helped to raise the profile of formative uses of assessment and focused attention on the essential feedback loop linking assessment to teaching and learning. We welcome that trend, and we strongly endorse the objective of the AfL pioneers to promote policymaking based on evidence and making use of research. We hope that this book will help to provide routes for policymakers to be guided to evidence and research relevant to current concerns. However, AfL has had less of an impact on thinking about assessment which is primarily used for summative purposes. In our view, it is time for a similar re-think, but focused on assessments involving a summative judgement of the knowledge and skills of the learner.

Chapter 2 also contains the first of several references in this book to the rise of generative AI – arguably the most spectacular and fast-moving technological change in the 2020s. The questions raised for assessment are frequently debated, but no less important for that: What are the implications for the knowledge and skills that are needed for learning and the world of work and for how they should be assessed? What part (if any) should AI play in the production by learners of evidence for assessment? Is there a new (or differently presented) need to ensure the integrity of work produced for assessment and how should that be done? Could the role of assessor be taken over by AI? Might it do a better job than human assessors do? Or is it a threat to the professionalism of teachers and assessors?

AI is already a major part of the context in which much teaching and learning takes place, and it will rapidly become even more so. This will require an open-minded rethinking of many of the constructs and methods of assessment, as well as of approaches to teaching. It would be naive to ignore or underestimate the risks to the integrity and security of the evidence submitted for assessment. But we have some sympathy with the view that AI has drawn attention to issues around integrity and honesty in assessment that were there before AI and are long overdue to be considered more rigorously and arguably more realistically. In October 2023, Stanford University reported:

> For years, long before [generative AI] hit the scene, some 60 to 70 percent of students have reported engaging in at least one "cheating" behavior during the previous month. That percentage has stayed about the same or even decreased slightly in our 2023 surveys, when we added questions specific to new AI technologies . . . and how students are using [them] for school assignments.[4]

In Chapter 3 ("New priorities and an unexpected shock"), we considered two issues that were long-standing but had risen in priority and attention in the first quarter of the 21st century – climate change and well-being. Each has implications for education – notably for curriculum as well as assessment – and there is a link between the two, with increasing references to "ecoanxiety", particularly in young people (Clayton et al., 2017). The implications for the curriculum as experienced by learners of all ages range well beyond formal schooling, but there are questions about the designed curriculum as taught in schools. How much (if at all) should climate change feature in the teaching of "subjects", such as geography, history, biology or literature? Or should the subjects – which structure so much of the curriculum for older children, if less so for their younger siblings – be combined when addressing climate change? Climate change does seem particularly suited to interdisciplinary study. That means that time needs to be provided for such study – perhaps at the cost of some more detailed subject-specific work – and it should be reflected in the tasks required for assessments, which are regarded by students and others as important. Assessing project work on interdisciplinary subjects may raise technical challenges regarding the setting of assessment criteria and applying them consistently, but these challenges need to be recognised and met. And there is a need to pay attention to the unspoken messages given to young people by the way assessments are carried out. What will they think of a project report on climate change that is required to be submitted on paper and then driven in a petrol-fuelled van to a marking centre?

The importance of well-being also raises questions for assessment. The first is whether it is necessary or appropriate to assess well-being and, if so, how to do that. We suggested that there might be lessons from the techniques drawn up in medicine to diagnose multi-factorial conditions. There is also a long-standing problem with assessment: how to assess emotions. How do we know what the person being assessed "really" feels? And is it right to seek to do so? Furthermore, should we assume that well-being is best assessed at the individual or group level? We suggest that both may be appropriate, though very little has been written in the realm of educational assessment about assessing groups,[5] or about how any such assessments should be used.

The shock of the Covid-19 pandemic showed up in a sharper focus on existing problems affecting education and educational assessment, notably inequalities in access to learning. We discussed the reactions in many countries to the perceived practical impossibility, during pandemic restrictions, of carrying out high-stakes assessments in the customary way. The jury is out on whether the improvisation in assessment that some countries felt they had to make in quick time will have a lasting effect – for example, persuading risk-averse assessment organisations and national governments to make greater use of technology.

In Chapter 4 ("Changes to thinking about society"), we looked at theoretical challenges from critical theories, and in particular, from Critical Race Theory (CRT). It is important to note here that the founding papers for CRT arose from a realisation by legal academics in the USA that the anti-discrimination movement in the late 20th century had not succeeded in reducing inequality and injustice. That led to challenges to the theoretical basis of a long succession of anti-discrimination measures aiming for "color-blind" judgements and spelling out in legal instruments and guidance detailed processes to exclude racial bias.

Many of the instruments rejected by the critical race theorists are familiar to educational assessment. The late 20th century has seen much development of good assessment practice involving scrutiny of tests before and after they are taken to try to exclude, or at least minimise, bias reflecting construct-irrelevant factors such as race (AERA et al., 2014; Qualifications Wales/CCEA, 2019). And yet, racial and socio-economic inequalities in achievement persist and arguably have worsened in recent years rather than being reduced. That raises the question of whether assessment thinkers need to step back and question their assumptions, just as the US legal academics did when developing CRT.

One answer to our question might be that the persisting inequalities and injustices are not the "fault" of education, let alone of educational assessment, but reflect wider problems in society. To that, we would respond that the same answer could have been given to the CRT legal academics about the law. We would argue, as they do, that educational assessment is part of an interlocking tapestry of factors, each influencing the others – a situation recognised by the critical theorists in their concept of "intersectionality". Assessment has its part to play in social change, and its interrelationship with other factors cannot be set aside. A further counterargument is that assessment should not be about bringing about social change but about measuring it accurately. We would challenge the distinction expressed in that view between having an active role in society and measurement. Tests, examinations and assessments have a huge influence on learners' life chances.

Chapter 4 also contained two case studies – about the convoluted attempts in US law to allow or outlaw race-conscious college admissions policies and about decolonising the university curriculum in the UK. They have implications for what is assessed, how assessments are done and how the results of assessments are used. All the examples discussed in Chapter 4 are controversial, and we expect that readers will reject some of the positions taken, as we do. However, we do argue here that there are important theoretical challenges to the assumptions that "blindness" to context can be justified at any stage in education or educational assessment.

Chapter 5 ("Changes to thinking about education and assessment"), discussed trends in thinking about the purposes of education and learning theory. We charted the development of constructivist views of learning and challenges to these views, including a revival of support for "knowledge", with the related concept of "powerful knowledge". We observe here in passing that, contrary to the accusations of some opponents of "powerful knowledge", its champions are motivated by concern about the context in which teaching and learning take place. Their contention is that teaching (often subject-specific) knowledge rather than an emphasis on generic skills enables disadvantaged young people to have successful lives.

However, we do criticise some of the arguments used both by the knowledge – revivalists and by their opponents. And we criticise two common dichotomies – between knowledge and skills and between generic and subject-specific knowledge. In our view, the extremes on both sides of those dichotomies are wrong and misleading. Most skills involve knowledge ("knowing why" as well as "knowing how"), and bringing together insights from different disciplines into generic understanding requires the learner to have insights to bring together.

Chapter 5 also discussed the impact on our thinking of the increased emphasis on "competence" as an objective of education, and the challenges from "big data", as well as from generative AI. There are significant feedback loops linking how we conceptualise assessment with the capabilities made possible by technological advances. Our ideas about assessment influence the uses we seek from technology, but technologists can present assessment options that were not before available in a way that demanded that they be taken seriously by educationists.

Chapter 6 applied the "moral compass". We argued that it was time to revisit questions about the moral justification of education and of educational assessment. Taking a position on these is an essential prelude to considering the purposes of assessment – and, we suggested, for developing and applying the concept of validity in assessment. If there is no moral justification for assessing at all then such discussions are null and void. Challenges from descriptions of the early 21st century as being in "moral crisis" also need to be considered. We took a broadly Kantian view of the justification of education and derived a justification of assessment. Readers may disagree, but all theoretical thinkers about educational assessment need to consider their own position on these issues. We then proceeded to consider two possible moral challenges to assessment.

We concluded Chapter 6 by contending that the big moral questions facing assessment in the mid-21st century were twofold: "What evidence about learners, from the large amount now available from different sources, is it morally right to use to make educational assessments" and "What processes are morally justified to obtain that evidence?" We offered some suggestions of moral principles to inform assessment practice, but these are no more than initial examples, and more work is needed to identify and advocate relevant moral principles and to apply them to the practical realities of assessment.

Chapters 2 6 have yielded many lessons for assessment, and it may be rash to generalise from such a wide survey. However, we suggest three important linking themes. The first – perhaps the most important lesson to be learned from the critical theorists – is that context always matters. Context determines views on the purposes and practicalities of education. Continual attention to context means challenging approaches to teaching, learning or assessment that seek to disregard context. As we shall see later in this chapter, this is a difficult message for some traditional approaches to assessment.

The second lesson is about the tension between constructs for assessment that are deemed relevant to the 21st century and traditional methods of assessment. The manifestation of this tension depends on the view taken about knowledge, skills and competences required for education in the decades ahead, and we have challenged some of the distinctions and concepts in those arguments. But the tension remains for many of the developments we have discussed, which have prompted the question "How can we assess *that*?"

The third lesson is the challenge of all these developments to the traditional caution and risk-nervousness of the assessment world, particularly those authorities and organisations concerned with summative assessments, which have great importance for the futures of those who sit them. We referred in Chapter 2 to wildly over-optimistic predictions by a lead regulator in England that most high-stakes examinations taken by 16-year olds in England would be taken online in the first decade of the 21st century. Very few are taken almost twenty years after the predicted date.[6]

There are good reasons for caution about change. Few parents want their children's assessments-that-really-matter to be novel or seen as experimental. Public confidence is important, and users of assessment outcomes, such as qualifications, need to understand and respect them. However, the result can be that assessment "limps along", to use Vicki Phillips' words (2024). And if the world changes but assessment does not, there are increasing threats to validity.

The path ahead

Tensions between approaches to assessment

We have stated in our comments on the "Assessment for Learning" movement that, in our view, it is time to take stock in a similar way on summative assessment, particularly those assessments that can influence the life chances of those who take them.

In our view, the developments and ideas that we have discussed in this book point to an underlying tension between two approaches to assessment. The first, which is common to much thinking and practice in the psychometric tradition and which is familiar in highly regulated assessments such as national examinations in the UK, can be labelled as "analytic and narrow". Assessments are tightly defined and quality controlled. Test items are scrutinised in advance for validity and absence of construct-irrelevant bias. All candidates take the test at the same time and answer the same questions, or have the same options (with adjustments to make tasks for candidates with disabilities as similar as possible). Criteria for marking/scoring are detailed, and there are processes of standardisation to ensure that they are applied in the same way to all. Markers do not take account of the context in which individuals or groups of candidates took the test and importance is given to distinguishing between the performances of candidates. There is an emphasis on reliability and consistency and the assessments are often perceived as fair – in the sense that all candidates are treated the same in relevant respects[7] – and often command public confidence. This approach is particularly good for assessments that are used to decide between applicants for a highly competitive benefit, such as a top job or a high-prestige university course.

The second possible approach, which is less familiar in the traditions referred to in the previous paragraph, can be described as "synthetic and wide". Its aim is to make evidence-based judgements on each candidate to produce as rich and informative an account of them as possible. Different kinds or amounts of evidence may be available for each candidate. Context can be taken into account at all stages – marking is not "blind" – and assessors may take into account the (different) circumstances in which the evidence was produced. The evidence submitted may include portfolios, which enable individuals to show what they can do (Walland & Shaw, 2022). This approach may be seen as good for validity, but less good for reliability and definitely poor on comparability. There are question marks about perceived (relational) fairness and public confidence. However, it can be particularly helpful for such purposes as identifying people who would benefit from a particular college course or looking for the right person for a particular job.

The comparative strengths of the two approaches are illustrated in this story, in which two university admissions officers meet:

Jim and Sheila meet in the bar

Jim and Sheila are attending a conference for university admissions officers. Over a drink they compare the problems of their respective jobs. Jim is in charge of selection for a medical school, which is in high demand. "The next few weeks are going to be really stressful", he says. "We have to select 20 for the course out of a long list of 100 applicants with excellent grades in national examinations. I have to make sure that the medics involved in the selection follow the criteria to the letter and that the evidence considered for each applicant is exactly the same. I am the one who has to answer the letters of complaint from the parents of unsuccessful candidates. That is so hard, when the lifetime ambitions of their sons and daughters have been ruined. At least I can say that the grades that the applicants presented were strictly comparable and validated by a regulator, and the processes we followed were rigorous and fair".

"I'm having a difficult time too", says Sheila, who works at a less prestigious university but one that has a strong reputation for offering life-changing opportunities to students from disadvantaged backgrounds. "I have targets for recruiting to our courses, but we need to try to find students who have the potential to benefit from the course, to complete it and get a degree. Many of them have not got good grades in the national examinations – or are now much older than when they took them – and we don't have as much recent information about them as we would like. We want examples of what they know and what they can do. It doesn't matter if the sources of the information differ from student to student. Without that our offers are sometimes really no more than ill-informed guesses. And if we lose students who can't cope with the demands of our courses, we are denounced for having poor completion rates. Recently I heard a rumour that we might be fined because too many students were dropping out of our courses – or that we might even be closed down. So my job's on the line because assessment doesn't give me enough information about our students".

Despite the difficulties involved, in our view, assessment in the mid-21st century should move from the analytic towards the synthetic approach. As we have illustrated, the analytic approach is good for the selection for highly competitive goods, such as entry into medical school. We acknowledge that in those circumstances, strict comparability may be required. But such highly competitive selections are comparatively few. Many college and university courses are described as "recruiting" rather than "selecting" students, and in our view, thinking about assessment has been skewed by the underlying assumption that the purpose of selection for a limited good is the paradigm on which norms and models for all assessment should be built.

Defenders of the importance (or even prevalence) of selection as a purpose of assessment[8] may argue, against us, that even where there is less competition for some university or college courses, it remains important to have a means of discriminating between those who want places on the course. If it is not possible to use applicants' end-of-school assessment results to do that, it might be necessary to impose an additional entrance test, which would simply move the problems we have raised from one assessment to another. Alternatively, the first year of a post-school course might be used as a kind of test bed, with large numbers dropping out after a year.[9] All of these options raise problems.

To some extent this is an empirical question of how recruitment for university or college courses is done in practice. Even in countries such as the UK, where the total number of home-based entrants to universities is lower than the total number of applicants,[10] there are still universities that do not meet their recruitment targets. We suggest that the cultural dominance of some highly selective university courses – at the same time as attempts have been made, for good reasons, to try to unify the assessments and qualifications taken by young people at the end of compulsory schooling – may have had the effect of skewing the approach to assessments-for-all to reflect the values of selection-for-a-few.

Linked to this may be an unstated wider assumption that discrimination between the performance of test-takers is the primary purpose of all assessment. That is sometimes expressed by seeing the desired expression of assessment outcomes in terms of rank-orders of candidates. We accept that there are contexts where such rank-ordering may be seen as necessary. An example might be the US Medical College Admissions Test (MCAT),[11] which shortlists applicants from a field of over 85,000 each year. However, in our view, it is always necessary to ask the question "Why does it matter how well candidates have done *compared with other candidates*?" It may be more important to find out what individuals know or can do.

There are four possible counterarguments to our position. The first is that rank-ordering of candidates can be a good method of defining standards of assessment more precisely. It is common practice to compare scripts at around the same level as a means of deciding on a grade boundary. Recent interest in marking systems using "matched pairs" (see, e.g. Coe & Kime, 2013; Bavarian et al., 2013; Rosenbaum, 1986) can be justified in these terms, and we have no problem with suggestions that rank-ordering is a means to an end. Our argument is with those who suggest that rank-ordering is an end in itself.

The second counterargument is that the wider, synthetic approach may be suitable for some contexts, such as non-competitive selection for college courses, but it is less suitable for others, such as state or national examinations or tests for professional qualifications, where there is a requirement for relational fairness and comparability. In reply to this, we accept that an element of comparability in the meaning and interpretation of information from assessments about individuals is desirable for national or state assessments and for meeting the requirements of professional bodies for licences to practise. However, a balance needs to be struck between those requirements and the importance of enabling candidates to show the full extent of what they can do. And some professions, such as medicine, are putting more emphasis on attributes that are difficult to assess in the narrow/analytic tradition. For example, the Medical Schools Council in the UK lists attributes that those who want to be doctors should be able to demonstrate. Their list includes "honesty", "teamwork", "treating others with respect" and "empathy".[12]

The third counterargument is a defence of the centrality of "discrimination" in assessment. The objector might say that all assessment should be about discrimination – discriminating between those who meet the required assessment objectives or standards and those who do not. Our reply is that this objection is really a linguistic point about what the object of discrimination is. Assessments where all candidates are expected to meet the standard (e.g. an assessment of whether all the children in a class are able to swim for at least 10 yards) involve making a judgement on whether the requirement can be met by each child. But the primary objective is not to distinguish between the children, but rather to find out whether each child can swim. And an assessment involving a single candidate requires judgements on whether the standard has been met. There are examples in most countries of national or state examinations for highly specialised minority subjects, where it is not uncommon to have a single candidate. And the assessment of a single candidate is a common experience for those who assess postgraduate work at the doctorate level. The objector might claim that these assessment judgements are implicit comparisons between the single candidate and hypothetical other candidates who might score differently against the assessment objectives. However, it seems bizarre to us to claim that the primary purpose of assessment is to compare candidates with people who do not exist – ghosts in the examination room.

In our view, the strongest counterargument to our approach is the fourth: that it can create a new kind of inequality. In *Our Kids: The American Dream in Crisis*, Robert Putnam (2015) illustrates, drawing on examples from his own hometown, how many more opportunities rich kids have than their poorer contemporaries to gain wider experience, outside school as well as inside, and develop rich portfolio material to champion their progress (Putnam, 2015). Rich kids can obtain (and afford) unpaid internships with their father's friends and are more likely to be members of sports clubs and voluntary associations.

In the USA, after a period when many universities rejected the use of tests such as the SAT in selecting undergraduate entrants, on the grounds of lack of equity (particularly between races) in test outcomes, there are recent signs that the tests may be staging something of a comeback. In February 2024, Yale announced that it was reverting to including results from a range of standardised tests (not just the SAT) to be presented by applicants. Tellingly, they said that they had concluded that "inviting students to apply without *any* test scores can, inadvertently, disadvantage students from low-income, first-generation, and rural backgrounds" [emphasis in original].[13]

We think that the danger of creating a new kind of inequality through diversity of assessment sources is an important one, but it is not decisive. The challenge to education is to widen the opportunities for all to provide the rich information that assessment should be seeking. This should not exclude information provided by highly controlled tests, particularly, as Yale has discovered, where it provides a balancing factor against inequalities presented by other forms of evidence. It would be pointless – and wrong – to try to narrow assessment to a common denominator, excluding the areas of advantage for the rich (or for particular ethnic groups). As well as being self-defeating, such an enterprise would risk increasingly taking assessment away from factors that are most important for the needs of the 21st century.

Reviewing the theoretical assessment model

We contend that assessment theoreticians will need to develop a new approach to the "assessment argument". This is a way of modelling the journey from obtaining evidence, evaluating it against rubrics (or criteria) and producing a "claim", or outcome, usually related to a student's learning, or to their demonstrated performance. The journey from evidence to claim is the argument. Gorin argues that the clarity, coherence and plausibility of an (assessment) argument are fundamentally a function of the evidence used to support the argument (Gorin, 2012, p. 3; see also, Kane, 2013).

Mislevy (2012), in a paper for the Gordon Commission on the Future of Assessment in Education, outlined four metaphors required for understanding assessment, one of which was the metaphor of assessment as an evidentiary argument about students' learning and abilities based on their behaviour in particular circumstances.[14] Since the turn of the century, the educational assessment argument has been increasingly conceived of as a "special case of evidentiary reasoning, which in turn is a special case of argument" (Mislevy, 2018, p. x): an assessment being a form of evidential argument about students' learning and abilities given their behaviour in particular circumstances (Gorin, 2012; Mislevy, 2012).

Gorin (2012, 2014) argues that assessments able to draw upon multiple, more novel evidence sources derived from richly situated learning environments offer a more fully developed articulation of "assessment". Such assessments, Gorin contends, will enhance the capacity to make more valid and accurate decisions about student learning and pedagogy. The kinds of unconventional data that can potentially contribute to an assessment argument, listed in Gorin (2012) and elsewhere, include the use of digitally enhanced assessments that reinforce assessment arguments by generating a task environment that elicits skills and processes designed to reflect 21st-century thinking – for example, student engagement, motivation, opportunity-to-learn and sociocultural experiences. The use of psycho-sensory data has the potential to measure student engagement and attention during the learning and testing experience (Sanchez et al., 2011). More recently, the utility of physiological data is being explored, such as eye tracking, which can provide detailed information on respondent gaze in assessment that can be used to inform test design and the analysis of test performance and validity (Bax, 2013; Oranje et al., 2018; Maddox et al., 2018). Video-ethnography can involve recording students in test-taker environments and observing their behaviours and interactions.

For the reasons stated earlier in this section, we support the view of Gorin (and others) that the evidence used as the basis of the assessment argument should be widened to include the kinds of rich data that will contribute to a more informed view of the individual. We also agree that new developments in providing ways of obtaining information about learners' motivation and feelings may be relevant and important, although we feel strongly that rigorous ethical guidelines would be required for the use of psycho-sensory data and techniques such as eye-tracking. Would the reader want their son or daughter to attend a school where their eyes were traced for assessment purposes?

In our view, thinking about the assessment argument will need to be extended to embrace the relevance of *context* at all stages. Context should be able to affect the evidence used, the rules or warrants applied to it, the resulting claim and the way that it is used. Despite the interesting thinking by Gorin and others about novel sources of evidence, the formulation of the argument needs to be able to allow for different contextual factors to affect (otherwise similar) evidence, the rubrics applied to it, the resultant claim, and the uses to which it is put.

We suggest that the path ahead for work on assessment in the 21st century should include theoretical work to adapt the assessment argument to apply to assessments that use more of the synthetic/wider approach and allow for the relevance of context at all stages. This will require extended work beyond the purview of this book, but we hope that the discussion here will stimulate that work.

The second quarter of the 21st century may also require a rethink of the concept of validity as applied to assessment. The wider, synthetic approach to assessment requires the balance between reliability and validity to be tilted more towards validity, as more individualised approaches and variable uses of evidence can come at the cost of aspects of reliability. The approach that we are recommending puts an increased weight on the importance of validity – the fit between different components of the assessment and between the assessment as a whole and its interpretation and use.

At the end of Chapter 6 ("The moral compass") we quote Messick's view that:

> The primary measurement standards that must be met to legitimize a proposed test use are those of reliability, validity, and fairness, which are also value-laden concepts.
>
> *(Messick, 1998, p. 1)*

And we ask whether validity can be regarded as a *moral* value. Here, we suggest that some applications of the concept of validity do have moral significance. Examples might include the link between the assessment outcomes and their intended use and the way in which they are reported. Also, morally relevant differences between the contexts in which assessments are taken by different users may affect the validity of the processes applied to the assessment evidence derived in these different contexts. Other validity issues – for example, the fit between particular assessment tasks and the constructs being assessed or between the construct and the objectives of the test – may be regarded as more technical and of less moral interest. But we can envisage circumstances in which even the more apparently technical validity issues can have moral significance – for example, if a lack of fit between constructs and objectives leads to misleading or harmful interpretations of the test outcome. It is always relevant to ask about the moral significance of attributions of validity or invalidity to an assessment.

. . . .

In this book, we have attempted to reconceptualise assessment thirty years on from the reconceptualisation by Caroline Gipps that we have quoted at the beginning of the book and at the beginning of this chapter. We have surveyed developments and changes in thinking about education and assessment over the past quarter-century. In our view, these developments warrant a reset of our approaches to educational assessment, both in theory and in practice. In this chapter, we have suggested directions for the future – a different approach to assessment, new theoretical work on the "assessment argument" and a revisiting of validity, allowing that aspects of validity can be seen as moral arguments. In Chapter 6, we have also asked for work to identify moral principles that should inform assessment practice.

In recent years, thinking about education and assessment – as well as many other aspects of society – has frequently been polarised and heated. Readers may disagree with some of our conclusions, but we hope that exploring their reasons for disagreeing with us will enable all of us to move forward. Perhaps the most important lesson learned from the very different material that we have brought together is the importance of context in every part of educational assessment. Although the directions we are advocating are challenging, it is no longer acceptable to narrow the scope and approach of assessment to exclude contextual factors.

We hope that a further reconceptualisation can be done a quarter of a century later. By 2050, will there still be high-stakes tests or examinations used for summative purposes? Will there still be tests taken using pen and paper? Will the purposes of assessment be the same as they are now? And are there assessment practices in the 2020s that will be thought morally wrong a quarter of a century later?

Whatever the eventual answers to these and other questions prompted by this book, the educational assessment profession, and those who support it with theoretical work and research, cannot continue to "limp along" from year to year. There is a lot to be done.

Notes

1 www.federalreservehistory.org/essays/great-recession and its-aftermath
2 www.bbc.co.uk/news/entertainment-arts-63458467
3 "Things fell apart", BBC Radio 4. www.bbc.co.uk/programmes/m0011cpr
4 https://ed.stanford.edu/news/what-do-ai-chatbots-really-mean-students-and-cheating
5 That is different from assessing the performance of individuals *in* groups, which has been the subject of some studies (e.g. Webb, 1997).
6 It has been pointed out to us that this may reflect a lack of finance as well as nervousness about change.
7 Elsewhere, we call this sense of fairness "relational fairness" (Nisbet & Shaw, 2020), as opposed, for example, to "retributive fairness" where each individual candidate is seen to get what he or she deserves.
8 We are very grateful to Paul Newton for raising some of the questions that we address here.
9 Much more is a feature of colleges in the USA – see www.usnews.com/best-colleges/rankings/national-universities/freshmen-least-most-likely-return.
10 In 2023, in the UK, 554,000 home-based applicants for undergraduate courses were accepted through the main national system (UCAS), out of 757,000 applications. That difference would have narrowed through "clearing" discussions with students who had not achieved their expected grades. See Bolton (2024). https://researchbriefings.files.parliament.uk/documents/CBP-7857/CBP-7857.pdf.
11 https://students-residents.aamc.org/choosing-medical-career/what-you-need-know-about-mcat-exam#
12 www.medschools.ac.uk/media/2368/msc-infosheet-good-doctor.pdf
13 https://admissions.yale.edu/test-flexible.
14 The four metaphors proposed by Mislevy (2012) are: Assessment as Practice; Assessment as Feedback Loop; Assessment as Evidentiary Argument; and Assessment as Measurement.

References

American Educational Research Association, American Psychological Association, and National Council on Measurement in Education. (2014). *Standards for educational and psychological testing*. American Educational Research Association.

Bavarian, N., Lewis, K. M., Dubois, D. L., Acock, A., Vuchinich, S., Silverthorn, N., Snyder, F. J., Day, J., Ji, P., & Flay, B. R. (2013). Using social-emotional and character development to improve academic outcomes: A matched-pair, cluster-randomized controlled trial in low-income, urban schools. *Journal of School Health, 83*(11), 771–779. https://doi.org/10.1111/josh.12093

Bax, S. (2013). The cognitive processing of candidates during reading tests: Evidence from eye tracking. *Language Testing, 30*(4), 441–465. http://doi.org/10.1177/0265532212473244

Bolton, P. (2024, January 2). Higher education student numbers. *Research Briefing*. House of Commons Library. Number 7857. https://researchbriefings.files.parliament.uk/documents/CBP-7857/CBP-7857.pdf

Brown, G., El-Erian, M. A., Spence, M., & Lidow, R. (2023). *Permacrisis: A plan to fix a fractured world*. Simon & Schuster.

Clayton, S., Manning, C. M., Krygsman, K., & Speiser, M. (2017). *Mental health and our changing climate: Impacts, implications, and guidance*. American Psychological Association, and ecoAmerica.

Coe, R., & Kime, S. (2013, January). The DIY evaluation guide. *Education Endowment Foundation (EEF)*. https://johntomsett.com/wp-content/uploads/2013/09/eef_diy_evaluation_guide_2013.pdf

Gipps, C. C. (1994). *Beyond testing: Towards a theory of educational assessment*. The Falmer Press.

Gorin, J. S. (2012). Assessment as evidential reasoning. *White paper commissioned by The Gordon Commission on the Future of Educational Assessment*. https://www.ets.org/Media/Research/pdf/gorin_assessment_evidential_reasoning.pdf

Gorin, J. S. (2014). Assessment as evidential reasoning. *Teachers College Record, 116*(11), 1–26. https://doi.org/10.1177/016146811411601101

Kane, M. T. (2013). Validating the interpretations and uses of test scores. *Journal of Educational Measurement, 50*(1), 1–73. https://doi.org/10.1111/jedm.12000

Maddox, B., Bayliss, A. P., Fleming, P., Engelhardt, P. E., Edwards, S. G., & Borgonovi, F. (2018). Observing response processes with eye tracking in international large-scale assessments: Evidence from the OECD PIAAC assessment. *European Journal of Psychology of Education, 33*(3), 543–558. https://doi.org/10.1007/s10212-018-0380-2

Messick, S. (1998). Consequences of test interpretation and use: The fusion of validity and values in psychological assessment. *ETS Research Report RR-98-48*. www.ets.org/research/policy_research_reports/publications/report/199/ihem.html

Mislevy, R. J. (2012). *Four metaphors we need to understand assessment*. Gordon Commission on the Future of Assessment in Education.

Mislevy, R. J. (2018). *Sociocognitive foundations of educational measurement*. Routledge.

Nisbet, I., & Shaw, S. D. (2020). *Is assessment fair?* SAGE Publications Ltd.

Oranje, A., Gorin, J., Jia, Y., & Kerr, D. (2018). Collecting, analysing, and interpreting response time, eye tracking, and log data. In K. Ercikan & J. Pellegrino (Eds.), *Validation of score meaning for next generation assessments* (pp. 39–51). Routledge.

Phillips, V. (2024, January). In 2024, 5 big issues will shape education. *Forbes*. www.forbes.com/sites/vickiphillips/2024/01/03/in-2024-5-big-issues-will-shape-education

Putnam, R. D. (2015). *Our kids: The American dream in crisis*. Simon & Schuster Inc.

Qualifications Wales & CCEA (Regulation). (2019, July). *Fair Access by Design: Guidance for awarding organisations on designing high-quality and inclusive qualifications*. www.qualificationswales.org/media/4739/fair-access-by-design.pdf

Rosenbaum, P. R. (1986). Dropping out of high school in the United States: An observational study. *Journal of Educational Statistics*, *11*(3), 207–224. https://doi.org/10.3102/10769986011003207

Sanchez, J. G., Christopherson, R., Echeagaray, M. E. C., Gibson, D. C., Atkinson, R. K., & Burleson, W. (2011). How to do multimodal detection of affective states? *ICALT*, 654–655. http://doi.org/10.1109/ICALT.2011.206

Walland, E., & Shaw, S. D. (2022). E-portfolios in teaching, learning and assessment: Tensions in theory and praxis. *Technology, Pedagogy and Education*, *31*(3), 363–379. http://doi.org/10.1080/1475939X.2022.2074087

Webb, N. M. (1997). Assessing students in small collaborative groups. *Theory Into Practice*, *36*(4), 205–213. http://doi.org/10.1080/00405849709543770

Yeats, W. B. (1920). The second coming. In *The Dial Magazine* (Vol. 69). University of Virginia. https://www.poetryfoundation.org/poems/43290/the-second-coming

AFTERWORD

One key challenge in R&D in assessment and education is keeping a balance between drilling down into specific issues and maintaining a sense of the broad sweep of change. Ideally, change should be driven by meticulous research – it should be evidence-driven, stepwise, rational and progressive. We absolutely need work that pores over the specific implications of research on working memory, on how skills in reading develop and on the validation of specific assessments. But we also need to understand the wider sets of values and assumptions that should underpin policy in assessment and education – ideas of ability, equity, routes and progression.

This book admirably moves between these different levels of enquiry and analysis – and adds a further vital element: events. It has transpired that Harold Macmillan never said "Events, dear boy, events" in response to a question about challenges to effective policy, but the point still remains. What we ACTUALLY experience as the reality of education – with assessment being a crucial part – is created by a cauldron of evidence, thought, reaction, judgement, imagined futures and historical pressures.

This book helps us to move from anxiety about "what next?" to a more considered understanding of "that's why things are as they are", which I, for one, hope leads to a greater sense of control over next steps: an accumulation of collective expertise in refining education rather than a buffeted reaction to vaguely framed worries and ill-informed futurology.

It is very demanding to write about broad sweeps of history and the specifics of things. It is even more demanding for practitioners and policy makers to hold this all in their heads simultaneously. But this book provides both the overview and the detail to support them in doing exactly that.

Tim Oates, CBE
Group Director – Research
Cambridge University Press & Assessment

INDEX

The 1619 Project 101–102

About Our Schools (Brighouse and Waters) 182
Abulafia, D. 111
academic integrity 47n49, 158n31
achievement gap 103–104
Action for Climate Empowerment 61
admissions, race-conscious 104–112
adult education and learning *see* lifelong learning
Advance HE 159n39
AfL *see* assessment for learning (AfL)
Akrofi, M. M. 68
Aloisi, C. 40
American capitalism 101
anti-racist education 114
anxiety 71, 74, 76–77; ecoanxiety 194; examination 184
Arab Spring 7
Aristotle 170
Armstrong, J. 113
Arnold, M. 112
Arrhenius, S. 59
artificial intelligence (AI) 30, 31, 193–194; and academic integrity 158n31; and assessment 39–40, 43; CAT 148; definition 142; in education 39, 142–145; generative powers 38; human rights and 144; JCQ guidance 42; risks 144–145
assessment 3, 8; argument 202–203; context 185, 197, 203, 204; digital inequality 150; e-assessment 36, 148; formative 32–33, 46n38, 78, 128, 152, 158n37; immersive 149; inclusive 152–154; innovation in 147–151; moral challenges 180–183; overassessment 185; and pandemic 81–86; paper-based 69; and power 180–182; purposes of 177–178; socioculturally responsive 154–156; summative 65, 77; tension between approaches 197, 198–202; traditional 43; validity 203–204; vocational 183; *see also* developments in assessment; formative assessment
assessment for learning (AfL) 11, 32–33, 46n37, 46n41, 152, 193
Assessment in Education: Principles, Policy and Practice 145
Assessment Reform Group (ARG) (UK) 11, 32–33, 152
augmented reality (AR) 149
automation 20, 30

Baird, J. A. 12, 126, 128
Bakke, A. 106
Barber, M. 18, 22
Barnard, A. 79
basic education 22, 23
behaviourism 126–127, 157n3
Bell, D. 100
benchmarking 178
Bennett, R. E. 36–37, 147, 149, 150, 152, 155, 156

Bermingham, D. 65
Bersin, J. 25, 26
Beyond Testing (Gipps) 2, 191
big data 37, 138–142
Bimpeh, Y. 158n33
Blackburn, S. 174
Black Lives Matter 100, 116n5
Black, P. 11, 33, 46n38, 46n41, 145
Bloom, B. S. 26–27, 146
Blum, E. 105–106
Boston, K. 36, 148
Brassler, M. 135
Brighouse, T. 182, 183
Bringing Knowledge Back In (Young) 129
Broadfoot, P. 38, 145, 146
Broecker, W. 59
Brown, G. T. L. 33
Brown, M. 100, 112
Brown v. Board of Education 104
Bruner, J. 128, 157n4
bullying 74–75

Cameron, D. 70
Carnie, F. 64–65
CDAs *see* cognitive diagnostic assessments (CDAs)
Centre for Evaluation and Monitoring (CEM) (Cambridge) 158n32
certification 178
Chainey, J. 65
Chami, G. 145, 158n31
ChatGPT 41
child in learning poverty 79
Childline (UK) 71
Chomsky, N. 112
Clesham, R. 40
climate change 4, 58, 194; attitudes towards 68; education 59–65; educational assessment 65–68; environmental impacts 66, 67; greenhouse effect 58–59; impact of 59–60
Clinton, B. 1, 192
Coe, R. 33
cognitive apprenticeship 128
cognitive constructivism 125, 128
cognitive development 127
cognitive diagnosis 11
cognitive diagnostic assessments (CDAs) 35
cognitive learning 127–128
cognitive psychology 10, 11, 34–35, 125, 152

Colburn, B. 187n2
Coleman, V. 150
competence 5, 134, 196; behavioural 135; cognitive 135; definition of 135; generic 135, 136; Gillick 158n30; workplace 134, 136
competencies 27–28, 134; interdisciplinary 135
competency frameworks 136
computer adaptive testing (CAT) 148, 158n33
computer-based assessment 148; guidelines 149; migratory strategy 150; transformational strategy 150; *see also* e-assessment
Confucius 181
constructivism 125, 127–128, 157n1
COP26 87n7
Cope, B. 141
Cordero, E. C. 61
Cotton, D. R. F. 40
COVID-19 pandemic 4, 89n36, 195; assessment and 81–86; educational impact of 80–81; learning poverty 78–80; remote learning 80; school closure 81
Crenshaw, K. 103
Critical Race Theory (CRT) 5, 97–104, 195
critical theory 98
Critical Theory (Frankfurt School) 98
critical thinking 138
Cultural Literacy: What Every American Needs to Know (Hirsch) 133
culturally sustaining pedagogy 154
culture wars 5, 97–104
Curriculum for Excellence 87n6
Curriculum for Wales 132
curriculum-pedagogy-assessment triad 151

Dada, F. 66
D'Agostino, S. 43
data ethics 38
Dawson, P. 41
decolonisation in education 112–116
deep technologies 8, 13n8, 46n31
DeFunis, M. 106
degree awarding gap 104
Delgado, R. 99
Desmond, M. 101, 102
Dettmers, J. 135
developments in assessment 4, 32; artificial intelligence 39–40;

assessment for learning 32–33;
Assessment Reform Group 32–33;
ChatGPT 40–43; cognitive
psychology 34–35; technology
and 35–38
developments in education 4, 17;
artificial intelligence 39; basic
education 23; ChatGPT 41;
competency 27–28; Fourth Industrial
Revolution 29–30; Generation
Alpha 28–29; Generation Z 28;
globalisation 18–19; information
deluge 30–32; Jomtien Declaration
21; knowledge and skills 27;
knowledge economy 19; lifelong
learning 24–26; literacy 21–24;
MDGs 21–22; Skills for Life 23; 21st
century skills 26–27
Dewey, J. 97, 98, 131
Didau, D. 33
digital divide 29, 31, 38
digital inequality 150
digital native 28, 150
digital technologies 9–10; *see also*
technology
*Discipline and Punish: The Birth of the
Prison* (Foucault) 180
discrimination 201
distress 71, 74
diversity, educational benefits of
108–109
Donaldson, G. 132
Downie, R. 72
Drucker, P. 123
Duncan, O. D. 104

Earth Warriors 61
e-assessment 36, 148; *see also*
computer-based assessment
ecoanxiety 194
education 3; climate change 59–65;
moral justification 176–177;
purposes of 122–124; right to 177;
and training 175
educational assessment 3, 13n6;
changing context 7–8; cognitive
diagnosis 11; technology 7–10
Educational Data Mining (EDM) 139
educational debt 104
Education for All 9, 18, 44n5
Education for Sustainable Development
(ESD) 80–81
The Effective Executive (Drucker) 123

England: adult education 22;
Assessment for Learning 32, 33;
Assessment Reform Group 11, 32;
climate change education 62–64;
COVID-19 impact on grading system
83–85, 89n40; curriculum 132;
mental illness 71; national curriculum
45n11; Office for Students 42,
103–104, 150; Ofqual 83; *see also*
United Kingdom (UK)
ESD for 2030 61
ethical discourse 172
ethics 184; medical 171, 184; morality
and 170–172
EU Kids Online 28
European Union (EU), Economic and
Social Strategy 19
examination 180–181; anxiety 184; cold
shower theory of 184; stress 184–185
extended reality (XR) 149

Faces at the Bottom of the Well
(Bell) 100
fairness 82, 105, 110, 205n7; inclusivity
and 153–154
FairTest (US) 174, 177
Finland 24
Fioramonti, L. 62
First Industrial Revolution 46n32
Fisher, A. 107–108
Flew, A. 179, 186
Floyd, G. 100
Ford, R. T. 105, 110
formative assessment 32–33, 46n38, 78,
128, 152, 158n37
forms of knowledge 129–130, 132
Foucault, M. 180
Fourier, J. 58
Fourth Industrial Revolution 29–30
France, Universities of the Third
Age 25
Fundamental Values of Academic
Integrity 47n49
The Future of Education and Skills -
Education 2030 (OECD) 134

Gates, B. 142, 145
Generation Alpha 28–29
Generation Z 28
Gibson, D. C. 142, 158n26
gig economy 46n33
Gillick competence 158n30
Gipps, C. 2, 191, 204

Global Action Programme on ESD (2015–2019) 61
globalisation 18–19
Goodlad, L. M. E. 43
Gordon Commission on the Future of Assessment in Education 36, 202
Gorin, J. S. 202–203
grade inflation 83–85, 89n41
grade point average (GPA) 89n43
grading system, COVID-19 impact on 81–86
Gratz, B. 107
Gray, C. 60
greenhouse effect 58–59
Groundwork of the Metaphysic of Morals (Kant) 170
Grutter, B. 107
Grutter settlement 107, 108

Habermas, J. 172
Hague, W. 132–133
Hamilton, L. S. 147
Hand, M. 173
Hanesworth, P. 153, 154
Hannah-Jones, N. 101, 102
Happiness: Lessons from a New Science (Layard) 70
Hare, R. M. 173; overridingness 173
Heaven, W. D. 41
higher-order thinking skills 127, 146–147
Hippocrates 184
Hirsch, E.D. 27, 131–133, 138
Hirst, P. H. 123, 129–132, 138, 173, 177; *see also* forms of knowledge
Hockings, C. 153
Hodgen, J. 80
Holmes, W. 144
Horkheimer, M. 98
Hughes, S. 150
Hughes, T. 75
human capital 123
human rights 144, 177

identify 116n1
illiteracy 21, 22
immersive assessment 149
Implementation of the National Literacy Strategy 22
inclusive assessment 152–154
Industry 4.0 *see* Fourth Industrial Revolution
inequality 201, 202

information deluge 30–32
information revolution 30
Intergovernmental Panel on Climate Change (IPCC) 87n1
internal colonization 112
International Association for Educational Assessment (IAEA) 81
International Baccalaureate Organization 42
International Centre for Academic Integrity 47n49
International Computer and Information Literacy Study (ICILS) 28
International Conference on Artificial Intelligence and Education (Beijing, 2019) 143
intersectionality 100
Ixer, G. 146, 147

James, M. 13n6
James, W. 99
Jankowski, N. 153
Jerrim, J. 77
Johnson, L. B. 105
Joint Council for Qualifications (JCQ) (UK) 42, 47n56
Jomtien Declaration 21, 44n6
Just What Is Critical Race Theory and What Is It Doing in a Nice Field Like Education? (Ladson-Billings) 100

Kalantzis, M. 141
Kane, M. T. 12
Kant, I. 174, 186; categorical imperative 173; *Groundwork of the Metaphysic of Morals* 170; justification of education 182; *Lectures on Pedagogy* 176, 181
Kennedy, J. F. 104–105
Kissel, A. 114
Kitchen, W. 181
knowledge: disciplinary and interdisciplinary 137–138; factual 133; forms of 129–130, 132; powerful 131–132, 157n10; revival 129–134, 157n15; and skills 27, 130, 137; types of 136
knowledge economy 19, 123
Kwanzaa 155, 159n42
Kwauk, C. 62

Ladson-Billings, G. 99–100, 104, 155
large language models (LLMs) 40

Lave, J. 128, 157n4
Layard, R. 70, 72, 73
Learning Analytics 139, 157n23
learning poverty 78–80
learning society 9
learning strategies 47n44
learning theory 124–129
Learning: The Treasure Within (Delors Report) 26
Learning to Be: The World of Education Today and Tomorrow (Faure Report) 26
Lectures on Pedagogy (Kant) 176, 181
lifelong learning 8, 9, 13n9, 24–26, 80
literacy 21–23
Liu, O. L. 105
Lohman, D. F. 125, 152
Loveless, T. 23
Lowman, R. 47n47
Lukes, S. 187
Lynch, M. 39

machine learning 40
Machlup, F. 123
Madgavkar, A. 123
Maimonides, perfection of body *vs.* soul 72
Manifesto for Education for Environmental Sustainability 63
mark scheme 182–183, 188n20
Mason, M. 172, 173
mathematics 102–103; student performance in 23, 34
McAthur, J. 154
McIntosh, P. 114
Medical College Admissions Test (MCAT) 200
Medical Schools Council (UK) 201
Meno (Plato) 129
mental illness 71, 74
Messick, S. 11, 12, 187, 204
meta-ethics 170, 187n1
Millennium Development Goals (MDGs) 21–22, 60
Mills, A. 43
Mislevy, R. J. 153, 202, 205n14
mixed reality (MR) 149
Montenegro, E. 153
Moore, G.E. 73
moral(ity) 5, 196–197, 204; challenges to educational assessment 180–183; ethics and 170–172; meaning of 173–174; principles 183–186

Moral Education in a Secular Society (Hirst) 173
moral justification: for education 176–177; for educational assessment 174–180
Moser, C. 22
Moser Report 45n13
Mulder, M. 27, 135
Muller, J. 157n10
Musk, E. 144

National Commission on Excellence in Education (US) 19
National Council of Labour Colleges (NCLC) (UK) 24
neuroscience 34, 152
neurotechnology 30
Newman, C. 129
New Skills Agenda for Europe 27–28
Newton, P. E. 12, 178
Nicomachean Ethics (Aristotle) 170
non-discrimination 105

OECD Learning Compass 2030 136
Office for National Statistics (ONS) (UK) 70, 76
Office for Students (OfS) (England) 103–104, 150
Ofqual (England) 83
Open University (UK) 24
operant conditioning 126
Organisation for Economic Co-operation and Development (OECD) 3, 9, 10, 13n12, 35, 47n46, 134; "Are Students Ready to Take on Environmental Challenges?" 64; human capital 123; Learning Compass 2030 136; PISA 2025 Science Framework 65–66
Our Kids: The American Dream in Crisis (Putnam) 201
out-of-school children 22, 45n9
overassessment 185

Paris Agreement 61, 81, 87n5, 89n38
Pavlov, I. 126
Pellegrino, J. W. 36
permacrisis 192
Perry, W. 127
Peters, M. A. 112
Peters, R. S. 123, 130, 131
Phillips, V. 197
Piaget, J. 125, 127

Pichai, S. 142
Pierce, C. S. 99
Plato 129
Plutzer, E. 63
Polanyi, M. 131, 181
Popper, K. 98
Porter, C. 59, 60
Postmodern Ethics (Zygmunt) 171
poverty, learning 78–80
powerful knowledge 131–132, 157n10
Prensky, M. 19–20, 29
Priestley, M. 82
Priestley Review 82
Principia Ethica (Moore) 73
Prinsloo, P. 157n23
Programme for International Student Assessment (PISA) 23, 65–66
progressive education movements 130–131
Pryor, J. 157n5
Putnam, R. 201

qualifications 42, 178–179
Qualifications and Curriculum Authority (QCA) (UK) 47n45
Quality Assurance Agency for Higher Education (QAA) (UK) 43, 112, 115

race-conscious admissions, in United States 104–112, 195–196; assessment and decision practices 110–111; *Brown v. Board of Education* 104; cases on 106–108 (see also Supreme Court cases on race-conscious admissions (US)); diversity and educational benefits 108–109; *Grutter* settlement 107; Prop 209 106; public opinion 110; race and social disadvantage 109; race-neutral alternatives 106; Top Ten Percent Rule 107
Race, Retrenchment, and the Reform of School Mathematics (Tate) 102
radical constructivism 125, 157n1
Randell, H. 60
rank order 188n18, 200
rational knowledge 115
Rebuilding Our Schools from the Bottom Up (Carnie) 64–65
reflection, student 146–147
Richardson, M. 40
right–good distinction 172
right to education 177

Roberts, J. 108
Roblin, N. P. 136
Rogoff, B. 128, 157n4
Roosevelt, R. 112
Ross, W. D. 172
Royal Society of Chemistry (RSC) 62
rubrics 182
Rushton, E. 63
Russell, B. 174

sapiential authority 181
Schleicher, A. 18, 20, 27, 74
Schmidt, F. L. 35
school mathematics 102–103
Schwab, K. 29
science education 66
Scotland: adaptive test 148; anti-racist education 114; Curriculum for Excellence 62, 87n6
Second Industrial Revolution 46n32
Shepard, L. 129, 157n3
Siarova, H. 136
Singapore 7, 24
Sitta, F. A. 67
situated learning theory 128
Skills for Life 23
Skinner, B. 126, 157n2
Slade, S. 157n23
slavery, in US 101, 102
Smith, R. 130
Snow, R. E. 125, 152
social justice 153, 154
socio-constructivism 125, 128
socioculturally responsive assessments 154–156
sociocultural theory 128
Sociology, Equality and Education (Flew) 179
Socrates 171
Sotomayor, S. 108, 109
special educational needs and disabilities (SEND) 6
standardised tests 154–155
"The State of the Global Education Crisis: A Path to Recovery" 80
Stecher, B. M. 147
stress, examination 184–185
summative assessment 65, 77
Supreme Court cases on race-conscious admissions (US) 106–108; *Bakke* case 106; *DeFunis* case 106; *Fisher* case 107–108; *Gratz* case 107; *Grutter* case 107

Surti, J. 78
Sustainable Development Goals (SDGs) 61, 81
Swiecki, Z. 43

Tate, W. F. 100; Race, Retrenchment, and the Reform of School Mathematics 102; Toward a Critical Race Theory of Education 99
Taylor, C. 13n9
technology: automation 30; deep 8, 13n8, 46n31; and educational assessment 9–10, 35–38; innovation in assessment 147–151; innovations 29–30; nanotechnology 30; neurotechnology 30; shifts in 7–8; transformative 13n8, 46n31
theories of learning 124–129
thinking skills 132; higher-order 146–147
Third Industrial Revolution 46n32
Third International Mathematics and Science Study (TIMSS) 23
Thomas, C. 108
Thorius, K. A. K. 154
Thorndike, E. 126
Timmis, S. 142, 147
Tom Brown's Schooldays (Hughes) 75
Top Ten Percent Rule 107
Torrance, H. 157n5
Toward a Critical Race Theory of Education (Ladson-Billings and Tate) 99
Trades Union Movement 24
training 130, 175–176
transformative technologies 13n8, 29, 46n31
Trump, D. 97
Tuhiwai Smith, L. 176
Twist, L. 146

UN Decade of Education for Sustainable Development (ESD) (2005–2014) 61
UNESCO 21, 22, 60, 80, 134; AI technologies 143; climate change education 63; ESD for 2030 61; Indicator 4.7.5 88n12; "Learning to Be: The World of Education Today and Tomorrow" 26
UN Framework Convention on Climate Change (UNFCCC) 61, 87n5
United Kingdom (UK): big data 141; climate change education 62, 67; COVID-19 impact on grading system 82; decolonising the university curriculum 112–116; examinations in 84; expenditure on education 175; Extension Movement 24; Gillick competence 158n30; Joint Council for Qualifications 42; Joint Information Systems Committee 148; Medical Schools Council 201; Quality Assurance Agency for Higher Education 43, 112; Russell Group universities 42; Skills for Life 23; University and College Admissions Service 111; *see also* England
United Nations 2030 Agenda for Sustainable Development 9
United States (US): achievement gap 104; American capitalism 101; Black Lives Matter 100; climate change education 62, 63; deaths of young black men 100; FairTest 174, 177; K-12 Climate Action Plan 2021 64; Medical College Admissions Test 200; National Commission on Excellence in Education 19; rubrics 182; slavery 101, 102; standardised tests in 154–155; student performance in mathematics 23; *see also* race-conscious admissions, in United States
Universal Design for Learning 154, 159n40
Universities of the Third Age 25
University and College Admissions Service (UCAS) 111
University College London (UCL) 67, 88n15, 112–113
University Extension Movement 24

validity 11–12, 203–204
Vayachuta, P. 45n9
virtual reality (VR) 149
Voogt, J. 136
Vygotsky, L. 125, 128, 157n4

Waitoller, F. R. 154
Wales: adaptive test 148; curriculum 132
Warwick-Edinburgh Mental Wellbeing Scale 76
Waters, M. 182, 183
Watkins, L. 13n9
Weale, S. 42
Webb, M. 142, 158n26

Weber, M. 98
well-being 4, 86, 123, 194; anxiety 71, 74, 76–77; bullying 74–75; definition 72; distress 71, 74; educational assessment 75–76; and happiness 72; mental illness 71, 74; in Moore's *Principia Ethica* 72; Office for National Statistics 70–71, 76; respect for evidence 77; at school 74–75; sense of proportionality 77; Warwick-Edinburgh Mental Wellbeing Scale 76
Wenger, E. 128, 157n4
West, D. 158n33
White, J. 70, 72–73, 132, 176, 179
white privilege 114
"Why is my curriculum white?" campaign 112–114
Wiek, A. 135
Wiliam, D. 11, 33, 46n38, 46n41
Williams, B. 171
Wilson, J. 173

Winthrop, R. 62
woke(ism) 101, 103
Woodson, C. 102
Workers Education Association (UK) 24
workplace competence 134, 136
World Conference on Education For All – Meeting Basic Learning Needs 21
World Education Forum 21
World Education Report (2000) 21
World Meteorological Organization 87n4
World Wide Fund for Nature 62
Worth, K. 63
Wyatt-Smith, C. 37, 149

Yosso, T. J. 155
Young Lives Foundation 87n3
Young, M. 129, 131, 132, 138, 157n10

Zahawi, N. 62
Zygmunt, B. 171